STRATHCLYDE

and the Anglo-Saxons in the Viking Age

STRATHCLYDE

and the Anglo-Saxons in the Viking Age

TIM CLARKSON

First published in Great Britain in 2014 by
John Donald, an imprint of Birlinn Ltd

Reprinted in 2016

West Newington House
10 Newington Road
Edinburgh
EH9 1QS

www.birlinn.co.uk

ISBN: 978 1 906566 78 4

British Library Cataloguing-in-Publication Data
A catalogue record for this book is available on request from the British Library

Typeset by Hewer Text UK Ltd, Edinburgh
Printed and bound in Britain by Bell & Bain Ltd, Glasgow

CONTENTS

List of Plates		vii
List of Maps		viii
Genealogical Tables		ix
1	Cumbrians and Anglo-Saxons	1
2	Early Contacts	20
3	Raiders and Settlers	44
4	Strathclyde and Wessex	57
5	Athelstan	75
6	King Dunmail	103
7	The Late Tenth Century	119
8	Borderlands	131
9	The Fall of Strathclyde	146
10	The Anglo-Norman Period	159
11	Conclusions	169
Notes		173
Bibliography		189
Index		199

LIST OF PLATES

1. Hogback gravestones in Govan Old Parish Church
2. Govan Old Parish Church
3. Dumbarton Rock
4. Bamburgh Castle
5. Govan in 1758: from Robert Paul's engraving *A view of the banks of the Clyde taken from York Hill*
6. Aethelflaed, Lady of the Mercians: commemorative statue erected at Tamworth Castle in 1913, showing Aethelflaed with her nephew Athelstan
7. The Gosforth Cross, Cumbria: a tenth-century monument displaying Anglo-Saxon and Norse influence
8. Anglo-Saxon cross near the east wall of All Saints Church, Bakewell
9. Eamotum: the confluence of the rivers Eamont and Lowther near Brougham Castle
10. Lowther Church, Cumbria
11. Dunmail Raise, Cumbria
12. St John the Baptist, Chester: ruins of the medieval church
13. The Giant's Grave, Penrith
14. Carham, 1018: view eastward along the River Tweed near the probable site of the battle

LIST OF MAPS

1. Early medieval Britain and Ireland
2. The North Britons in the Roman period
3. Northern Britain, sixth to eighth centuries
4. Govan in AD 900
5. The Solway region: Cumbric place-names of the Viking period [after Higham 1993, 181]
6. Britain in the time of Edward the Elder, c.920
7. Strathclyde and northern Northumbria in the early tenth century
8. The meeting at Eamotum, 927
9. The location of Brunanburh: five popular candidates
10. North Lancashire and the 'conflict zone' of 937
11. St Cathroe's pilgrimage
12. Strathclyde and Northumbria in the late tenth century
13. Hogback monuments in southern Scotland / northern England and sculpture of the 'Govan School'
14. Geographical context of the battle of Carham, 1018
15. Kingdoms and peoples, c.1050
16. Gospatric's Writ
17. Southern Scotland and northern England in the twelfth century
18. David's principality: 'Cumbria' in the Scottish kingdom, c.1120

GENEALOGICAL TABLES

Kings of Alt Clut, fifth to ninth centuries, based on
the Harleian pedigree of Rhun, son of Artgal. Names
in *italics* are from sources outside the pedigree.

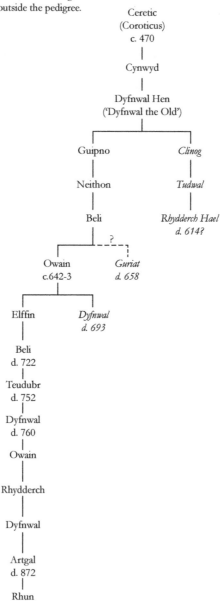

Ceretic
(Coroticus)
c. 470

Cynwyd

Dyfnwal Hen
('Dyfnwal the Old')

Guipno   *Clinog*

Neithon   *Tudwal*

Beli   *Rhydderch Hael*
d. 614?

?

Owain   *Guriat*
c.642-3   *d. 658*

Elffin   *Dyfnwal*
d. 693

Beli
d. 722

Teudubr
d. 752

Dyfnwal
d. 760

Owain

Rhydderch

Dyfnwal

Artgal
d. 872

Rhun

The royal dynasty of Strathclyde

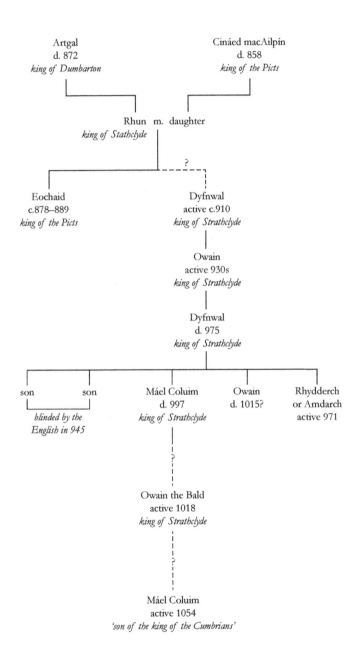

The royal dynasty of Wessex

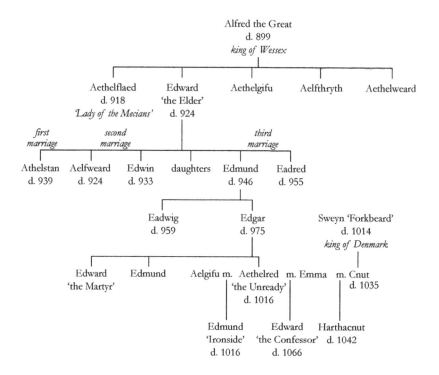

The royal dynasty of Alba to 1034

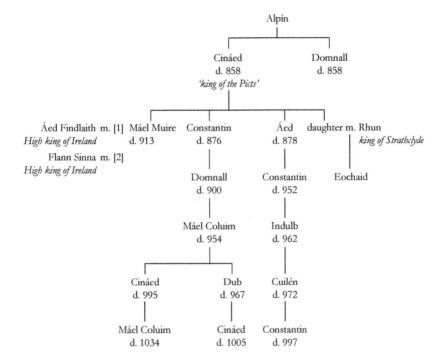

The royal dynasty of Alba,
11th to early 12th centuries

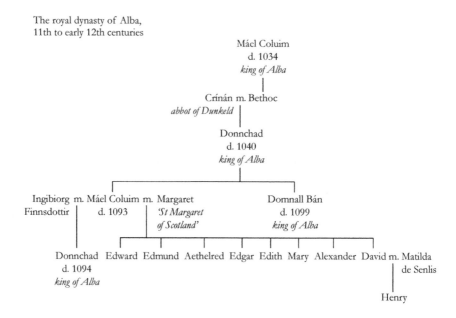

The royal dynasty of Viking Dublin
[after Downham 2007, 29]

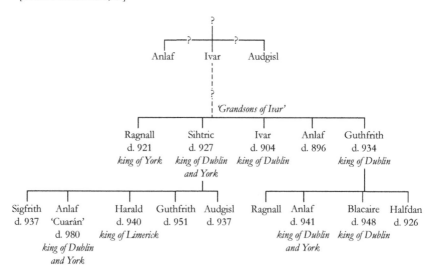

The dynasty of Bamburgh

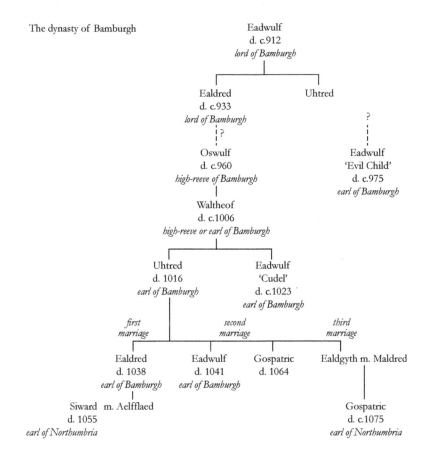

Eadwulf
d. c.912
lord of Bamburgh

Ealdred
d. c.933
lord of Bamburgh
?

Uhtred

?

Oswulf
d. c.960
high-reeve of Bamburgh

Eadwulf
'Evil Child'
d. c.975
earl of Bamburgh

Waltheof
d. c.1006
high-reeve or earl of Bamburgh

Uhtred
d. 1016
earl of Bamburgh

Eadwulf
'Cudel'
d. c.1023
earl of Bamburgh

first marriage   *second marriage*   *third marriage*

Ealdred
d. 1038
earl of Bamburgh

Eadwulf
d. 1041
earl of Bamburgh

Gospatric
d. 1064

Ealdgyth m. Maldred

Siward m. Aelfflaed
d. 1055
earl of Northumbria

Gospatric
d. c.1075
earl of Northumbria

MAP 1 Early medieval Britain and Ireland

1

CUMBRIANS AND ANGLO-SAXONS

Introduction

One thousand years ago, at the beginning of the eleventh century, the valley of the River Clyde was the heartland of a powerful kingdom. In those days, the river flowed through a rural landscape devoid of towns and cities. From its sources in the hills, it meandered north-westward for many miles before widening to form the estuary we know today as the Firth of Clyde. Eleven miles upstream from the head of the firth, and two miles downstream from the site of modern Glasgow, an important ford provided a crossing-point. Here, at Govan, travellers on foot could traverse the river at low tide. It was here, too, that the Clyde was joined by the River Kelvin coming down from the north. Directly opposite the confluence, on the southern bank of the Clyde, the ford was overlooked by a huge mound with two levels and a flattened summit. Further along the southern bank, no more than a stone's throw from the mound, stood a small wooden church in a heart-shaped enclosure. The mound has long since disappeared, a casualty of nineteenth-century industrialisation, and no trace of it remains today. But a church still stands nearby, the most recent successor of the wooden church of a thousand years ago. This impressive Victorian building, known today as Govan Old, is home to a remarkable treasure: an internationally renowned collection of early medieval sculpture. Visitors come from far and wide to admire the finely carved monuments, all of which formerly stood in the churchyard amidst the gravestones of later times. Among the collection are an ornate sarcophagus, three broken cross-shafts, five hogback gravestones and more than twenty recumbent slabs. Each of the thirty-one stones at Govan Old is a reminder of the skill and artistry of local craftsmen who developed their own distinctive style of carving.[1] The patterns and motifs on these stones are similar to those on contemporary sculpture in other parts of the Celtic world – panels of interlace, figures of humans and animals, religious symbols – but the art of the Govan monuments is otherwise unique. This remarkable collection bears witness to the wealth and power of the long-vanished kingdom of Strathclyde.

Strathclyde is the modern, Anglicised form of a name recorded in ancient sources as *Strat Clut* or *Strad Clud*.[2] As the name indicates, the kingdom's core territory was the *strath* or lower valley of the River Clyde. Its inhabitants were referred to by various names: *Clutinenses* (Latin: 'Clyde-folk'), *Britones* (Latin: 'Britons'), *Cumbrenses* (Latin: 'Cumbrians') and *Straecledwealas* (Old English: 'Strathclyde Welsh'). They probably called themselves *Cumbri*, meaning 'fellow-countrymen' or 'compatriots', a name related to Modern Welsh *Cymry*.[3] Both names share the same meaning and a similar pronunciation, having been formed in what was essentially the same ancestral language. This book is chiefly concerned with one aspect of the story of the *Cumbri* or 'Cumbrians', namely their relations with the Anglo-Saxons or English who dwelt beyond their southern and eastern borders.

Chronological scope

The following chapters are chiefly concerned with a 350-year period running from the middle of the eighth century to the beginning of the twelfth. This corresponds roughly to the second half of the early medieval period or 'Dark Ages'. It contains the main era of Viking raiding and colonisation (ninth to eleventh centuries), the emergence of the kingdom of Alba (late ninth to early tenth) and the Norman conquest of England (late eleventh). Earlier centuries are covered more briefly, to provide a necessary historical background for the main narrative. In Chapter 2, the origins of the kingdom of Strathclyde are discussed and the kingdom's history is traced as far as the eighth century. The same chapter deals with the earliest contacts between the Clyde Britons and their Anglo-Saxon neighbours and with the founding of the kingdom of Northumbria. This sets the scene for the first clearly documented conflict between the two peoples, an eighth-century war in which the Picts were also involved. In Chapter 3 the story reaches the Viking Age, a period of profound upheaval which saw the emergence of Strathclyde as a major political force. Two significant events of the late ninth century are highlighted: the collapse of Anglo-Saxon Northumbria and the Viking assault on Dumbarton. Subsequent chapters give detailed coverage of the tenth and eleventh centuries, both of which are fairly well documented in comparison with earlier periods. The end of the kingdom of Strathclyde is examined in Chapter 9, while Chapter 10 looks at the kingdom's re-emergence in the early twelfth century as a Scottish principality. Chapter 10 also explores the origins of the English county of Cumberland and the survival of 'Cumbric' speech and traditions on either side of the Anglo-Scottish border. For the entire period spanned by the book, the term 'early medieval' is generally preferred to 'Dark Age', chiefly because the latter can all too easily conjure negative images of barbarism. Both terms refer to a period of roughly six or seven hundred years following the collapse of the Western Roman Empire in the fifth century AD.

Terminology

Throughout this book, the people of Viking-Age Strathclyde are frequently referred to as 'Cumbrians'. In modern usage this is, of course, a term more commonly applied to the inhabitants of the English county of Cumbria. Applying the same term to a people whose kings dwelt a few miles west of Glasgow might seem puzzling, but no confusion or anachronism is intended. In this book, 'Cumbrians' is used in its early medieval sense, as a synonym for 'North Britons', rather than in relation to any modern administrative entity. In medieval chronicles in which the history of the ninth to eleventh centuries is preserved, *Cumbria* was a Latin term denoting an extensive territory ruled by the kings of Strathclyde. It was used as a collective name for all lands inhabited by the Cumbrians or North Britons and was not restricted, as it is today, to a region south of the Solway Firth. The language spoken by the Cumbrians was a Celtic language similar to Old Welsh. Specialist scholars now refer to it as 'Cumbric', to distinguish it from related languages such as Cornish, Breton and Welsh. These four languages, together with Pictish, belong to a group known as Brittonic or Brythonic because they evolved from the common speech of the Britons, the ancient inhabitants of the whole island of Britain.[4] A second group of Celtic languages includes the Gaelic speech of Ireland, Scotland and the Isle of Man. In this book, the main language of the kingdom of Strathclyde is usually referred to as Cumbric, occasionally as 'British', but never as Welsh. Although their English neighbours regarded the Cumbrians as *wealas* ('Welsh') like the Britons of Wales, it would be quite confusing if the same terminology was followed in this book. Some of the early English chroniclers did, however, distinguish the Cumbrians from the Britons of Wales by describing them as *Straecledwealas* ('Strathclyde Welsh'). This term, in its modern English form, is sometimes used by present-day historians, but has generally been avoided here.

The oldest reference to Strathclyde as a political entity is in an Irish chronicle which notes the death in 872 of a ruler described as *rex Britanorum Sratha Cluade*, 'king of the Britons of Strathclyde'.[5] Earlier references associate this king and his predecessors with a place called *Alt Clut*, 'Rock of Clyde', rather than with the *strath* or lower valley of the river. The rock in question is the distinctive twin-peaked 'volcanic plug' at Dumbarton, now the site of Dumbarton Castle. In the early medieval period a fortress on the summit of the Rock was the principal stronghold of a royal dynasty whose origins may have reached as far back as Roman times. Many historians refer to the kingdom ruled from Dumbarton as 'Strathclyde' but this name more correctly belongs to the successor kingdom that arose further upstream after the destruction of the fortress of Alt Clut in 870.[6] The earliest English text to mention Strathclyde is the *Anglo-Saxon Chronicle* (hereafter *ASC*) in a reference to Viking forces who are said to have 'often ravaged among the Picts and the Strathclyde Britons'.[7] In the same source we find the first use of 'Cumberland' as an English term for all the lands ruled by the kings of Strathclyde. The first element of 'Cumberland' probably originated as the Anglicised form of a lost Cumbric word similar to *Cymry* (pronounced 'Cum-ree'), a medieval Welsh name for the people of Wales. Although no equivalent of *ASC* has survived from the kingdom of Strathclyde, it is likely that at least one such chronicle was maintained in a major monastery within the kingdom, by scribes writing in Latin. It also seems likely that these scribes referred to their country as *Cumbria*, a Latinised form of 'Cumberland' found in later Scottish texts. Both *Cumbria* and *Cumberland*, together with Welsh *Cymry*, derive ultimately from *Combrogi*, a much older term in an ancestral tongue that was once common to all Brittonic-speaking peoples. *Combrogi* meant 'compatriots' and undoubtedly expressed a belief that those whom it encompassed belonged to one nation, regardless of where in Britain they lived. In the lands of the North Britons *Combrogi* evolved into a form from which neighbouring English-speakers derived *Cumber*, as in 'Cumber-land'.[8] When we first encounter the name Cumberland in *ASC* the context is a military campaign by an English king who ravaged the area in 945. There is no doubt that the target of this onslaught was the kingdom of Strathclyde, for the same campaign is noted in another chronicle – the Welsh Annals – as *Strat Clut vastata est a Saxonibus* ('Strathclyde was laid waste by the Saxons'). Further confirmation of the synonymity between the terms Cumbria, Cumberland and Strathclyde comes from Scotland, from the early twelfth century, when the future king David I held lordship over a large swathe of territory between the firths of Clyde and Solway. By then, the kingdom of Strathclyde had disappeared, having been absorbed into Alba, the kingdom of the Scots. Contemporary documents describe David as *princeps Cumbrensis* ('Prince of the Cumbrians') and *Cumbrensis regionis princeps* ('Prince of the Cumbrian kingdom').[9] Although nominally a subordinate of the Scottish king – his own elder brother – David ruled a large part of southern Scotland as a semi-independent principality. He commissioned a survey or 'inquest' of ecclesiastical property throughout his domain, obtaining information on church landholdings in what had once been the heartland of the kingdom of Strathclyde.[10] The accuracy of the resulting data was confirmed by five of 'the older and wiser men of all Cumbria'.[11] In spite of this type of clear evidence that Cumbria and Cumberland were synonyms for the kingdom of Strathclyde in early medieval times, some modern historians take a different view by envisaging a separate 'Cumbrian' realm centred on what later became the English county of Cumberland.[12] This is an erroneous idea based on a vision of history presented by the Scottish chronicler John of Fordun in the fourteenth century. According to Fordun, 'Cumbria' was simply the English county, ruled in the tenth century by kings who were Scottish crown-princes.[13] The basis of Fordun's scenario was comprehensively demolished in an important paper, published nearly forty years ago, which demonstrated beyond doubt that early medieval Cumbria and the kingdom of Strathclyde were one and the same.[14]

The terms 'Anglo-Saxons' and 'English' are also synonymous in early medieval contexts. Although the former appears in the title of this book, the latter is used more frequently in the following chapters. 'Anglo-Saxons' seems to have been coined in the eighth century to distinguish the descendants of Germanic settlers in Britain from the 'Old Saxons' who still dwelt in the ancestral homelands across the North Sea.[15] It is a useful term for distinguishing between the English of the fifth to eleventh centuries and those of later times. For example, 'Anglo-Saxon England' is often used as an umbrella name for the territories under English rule before the Norman conquest of 1066. Similarly, 'Anglo-Saxon Northumbria' refers to a powerful English kingdom whose kings held sway over much of northern Britain from the seventh century onwards, until their eventual overthrow by Viking warlords in the ninth. The name 'Northumbria' was also borne by this kingdom's successor, which was under Scandinavian rather than English rule. In the following chapters, 'Northumbria' usually appears without any qualifying term unless the context requires it, in which case a prefix such as 'Anglo-Saxon' or 'Anglo-Danish' is added for clarity. Beyond the northern borders of Northumbria lay what is now Scotland, although this did not become a recognisable political entity until the end of the Viking Age. The great medieval kingdom of Scotland was preceded by the kingdom of Alba which emerged in the ninth century under the leadership of Gaelic-speaking monarchs who ruled a mixed population of Scots and Picts. These two peoples had formerly been politically and culturally distinct but, from the eighth century onwards, they began to converge. After c.900, the notion of a separate Pictish identity had almost disappeared and all the people of Alba had become 'Scots'.[16] It is therefore accurate to describe the rulers of tenth-century Alba as 'Scottish' kings, even if their ancestry only a few generations earlier had been Pictish. A measure of caution does, however, need to be shown when the terms 'Britain' and 'British' are used in an early medieval context. No political connotation whatsoever can be attached to 'Britain', a purely geographical term in any historical period before the modern era. Similarly, although 'British' and 'Britons' are now used as umbrella terms for all the inhabitants of Britain, this was not the case a thousand years ago. To anyone displaying an English or Scottish identity in those days, the Britons were a distinct group who had their own language and culture. In contemporary Latin chronicles they appear as *Britones* or *Britanni*, while Gaelic texts refer to them as *Breatain*. At the beginning of the eleventh century, the last remaining kingdoms of the Britons lay in Wales and on the Clyde. The inhabitants of these areas were, respectively, the Cymry and the Cumbri or, to their English neighbours, the Welsh and Strathclyde Welsh. A tenth-century poem from Wales suggests that, to some extent, both groups still thought of themselves as a single nation sharing a common language.[17] Such sentiments did not, however, deter Welsh soldiers from joining English allies in a rampage across Strathclyde in 945. The campaign in question took place at the height of the Viking Age, a period in which new cultures and new identities arrived in Britain and Ireland. The Vikings themselves were warriors and colonists of Scandinavian origin, mostly from Norway and Denmark, who sailed abroad – in search of loot and territory – from the eighth century to the twelfth. Some of them are identified in the early chronicles as 'Northmen' (Norwegians) and 'Danes' but historians are increasingly sceptical about the accuracy of these ethnic distinctions.[18] In this book, Norwegian Vikings are referred to by the conventional term 'Norse', while those who colonised Ireland are distinguished as 'Hiberno-Norse'. The label 'Danes' is likewise applied to Viking forces who took control of Northumbria in the late ninth century and whose leaders were regarded by contemporary observers as being of Danish origin.

Fordun and Strathclyde

The erroneous belief that early medieval Cumbria and Strathclyde were not one and the same can, as noted above, be traced back to John of Fordun in the fourteenth century. Fordun is the source of two other misconceptions, namely that Strathclyde was part of the kingdom of Alba from the end of the ninth century, and that all kings of Strathclyde thereafter were not Britons but Scots. Unfortunately, his depiction of 'Cumbria' as a subjugated territory under Scottish rule has profoundly influenced the views of modern historians. He asserted that any individual described as 'king of the Cumbrians' in the tenth and eleventh centuries should be seen as a prince of the Scottish royal house and as heir-apparent to the throne of Alba.[19] The kings in question were actually those of Strathclyde, but this historical fact did not fit with Fordun's vision. He described a system of royal succession called 'tanistry' in which the tanist or designated heir of a kingdom gained experience of government by ruling a subordinate realm. Central to this vision was Fordun's belief that tenth- and eleventh-century 'Cumbria' was the area known in his own time as the English county of Cumberland. He claimed that this had been a subordinate realm under the authority of the kings of England, by whom Scottish princes were permitted to govern it in exchange for an oath of allegiance. Some modern historians, while believing that Fordun misunderstood the broader meaning of the term 'Cumbria', have nonetheless accepted the rest of his testimony as reliable. For them, his depiction of Cumbrian kings as princes of Alba must be an accurate reflection of his sources. This is why the tanistry scenario has long formed part of the bedrock of modern scholarship on Strathclyde, and why many people assume that the kingdom was little more than a province of Alba from c.900 onwards. Fortunately, not everyone puts so much faith in Fordun. The doubters are right to be sceptical, for there is no reason to believe that he approached his sources objectively.[20] None of the older chronicles written in the tenth to twelfth centuries implies that the kings of Strathclyde were Scottish princes. On the contrary, they indicate that the land of the Cumbrians – including Clydesdale itself – remained independent until the eleventh century. Only one period of Scottish domination in the tenth century is recorded but this was fairly brief and seems to have had no major impact on the system of royal succession in either Strathclyde or Alba.[21] Fordun is not, in fact, a reliable witness for any period before his own time. His information on the Cumbrian kings seems rather to reflect his own preferred version of the past.[22] Much of what he wrote about these kings is linked to his identification of one of them, a certain Owain, as the son of a Scottish king called Domnall who died in 900. While there is absolutely no warrant for making the identification in the first place, it is possible that Fordun found it in a work compiled some years before his own, a source that evidently formed the basis for his chronicle.[23] In reality, Owain's father was a king of Strathclyde rather than a king of Alba and would have borne a Cumbric form of the Welsh name *Dyfnwal* rather than the Gaelic name *Domnall*. An older Scottish source, the *Chronicle of the Kings of Alba*, places the death of *Doneualdus* 'king of the Britons' between 906 and 915 and this may be Owain's father.[24] While it now seems logical to identify father and son as Britons rather than as Scots, it plainly did not suit Fordun's purposes to do so.

Sources: the English chronicles

Fordun's chronicle is not a reliable source for the history of Strathclyde. It was, in any case, compiled in the late fourteenth century, three hundred years after the kingdom's demise. More useful are a number of older texts written when the kingdom was still in existence or shortly afterwards. These are a mixed bag of chronicles, poems, charters, stories and genealogies, none of which was produced by the Cumbrians themselves. The historical value of these texts depends largely on the age and provenance of the manuscripts in which they are preserved. Some, for instance, survive only in very late copies. Others survive in older manuscripts riddled with scribal errors. In some cases the work itself is less concerned with history than with promoting political or ecclesiastical interests or, in the case of poetry, with literary techniques such as rhyme and alliteration. One of the fundamental truths of early medieval studies is that none of the so-called 'primary sources' can be taken at face value. All must be approached with caution, even after having been thoroughly dissected by specialist scholars.

This book, of course, is not only about the Strathclyde Britons or 'Cumbrians'. It is also about the Anglo-Saxons or English, a people with whom the Cumbrians had a great deal of contact during the Viking Age. Indeed, much of our information on Strathclyde in this period comes from texts of English origin. Of these, the earliest is the *Anglo-Saxon Chronicle* (*ASC*), a collection of year-entries or annals from 60 BC to the twelfth century. The first version was written in Wessex, the kingdom of the West Saxons, in the late ninth century.[25] Most early medieval chroniclers wrote in Latin but the scribes of *ASC* wrote in Old English, their own everyday speech. The West Saxons continued to update the text with new annals during the tenth century and onwards into the eleventh, by which time a number of copies had been made. Sadly, the original chronicle no longer exists, but some of the copies have survived. These had been distributed among various English monasteries to be maintained and updated and, inevitably, their annals often reflect local interests rather than those of Wessex. Of the nine survivors, the oldest is the 'A' text, otherwise known as the Parker or Winchester Chronicle, a manuscript written in various hands from the late ninth to the late eleventh centuries.[26] It forms the basis of most modern editions of *ASC* and is generally regarded as the standard version. Although it has a geographical bias towards West Saxon affairs, the 'A' text is nonetheless where we find *Straecledwealas*, the Old English name for the Cumbrians or 'Strathclyde Welsh'. However, for a generally more northern perspective we turn to the 'D' text, a manuscript of the mid-eleventh century whose compilers had access to a separate chronicle from Northumbria.[27] Drawing on this now-lost Northumbrian source, the scribes of 'D' were able to give detailed information on contacts between the West Saxons and the peoples of northern Britain. A similar perspective is found in the 'E' text, a manuscript written at Peterborough in the early twelfth century to replace an earlier copy lost in a fire.[28] Known as the 'Laud Chronicle', it can be used alongside 'D' as a source for northern information not otherwise found in 'A'. Sometime around 980, a Latin translation of *ASC* was written by Aethelweard, a high-ranking English nobleman connected to the royal family of Wessex. Sadly, the only known copy of his *Chronicon* was severely damaged by fire in 1731. Fragments still survive but much of the original manuscript was destroyed, leaving modern scholars dependent on an edition of the complete text published in the sixteenth century.[29] As a contemporary witness of tenth-century events, in some of which he played a prominent role, Aethelweard is obviously a valuable source. However, his *Chronicon* was based on a version of *ASC* similar to the 'A' text and therefore lacks the northern detail found in 'D' and 'E'.

In addition to *ASC*, the English sources include a number of chronicles written in Latin during the twelfth century which provide useful detail on relations between the kings of Strathclyde and their English neighbours. Among these is a collection of annals begun in the closing years of the eleventh century and completed between 1140 and 1145. It is usually attributed to John of Worcester, one of its principal compilers, although an alternative attribution to another Worcester monk called 'Florence' was popular until fairly recently.[30] This chronicle traces the history of the world from the Creation onwards and, although drawing heavily on *ASC*, it includes material from several sources that are no longer extant. Among its annals are points of detail relating to Strathclyde not found in the equivalent year-entries in *ASC*. These were almost certainly drawn from lost Northumbrian chronicles, probably originating at Durham where the monks of St Cuthbert of Lindisfarne established their headquarters in 995. Thus, although John and his colleagues were writing in the twelfth century, they were consulting older texts compiled much closer in time and place to the era of the Cumbrian kings.[31] The Durham monks themselves have bequeathed a number of texts that add considerably to our understanding of northern history in the Viking Age. Central to their work was the story of their own community from its seventh-century beginnings to the founding of Durham Cathedral. The community traced its origins back to the Anglo-Saxon kingdom of Northumbria, of which Cuthbert of Lindisfarne (died 687) was a revered patron saint. He was an older contemporary and fellow-countryman of Bede, a monk at Jarrow on the River Tyne, whose *Historia Ecclesiastica Gentis Anglorum* ('Ecclesiastical History of the English People') is one of the key sources cited in the second chapter of this book. Bede had much to say about Cuthbert and wrote two hagiographical accounts of his life, thus playing an important part in the beginnings of a saintly cult. The monks at the monastery on Lindisfarne developed the cult still further by promoting Cuthbert as the premier saint of northern Britain.[32] This devotion spread throughout Anglo-Saxon Northumbria, in churches and monasteries in every part of the kingdom. In 793, however, the entire community reeled in shock when Lindisfarne was brutally attacked by Viking raiders. In the wake of this distressing event, Cuthbert's holy remains were removed to keep them from harm. A safe repository proved elusive and the relics were moved around Northumbria for almost a hundred years until, in 882, the monks settled at Chester-le-Street on the River Wear. In 995, they moved to a new base at Durham where the tomb of the saint can still be seen in the eastern apse of the cathedral. In the early twelfth century, a Durham monk wrote a history of the community from its origins to 1096. Modern scholars refer to this work as *Libellus de exordio* ('Tract on the Origins') or as *Historia Dunelmensis ecclesiae* ('History of the Church of Durham').[33] The latter title, hereafter abbreviated to *HDE*, is the one most commonly cited in the following chapters. As with John of Worcester's chronicle, *HDE* gives a number of interesting details about the kingdom of Strathclyde. For example, it identifies by name the 'king of the Cumbrians' who fought in the great battle of Brunanburh in 937. The oldest surviving manuscript of *HDE* was written between 1100 and 1115 but its writer remains anonymous. However, a later copy written in the twelfth century identifies the principal author of the original work as a Durham monk called Symeon and this attribution may be correct.[34] Symeon is also regarded as the main compiler of *Historia Regum Anglorum et Dacorum* ('History of the Kings of the English and Danes'), a collection of annals and other material drawn from

various sources.[35] The sources of *Historia Regum* (hereafter *HRA*) include identifiable works such as *HDE*, John of Worcester's chronicle and a northern
version of *ASC*, together with a number of texts whose existence can only be
inferred. Among the lost materials was a set of Northumbrian annals containing
information not found elsewhere but providing unique insights into the history
of northern Britain in the ninth to eleventh centuries.[36] Two other Durham
texts, the eleventh-century *Historia de Sancto Cuthberto* ('History of St
Cuthbert') and *De Obsessione Dunelmi* ('On the Siege of Durham') of c.1100,
are also cited in the following chapters, but the twelfth-century tract *De Primo
Saxonum Adventu* ('On the Coming of the English') has not been used.

From southern England in the twelfth century come the works of William of
Malmesbury and Henry of Huntingdon, both of whom wrote detailed histories
up to their own time.[37] Like their contemporaries at Worcester and Durham,
William and Henry provide unique information relating to Strathclyde and
must have had access to older texts that no longer survive. The challenge facing
modern scholars is the value of such information when its very uniqueness puts
its reliability in doubt.[38] This applies to any twelfth-century text containing
historical details that cannot be verified in an earlier source. Not even the
Durham material, written at no great geographical distance from what had once
been the southern frontier of Strathclyde, is immune from such scrutiny.
Scepticism inevitably deepens when we turn to texts produced even later, in the
thirteenth and fourteenth centuries, for we then move into a period that
produced the fictionalised histories of Fordun. Some writers of this later period
are nonetheless worthy of consideration, an example being Roger of Wendover
who wrote a chronicle called *Flores historiarum* ('The Flowers of History') in
the early thirteenth century.[39] Roger is our source for one small but significant
piece of information relating to contact between a king of Strathclyde and an
English counterpart. By then, of course, the Clyde kingdom was already a
distant memory and its history was ripe for manipulation.[40] Fordun, as we have
seen, repackaged its kings as Scottish princes because it suited his purposes to
do so. His contemporaries in England were at liberty to make similar alterations
of their own.

Sources: Ireland, Wales and Scotland

The Celtic areas of Britain and Ireland have bequeathed a rich assemblage of
early medieval literature ranging from annals and genealogies to poetry and
hagiography. It is thus a matter of regret that so little of this material is from

Strathclyde. No chronicles or king-lists survive from the Cumbrian kingdom. No hagiographical account of any local saint written before the kingdom's demise in the eleventh century has been preserved. A twelfth-century *vita* or 'life' of Kentigern or Mungo, the patron saint of Glasgow, does seem to incorporate older material but it remains a difficult and controversial text.[41] Snippets of information on other early saints who supposedly founded churches and monasteries in Strathclyde are scattered among a variety of later Scottish works but their historical value is questionable. A single stanza of heroic poetry, probably composed at Dumbarton in the seventh century, appears in a collection of medieval Welsh verse of uncertain date and provenance.[42] This fragment may be the only surviving literature from the kingdom of the Cumbrians, which is why so much of the raw data for this book comes from other lands.

The English chronicles have already been discussed. Our focus now switches to sources of Celtic origin, and we begin with the Irish annals. Although these obviously have a primary focus on Ireland, they provide a wealth of information on Britain too, much of it not repeated in texts of English, Scottish or Welsh origin. Two of the Irish annalistic compilations are of particular interest: the *Annals of Tigernach* (hereafter *AT*) and the *Annals of Ulster* (hereafter *AU*).[43] Although these survive, respectively, in manuscripts of the fourteenth and fifteenth centuries, both are based on much older chronicles and are regarded by modern specialists as generally reliable. Many of their year-entries are the same, a clear indication that their respective compilers had access to similar source material, but the two compilations are sufficiently distinct to show that they do not derive from a single work.[44] Each took information from older chronicles, now no longer extant, of which one was a set of annals compiled at the Hebridean monastery of Iona. Many of the entries in *AU* and *AT* relating to northern Britain were taken from this 'Iona Chronicle', especially for the period up to c.750, while those for the ninth to eleventh centuries seem to have originated in Ireland. This means that although both *AU* and *AT* note the deaths of two tenth-century kings of Strathclyde, there is no indication that the information came from a written source in Britain, still less from a chronicle compiled in the Cumbrian kingdom itself. News of both deaths may have come directly to Ireland via travellers passing to and fro on the seaways in between. Other Irish chronicles giving useful data on northern Britain in this period are the *Annals of Clonmacnoise* (hereafter *AClon*), the *Annals of the Four Masters* (*AFM*), the *Annals of Inisfallen* and the *Fragmentary Annals of Ireland* (*FAI*). All four contain items of unique information not found in *AU* or *AT*. *AClon* is a seventeenth-century translation, into English, of a chronicle traditionally believed to be a product of the monastery of Clonmacnoise in County Offaly.[45] The original chronicle is lost but the translator's description of it as an 'old Irish book' indicates that its year-entries were written in Irish Gaelic not Latin. Although the translation is a rather curious work containing unfamiliar spellings of names, it is thought to be a fair rendering of its source and a useful witness of early medieval events. Also from the seventeenth century comes *AFM*, the four 'masters' of its title being its principal compilers.[46] As with other works produced in this period, *AFM* relied on older chronicles for information from early medieval times and its entries have much in common with those in *AU* and *AT*. From the fifteenth century come the *Annals of Inisfallen* and *FAI*, the former a chronicle originally begun in the 1100s, the latter surviving now in a seventeenth-century copy.[47] Of the two, *FAI* is of particular interest in the present context because it contains the only account of a military alliance in which the Cumbrians of Strathclyde agreed to help the English against the Vikings. Some modern scholars take a sceptical view of this account because it appears in a narrative tale added to a year-entry, a common feature of *FAI* that sets it apart from other Irish chronicles.[48] Although such stories do tend to be of uncertain provenance, they provide information not found elsewhere and are therefore worthy of consideration, even if their historical value is sometimes difficult to assess.

Turning now to Scotland, we possess no major collection of annals similar to those produced in Ireland. The so-called 'Iona Chronicle', commonly assumed to be an important source used by the Irish annalists, would have been a significant Scottish example had it survived to the present day. It is indeed unfortunate that no chronicles from the great monasteries of medieval Scotland have been preserved. We are left instead with a number of texts in various formats and of varying reliability. For the period covered by this book, one of the oldest and most reliable is the *Chronicle of the Kings of Alba* (hereafter *CKA*), a work of the tenth to twelfth centuries now preserved in a manuscript of the fourteenth.[49] As its name suggests, *CKA* is a record of early Scottish kings, beginning with Cináed mac Ailpín in the ninth century and ending with his namesake Cináed mac Mail Coluim in the tenth. Each king's reign is summarised in a brief account of important events including major battles and royal deaths. The original chronicle seems to have been compiled within a decade of the death of Cináed mac Mail Coluim in 995 so we are clearly dealing with a source of potentially high value. Like all ancient texts it does, however, require careful handling, not least because it has undergone several stages of transmission from original version to surviving copy.[50] It nevertheless provides unique insights into

relations between the kings of Alba and their neighbours, including those on
the Clyde. Somewhat more problematic is the *Prophecy of Berchan*, a long poem
on early Scottish kings which partly overlaps with *CKA* in its coverage.[51]
Berchan was a sixth-century Irish abbot but the poem itself was probably
composed in the twelfth century, its cryptic verses supposedly reporting his
prophetic visions. The prophecies are, in fact, retrospective allusions to events
that had already happened. Each verse refers to, but does not name, a Pictish or
Scottish king of the ninth to eleventh centuries, with a rather esoteric account
of his reign. Some parts make little sense at all, while others are corrupt, so the
work as a whole is somewhat frustrating. Nonetheless, despite its difficulties it
remains a useful source of early medieval Scottish history and, like *CKA*, makes
a number of interesting references to Strathclyde.

When the *Anglo-Saxon Chronicle* referred to the Clyde Britons as *Straecledwealas*,
'Strathclyde Welsh', it acknowledged their affinity with the inhabitants of Wales.
The Welsh themselves recognised this ancestral connection, for many of their
earliest poems and stories revered as illustrious heroes a number of North British
kings of the sixth and seventh centuries. Some of the most famous poems circulating among the royal courts of Wales in the Viking Age and later were
supposedly composed by northern bards such as Taliesin and Aneirin in the
period 550 to 650.[52] One verse attributed to Aneirin, who seems to have been
associated with the kingdom of Gododdin around Edinburgh, celebrates a
victory won by a king of the Clyde Britons over the Scots in 642 or 643. It is
almost certainly the sole surviving fragment of a longer poem composed at the
victor's royal fortress on Dumbarton Rock. No other poetry survives from the
heartlands of the Clyde kingdom, if indeed such literature was ever written
down. From further south, in territory ruled by the kings of Strathclyde in
Viking times, comes another stray verse also erroneously attributed to Aneirin
and likewise preserved in Wales. This curious item, apparently a child's lullaby,
appears to refer to the Lodore Cascade, a spectacular waterfall on the River
Derwent in what is now the Lake District in north-west England.[53] Whether it
was composed during the period of Strathclyde rule in the tenth and eleventh
centuries or in some earlier era of Cumbric speech has yet to be established.
From Wales itself a major chronicle known as *Annales Cambriae* or 'Welsh
Annals' has survived in a number of copies, the oldest being a compilation of the
tenth century preserved in a manuscript of the twelfth.[54]. Other, later manuscripts continue the sequence of annals beyond the tenth century to the
thirteenth. In comparison with the major Irish chronicles, the coverage of
Annales Cambriae is somewhat patchy, with brief entries and many gaps.

Although the history of northern Britain receives scant attention, the few entries relating to Strathclyde are valuable nonetheless. Among the other Welsh texts is *Historia Brittonum* ('History of the Britons'), a curious work of the early ninth century that appears to be a compendium of historical and legendary lore from a variety of sources.[55] Its information on a number of North British kings of the sixth and seventh centuries makes it a potentially useful resource for Chapter 2 of this book, but it is less helpful than we would wish. Some of these kings also appear in Welsh genealogies or 'pedigrees' which trace the ancestry of key figures from history and literature. Most of the pedigrees are fairly short, consisting of only a few generations, but one of the North British ones stands out as being far longer than the rest. It traces the paternal descent of Rhun, a ninth-century king of Strathclyde, through many generations back to shadowy forefathers who ruled from Dumbarton Rock in the fifth and sixth centuries.[56] Although some of Rhun's ancestors are unknown outside his pedigree, the historical existence of others can be verified by entries in the Irish annals recording their deaths. Either Rhun himself or his father Artgal was the first ruler of the new kingdom of Strathclyde after the Viking siege of Dumbarton in 870 which brought the old realm of Alt Clut to an end. Unfortunately, there is no pedigree for the period after 870 when the royal dynasty transferred its main centre of power to Govan, so the names of Rhun's descendants and successors have to be sought elsewhere.

Sources: hagiography

Hagiography was a type of religious literature, common throughout medieval Christendom, in which the achievements and virtues of famous saints were eulogised. A small number of hagiographical texts are cited in the bibliography at the end of this book, these being selected because they contain useful information on Strathclyde. Most hagiographical writing conformed to a standard template, namely the *vita* or 'life' of an ecclesiastical figure revered as a saint by his or her devotees. The subject was usually the founder of one or more monasteries that existed in the hagiographer's own time and who, in life, would normally have held the rank of bishop, abbot or abbess. Western Christendom produced a large number of saints and many were honoured with *vitae*, not all of which have survived in complete form. Some were produced within a few years of the saint's death, while others appeared much later – in some cases hundreds of years after the lifetime of the saint. To the present-day reader, a *vita* might seem to offer an authentic glimpse of the period when the saint was alive, but this is often a false hope. For a start, a hagiographical work cannot be described as biography in the modern sense.[57] The author of a *vita* was less interested in writing a factual life-story than in creating an idealised portrait of a paragon of Christian virtue. Moreover, the author probably had close links with a church or monastery founded by the saint and, in all likelihood, had been commissioned to write the *vita* as a publicity exercise for the place itself. Thus, a twelfth-century abbot or bishop might seek to promote the interests of his own monastery by commissioning a *vita* to enhance the fame of a long-dead founder. This was also a useful tactic for attracting pilgrims to the cult-centre of a saint, or for making one group of monasteries look more important than a rival group founded by a different saint. For the purposes of this book, the most useful hagiographical texts are two *vitae* of Kentigern, produced at Glasgow in the 1100s to honour a saint who died five hundred years earlier, and a tenth-century *vita* of St Cathroe of Metz who died c.971. One of the Kentigern *vitae* only partially survives, in a manuscript of the early fifteenth century. Its author is unknown but it was commissioned by Herbert, bishop of Glasgow from 1147 to 1164, and for this reason is usually referred to as the 'Herbertian Life'. The other *vita* survives in complete form in a manuscript of c.1200 but the version preferred by modern editors is in a manuscript from later in the thirteenth century. It was commissioned by Bishop Jocelin in the final quarter of the twelfth century and was written by his namesake Jocelin of Furness. Although both *vitae* deal mainly with the period of Kentigern's lifetime in the late sixth and early seventh centuries, their production is closely connected with the Scottish conquest of Strathclyde five hundred years later.[58] The *vita* of Cathroe, a Scottish saint who ended his days as abbot of Metz in France, is the work of a monk of Metz whose name was Reiman or Ousmann. It was written sometime around 980, just a few years after Cathroe's death. Sadly, the original tenth-century manuscript has not survived so scholars usually rely on a copy published by John Colgan, an Irish Franciscan friar, in 1645.[59] The *vita* includes an account of Cathroe's pilgrimage to the Continent, a journey that brought him face-to-face with a number of kings as he travelled southward through Britain. One of these was Dyfnwal, king of Strathclyde, whom the *vita* describes as a kinsman of the saint. Dyfnwal offered Cathroe the hospitality of his court and safe passage to his border, from where the pilgrim travelled onward to York, stronghold of the Viking rulers of Northumbria. In spite of its value as a contemporary source, this *vita* has often been neglected by modern historians, perhaps because it belongs to a genre traditionally regarded with scepticism. Also part of the same genre, but treated here as distinct from the *vitae* of Cathroe and Kentigern, are a number of shorter hagiographical works called *lectiones* ('readings'). An important collection of these is the *Aberdeen Breviary*, a sixteenth-century calendar in which information about Scottish saints was written under their anniversaries or 'feast days'. The *Breviary*, commissioned by the bishop of Aberdeen, was intended to be a definitive compendium of hagiography relating to all saints who had a connection with Scotland. Its sources included earlier *vitae*, most of which are now lost, together with oral legends relating to shrines and cult-centres. Among the saints commemorated are several obscure figures who had connections with Strathclyde but of whom we know almost nothing outside their *lectiones*.[60]

Sources: non-Insular texts

The term 'non-Insular' in this context refers to sources that were not written in the British Isles. The *vita* of St Cathroe is one such text, having been written at Metz in France. It is one of a small number of non-Insular sources providing information of relevance to the history of Strathclyde. One aspect of Cathroe's *vita* that makes it so useful to present-day historians is the fact that it was written within a few decades of the events it describes. The same can also be said of the chronicle of Ralph Glaber, a Burgundian monk who lived in the first half of the eleventh century. Although Ralph's *Historiarum Libri Quinque* ('History in Five Books') was primarily concerned with the ecclesiastical affairs of tenth- and eleventh-century France, it includes some interesting and unique references to Britain.[61] Indeed, Ralph is our only source for certain dealings between the kings of England and Alba that have a bearing on the last phase of Strathclyde's existence as an independent realm. Both he and Cathroe's hagiographer were geographically separated from Britain but fairly contemporary with the events they wrote about. This is not the case with a large group of non-Insular texts known collectively as the Norse or Icelandic sagas. These narrative tales deal with people and events of the Viking period but were written no earlier than the thirteenth century, predominantly in Iceland. Contrary to popular belief, they do not appear to preserve a record of real events of Viking times but seem rather to be imaginative tales composed by later storytellers.[62] Their creators were probably seeking to portray a nostalgic image of the past, often by using real figures from the ninth to eleventh centuries as the main characters in a story. Nevertheless, many historians in the nineteenth and twentieth centuries regarded the sagas as authentic sources, using them alongside the Insular chronicles to build a detailed picture of Viking activity in Britain and Ireland. Little trust is placed in the sagas today. They are now regarded as vivid, action-packed tales rather than as reliable historical texts, hence their absence from the bibliography at the end of this book.

Sources: charters

The final group of sources comprises legal documents relating to the ownership of territory or to the bestowing of rights and privileges. These are mostly in the form of charters confirming land-grants, the majority of which are 'diplomas' or royal charters issued by kings. A similar document was the 'writ' in which the rights and restrictions of certain individuals were defined by a king or high-ranking lord. Some charters and writs survive in their original form, while others are known only from later copies. Detailed study of these early legal texts is a scholarly discipline in its own right and much meticulous work has been done on understanding them. For historians the key issue is authenticity, especially where a document purports to give useful information about a particular king. Authentication by specialists is indeed crucial, for analysis has shown that some supposedly early charters were written much later, to provide fake evidence in disputes over land-ownership or to support a dubious claim. Under such scrutiny, the documents that have been identified as genuine become primary sources of the highest value. They can, for instance, give insights into the mechanisms of government in an age when loyal service to a king or lord was rewarded with land and privileges. Moreover, a charter issued at a place far from a king's core domain might tell us something about the real extent of his authority. Similarly, a charter's list of the dignitaries who witnessed it might include subordinate rulers who can thus be identified as vassals of the king who made the gift. Charters were issued by a number of Anglo-Saxon kings in the period covered by this book and some of these documents identify subordinate kings by name.[63] Two charters issued by the West Saxon king Athelstan are of special interest here because they appear to have been witnessed by a king of Strathclyde. Another charter, from the late tenth century, was witnessed by an individual who was almost certainly this same Cumbrian king's grandson. From the following century comes a fascinating document known as 'Gospatric's Writ', a charter relating to lands on the south side of the Solway Firth. It was issued by Gospatric, an English lord, who observes that these lands had formerly been under 'Cumbrian' control. In other words, they had been part of the kingdom of Strathclyde. As with the three earlier charters, Gospatric's Writ is discussed elsewhere in this book.

Whether or not the kings of Strathclyde issued their own charters is hard to say. Their English and Scottish neighbours certainly did, so perhaps they followed suit. If so, no such documents have survived. What we do possess is a survey or 'inquest' of ecclesiastical landholdings in what had once been the Cumbrian kingdom. As previously mentioned, this was commissioned by the Scottish prince David in the early twelfth century, a generation or more after his father's conquest of Strathclyde. The inquest is discussed more fully in Chapter 10 but here its value as a primary source can be acknowledged. David intended it to be a survey of ecclesiastical lands within *regio Cumbrensis*, 'the Cumbrian kingdom', a large area ruled by him as a semi-independent principality within the realm of Alba. What the inquest shows is the extent of the erstwhile kingdom of Strathclyde as perceived by David and the Scottish bishops of Glasgow in the early 1100s.

2

EARLY CONTACTS

Damnonii

The Roman conquest of Britain began in AD 43 with a full-scale invasion launched from Gaul (France). Within forty years, the entire southern half of the island had become part of the Roman Empire. The native Britons in the conquered area were assimilated and their lands garrisoned by imperial troops. By AD 79, Roman rule extended as far north as the isthmus between the firths of Forth and Clyde. Military campaigns beyond the Firth of Forth were undertaken in the early 80s by Agricola, the imperial governor, but failed to achieve long-lasting territorial gains. Other northern campaigns in the second and third centuries delivered similarly poor returns despite massive investment of resources, even on those occasions when the emperor himself took command. One outcome of this lack of success was that the peoples dwelling beyond the Forth–Clyde isthmus remained largely unconquered throughout the period of Roman rule in Britain.[1]

Early in the second century, probably in 122, work began on the construction of a huge stone wall between the Solway Firth and the mouth of the River Tyne. The project was commissioned by the emperor Hadrian as a physical embodiment of the imperial frontier, although how far it was intended to serve as a defensive line is debatable. As a display of Roman power it was, however, undoubtedly impressive. It functioned as the Empire's most northerly border for the next three hundred years, except for a brief interlude after the Antonine Wall was built across the Forth–Clyde isthmus. Unlike Hadrian's great monument of stone, the Antonine Wall was constructed in turf, which is why so little of it is visible today. It was garrisoned for a mere twenty years before being abandoned in the 160s.[2]

Between the two walls dwelt a population of native Britons who seem to have retained some measure of independence from Rome. Their status vis-à-vis the imperial administration is hard to discern but they appear to have had a stable relationship with the Roman army after their subjugation in the late first century, right up to the crises of the late 300s. They may have served as a 'buffer' between Roman Britain and the unconquered peoples further north, receiving payment or privileges as a reward. At times, no doubt, their relationship with the Empire broke down and old hostilities were rekindled, but there is no indication that they were accustomed to revolt.[3]

A map based on data compiled by the second-century geographer Ptolemy shows four large groupings of Britons in the 'intervallate' region between the two Roman walls. On the east, the Votadini probably inhabited large parts of Lothian and Berwickshire, although their territory may have reached as far south as Hadrian's Wall. Their immediate neighbours to the south-west were the Selgovae, a people whose heartland seems to have been Tweeddale. On the west, the Novantae lived in what is now the administrative area of Dumfries and Galloway. North of the Novantae, in the lower valley of the River Clyde, dwelt a people called Damnonii (or Dumnonii). How the four intervallate groupings came into being is unknown. It is possible that each was an amalgamation of smaller groups who, by force or mutual agreement, merged together to form large confederacies.[4] Within the intervallate zone a number of *loci* or places of importance are mentioned by Ptolemy. In the territory of the Damnonii, one such place was *Alauna*, a settlement or power-centre whose name means 'rocky place' in Brittonic, the ancestral language of the Britons.[5] The map based on Ptolemy's data suggests that *Alauna* lay slightly north of the Firth of Clyde, where the obvious candidates are the Iron Age fort on Carman Hill and the towering mass of Dumbarton Rock. At Carman, the site consists of a small enclosure, now defined by boulders, nestling within a larger enclosure marked by an encircling rampart. Although no archaeological excavation has yet taken place, the overall character of the fort suggests that it was a major settlement of the Damnonii. It may have been their chief centre of power in pre-Roman times, eventually being eclipsed by Dumbarton in the late Roman period or shortly after.[6] Either site might be the *Alauna* of Ptolemy, assuming that this name has been placed correctly on the map. Both sites could be described as 'rocky', so the name might even have been transferred from Carman to Dumbarton, especially if the latter replaced the former as the main Damnonian power-base.

The imposing bulk of Dumbarton Rock guards a river-confluence where the Clyde is joined by the Leven, the eponymous river of the Lennox district. The Rock's twin summits are a familiar sight to modern travellers on the busy A8 highway running along the opposite bank of the Clyde. On a clear day the Rock can even be seen from the Erskine Bridge four miles upstream. Dumbarton has

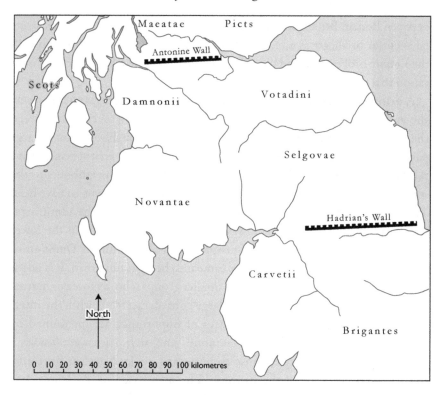

MAP 2 The North Britons in the Roman period

the honour of being the oldest continuously-occupied fortress in Britain and is today the site of a large castle, the latest in a series of strongholds reaching back through more than a thousand years of recorded history. Nothing of the ancient stronghold that preceded the castle is visible today but something of its character was revealed by an archaeological excavation in the 1970s. The fortress of the late Roman and early medieval periods probably occupied both summits and was defended by timber ramparts. Its occupants included people of high status who imported luxury goods such as Mediterranean pottery.[7] In strategic terms, these folk were the guardians of Clydesdale, controlling trade along the lower reaches of the river as well as access to the Firth of Clyde and the western seaways. This would have made them useful to the Roman Empire as friendly neighbours, not least because their lands bordered those of the Picts and Scots who emerged in the third and fourth centuries as fierce enemies of Rome. The Pictish heartlands lay north of the Forth–Clyde isthmus in unconquered territory beyond the Antonine Wall, while the Scots dwelt further west in Argyll and the Hebrides. Unlike the Picts and Britons, who spoke similar Brittonic languages, the Scots were Gaelic-speakers like the Irish, with whom they shared the seaways between Argyll and north-east Ireland. Attacks by Pictish, Scottish and Irish raiders on the coastlands south of Hadrian's Wall began to pose a serious threat to the security of Roman Britain from the late third century onwards. The occupants of Dumbarton Rock may have been expected to confront these predatory bands on Rome's behalf.[8]

Anglo-Saxons

Roman rule in Britain began to collapse in the late fourth century. A series of troop-withdrawals by ambitious generals seeking power on the European mainland depleted the island's imperial garrison to perilously low levels. Moreover, the Empire's ability to divert military and economic resources to outlying provinces began to weaken. At some point in the early fifth century, the reins of government in Britain passed to, or were seized by, a Romanised native elite in the southern part of the island. To what extent these Britons maintained a semblance of centralised authority is unknown. Given the archaeological evidence for economic downturn in the ensuing decades, it seems likely that the post-imperial leaders competed with one another for a diminishing pool of resources. Rather than strive for political unity they seem to have established themselves as independent kings in areas where their authority and status were already acknowledged by local populations. All of this would have happened against a backdrop of increasing political and economic uncertainty.[9] Raids by barbarian groups from outside the former imperial borders presented the most immediate threat, as had been the case for the late Roman administration in the fourth century. Roman officials had been able to rely on military assistance from other parts of the Empire but this was not an option in post-imperial Britain. The alternative chosen by the native leaders was to hire groups of barbarian raiders as mercenaries who would then fight off the rest. This was a tried-and-tested strategy that had been used by the Romans themselves. It offered a quick solution to a serious military problem. The barbarians hired by the Britons were Angles, Saxons, Jutes and Frisians from the coastlands of northern Germany. Attracted by promises of cash and land, they arrived in substantial numbers, bringing their families with them. This kind of resettlement of mercenaries and their dependents had long been standard practice in the Western Roman Empire and had often proved effective. In fourth-century Gaul, for example, the Roman authorities had bolstered their fading military strength by inviting Franks and other Germanic peoples to settle in vulnerable areas. In Britain, too, the Late

Roman garrison had been supplemented by barbarian warbands from outside the imperial borders. The Angles, Saxons, Jutes and others who arrived in the fifth century were hired primarily to fight the Picts, Scots and Irish. For a while, at least, these mercenaries performed their job adequately, until the growing political and economic turmoil created new opportunities for their leaders. Before the end of the century they began to revolt against their employers. By c.500, these 'Anglo-Saxons' were already seizing territory from the Britons and establishing kingdoms of their own.[10]

The Anglo-Saxons spoke a Germanic language which was the ancestor of modern English. It distinguished them from the Britons, many of whom probably used Latin as well as their own Celtic language in everyday speech. Relations between the two populations were not, however, defined by 'ethnic' tensions based on genetic heritage. Archaeological evidence, especially from southern Britain where Anglo-Saxon settlement was most concentrated, suggests that the new political divisions of the fifth century had a more complex set of origins. One factor was an individual's choice of cultural affiliation. Many Britons, it seems, chose to discard their ancestral language and customs in favour of an Anglo-Saxon identity or 'Englishness'. Outwardly, they became Englishmen and Englishwomen by changing their speech, dress and other cultural traits. Their political allegiance and, in the case of adult males, their military service, was transferred from British to Anglo-Saxon kings.[11]

Written sources for the history of fifth-century Britain are unreliable and problematic. Gildas, a British monk writing in the 540s, was the author of *On the Ruin and Conquest of Britain*, a complaint against immorality and corruption among his people. His work is essentially a religious sermon punctuated with historical information of varying reliability. In his account of the end of Roman Britain the chronology of the Hadrianic and Antonine walls is so muddled that it is hard for a modern reader to salvage anything useful. Nevertheless, it is from Gildas that we learn of the rise of native kings in the fifth century, and of their hiring of Anglo-Saxon mercenaries, a policy he regarded as foolish and dangerous. He saw the revolt of the hirelings as an inevitable consequence of the stupidity of the Britons. Although he noted that the expansion of Anglo-Saxon power had been halted by a British fightback in the early sixth century, he had little faith in the native leaders of his own day.[12]

By c.550, Britain had become a patchwork of kingdoms, some of which were ruled by Anglo-Saxon kings. These early English monarchs shunned the Christianity of the Britons by worshipping, and claiming descent from, pagan Germanic gods such as Woden. In the south, a rump of native authority lingered in western areas like Wales and Dumnonia (present-day Devon and Cornwall) but the south-east and south midlands lay firmly under Anglo-Saxon control before the end of the sixth century. Further north, British rule seems to have survived in the Pennine hills and in territories further west but the eastern vales and coastlands had already been taken over by English-speaking elites. The oldest Anglo-Saxon settlements in the north were established in Late Roman times, in areas deemed most vulnerable to seaborne Pictish raiders. These early colonies were most dense in fertile districts of Yorkshire where archaeologists have found large cemeteries of Anglo-Saxon graves dating from the late fourth century. By the middle of the sixth century, this area was ruled by a dynasty of English-speaking kings and was known as *Deira*, a name derived from a Brittonic word possibly meaning '(land of) waters'.[13]

Almost everything we know about the origins of Deira comes from *Historia Brittonum*, ('History of the Britons') a text hereafter referred to as *HB*. Written in Wales c.830, it purports to offer a narrative account of early British history in the period after the end of Roman Britain. Its author claimed to have 'made a heap' of the sources available to him. In reality, he assembled a collection of historical, pseudo-historical and legendary materials and cleverly wove them together. In doing so, he may have been attempting to compile a British coun-terweight to *Historia Ecclesiastica Gentis Anglorum* (hereafter *HE*), a monumental 'Ecclesiastical History of the English People' completed by Bede in 731. Although more reliable than the author of *HB*, Bede was not an objec-tive historian by modern standards and cannot, in spite of his reputation as a meticulous scholar, be trusted implicitly. As an Englishman and a northerner, Bede might have been expected to tell us a great deal about the beginnings of Anglo-Saxon Deira but, disappointingly, he adds little to the scattered frag-ments we find in *HB*.[14]

A genealogy preserved in *HB* traces the ancestry of the seventh-century Deiran king Edwin back to the god Woden, via a line of obscure forebears whose historicity is, in most cases, extremely doubtful. One of these figures may never-theless be a genuine ancestor of Edwin and a possible fifth-century founder of Anglo-Saxon Deira. His name was Soemil and he is said by the author of *HB* to have 'first separated Deira from Bernicia'. What this statement actually means is hard to say. Bernicia was the name of the most northerly of the Anglo-Saxon kingdoms, a realm whose heartland lay around a stronghold on the rocky eminence where Bamburgh Castle stands today. We have no idea why Soemil would have needed to 'separate' Deira from Bernicia, unless the former was under the latter's domination in the fifth century. Yet, we are told in an earlier section of *HB* that Bernicia's first Anglo-Saxon king was Ida whose reign, so Bede informs us, began in 547. If the information in *HB* has any historical value, it should mean that pre-English Bernicia, presumably when its rulers were native Britons, held Deira under subjection at some point in the fifth century, until an Anglo-Saxon leader called Soemil established a separate Deiran kingdom. It is possible, if not likely, that Soemil is a fictional character who has no role outside pseudo-history.[15]

With Ida we seem to be on fairly solid ground. His historical existence, while not fully guaranteed, is at least well-supported by Bede's mention of him. To Ida we may cautiously attribute the founding of Bernicia's first English dynasty, a remarkably successful line of kings who brought huge swathes of northern Britain under their authority. As with Deira, the beginnings of Anglo-Saxon Bernicia are dimly perceived through a mist of legend and pseudo-history. Bede tells us that Ida reigned from 547 to 559, but this might be no more than an eighth-century guess. In *HB*, a Bernician royal genealogy traces the lineage of Eadberht, an eighth-century king, back to Ida's great-grandson Oswiu, while another traces Oswiu's sons back to Woden. At the end of Eadberht's genealogy is the following note: 'Ida son of Eobba held the countries in the north of Britain, that is, north of the Humber Sea, and reigned 12 years, and joined Din Guayrdi to Bernicia.'[16]

Din Guayrdi (or Guoaroy) is the Brittonic name for Bamburgh, formed from *din* 'fort' and a second element of obscure meaning. As with Soemil's separation of Deira from Bernicia, Ida's joining of Bamburgh to Bernicia is bereft of context. Did Ida already rule some part of Bernicia before acquiring Bamburgh as his primary stronghold? Whatever the correct interpretation of this curious event, there is no doubt that Bamburgh was the chief fortress of Anglo-Saxon Bernicia by c.600. With such a large, imposing centre of power as their base, it is easy to see how Ida's descendants became one of the major powers of northern Britain.[17]

Rhydderch Hael

The Damnonii of the Clyde are known only from Ptolemy's geographical data. How long their name remained a meaningful political term is unknown, but it may have retained currency long enough to become fossilised in place-names. Dowanhill near Milngavie and Cardowan near Wishaw might preserve it, but the suggestion cannot be pressed too far.[18] By c.500, the name had faded into the background of history. The former heartland of the Damnonii became associated with the name of a fortress on Dumbarton Rock. This change from an ethnonym – the name of an entire people – to a toponym (place-name) associated with the ruling elite indicates a shift in the patterns of power, perhaps reflecting a new centralisation of authority around the king. Texts written in the seventh century mention kings of Dumbarton in the late 500s and, possibly, in the fifth century as well. By c.600, the fortress on the 'Rock of Clyde' was known in Latin as *Petra Cloithe*, in Gaelic as *Ail Cluaide* and in Brittonic as *Alt Clut*.[19] A royal genealogy or pedigree preserved in a Welsh manuscript of c.1150 traces the descent of a king called Rhun, who ruled the Clyde Britons in the late ninth century, through many generations back to the Roman period. Although the pedigree contains many figures whose existence is attested by other sources, the earliest names, those borne by Rhun's forefathers in the late-fourth to mid-sixth centuries, cannot be verified as belonging to historical rather than to legendary characters.[20] We are thus unable to say how many of them were real kings of Alt Clut. Our historical horizon, the point at which verifiable history begins, lies in the late sixth century, with a king called Rhydderch Hael.

Rhydderch's historicity is not in doubt: he is mentioned in *Vita Sancti Columbae*, a 'Life' of Saint Columba written at the end of the seventh century by Abbot Adomnán of Iona. This *vita* (hereafter *VC*) is regarded by modern historians as a fairly reliable source, rather more so than the pedigree of Rhun. Rhydderch is absent from Rhun's line of descent but appears in another pedigree, also preserved in the same Welsh manuscript, representing a branch from the main royal line of Alt Clut. A slightly different version of Rhydderch's pedigree is found in another text, but in both his father is called Tudwal, a figure whose own historicity is confirmed by Adomnán's mention of him. Adomnán has little to say of the Clyde Britons but was aware that they had been ruled by Rhydderch during Columba's abbacy of the monastery on Iona.[21] Columba founded this monastery in the 560s and died there in 597, so Rhydderch's reign can be associated with the same period. The epithet *Hael* ('Generous') appears in poetry preserved in Welsh manuscripts written no earlier than the twelfth century and was attached not only to Rhydderch but to several of his kinsmen in the pedigrees. Rhydderch also appears in a number of Welsh poems attributed to Myrddin, a precursor of the Arthurian wizard Merlin, who may have been a North British bard of the late sixth century. In these poems, Rhydderch sends soldiers to hunt down and capture Myrddin, at that time living as a fugitive in the wild Forest of Celidon. In his woodland refuge, Myrddin receives prophetic visions and is haunted by terrifying memories of a savage battle. Although much of the poetry attributed to him deals with supernatural themes, it does contain some historical elements, including Rhydderch himself. Nonetheless, the poems tell us little about the king, and the manuscript containing them is too late to be used as a valid source of sixth-century North British history. They should be regarded instead as literary compositions created in Wales from fragments of older tradition.[22]

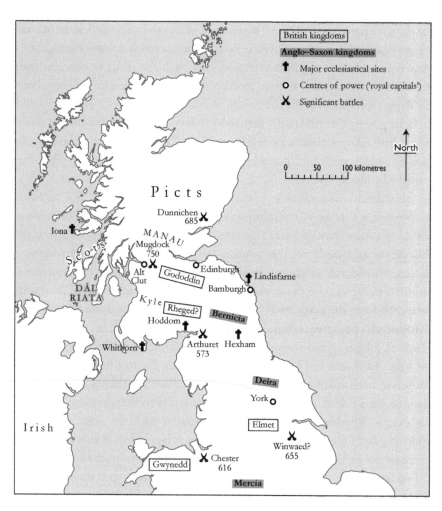

MAP 3 Northern Britain, sixth to eighth centuries

Rhydderch appears in *HB* only once, in the context of military campaigns against Anglo-Saxon Bernicia. The notice of these wars is our earliest record of conflict between the Clyde Britons and the English. The passage in question follows a list of early Bernician rulers, all but one of whom were sons of Ida:

> Four kings fought against them, Urien and Rhydderch the Old and Gwallawg and Morcant. Theodoric fought vigorously against Urien and his sons. During that time, sometimes the enemy, sometimes the Cymry were victorious, and Urien blockaded them for three days and three nights in the island of Lindisfarne. But during this campaign, Urien was assassinated on the instigation of Morcant, from jealousy, because his military skill and generalship surpassed that of all the other kings.[23]

Many historians have interpreted this passage as an account of a joint campaign by a coalition of British kings against their Bernician enemies. The leader of this four-pronged assault is usually seen as Urien who was then treacherously slain by another member of the coalition during a siege of Lindisfarne. A closer look at the passage reveals that this interpretation is highly speculative and possibly incorrect. Taken at face value, the sequence of events can be broken down into three separate elements:

1. A number of early Bernician rulers fought wars against four British kings.
2. One of these wars saw Theodoric, a son of Ida, being besieged on Lindisfarne by Urien.
3. The Lindisfarne campaign was still being fought when Urien was slain at the instigation of Morcant, another British king.

There is no warrant for assuming that Urien headed a military alliance in which his own forces and those of three other kings mounted a joint campaign against Bernicia. A simpler interpretation of the passage in *HB* is that each of the four British rulers waged separate campaigns of their own.[24] This liberates Rhydderch, Gwallawg and Morcant from the subordinate roles frequently assigned to them by modern historians. No part of the passage suggests that these kings joined forces with Urien, or that they were junior members in an alliance led by him. Only Urien and his sons are associated with a war against Theodoric and with a siege of Lindisfarne. Of the other British kings we are merely told that they fought wars against Bernicia, not that they fought together as allies in a single campaign.

It is a matter of regret that neither Gwallawg nor Morcant, nor indeed Urien himself, can be confidently associated with any place on a modern map. The locations of their kingdoms remain unknown, in spite of much guesswork by modern historians. Attempts to associate Gwallawg with Elmet, a British kingdom in Yorkshire, are based on a tenuous inference from a single line of Welsh poetry. Likewise, a belief that Morcant was a ruler of Gododdin – the former land of the Votadini of Roman times – is nothing more than a wild guess. The greatest optimism, however, is reserved for Urien, whom the Welsh poems associate with a place called Rheged. Generations of scholars have consistently identified Rheged as a large kingdom located on one or both sides of the Solway Firth. All of them are simply repeating a guess that has no real historical foundation. Rheged is named as one of Urien's principal domains in Welsh poetry supposedly composed by his personal bard Taliesin. Other places under his authority included Llwyfenydd, Goddeu, Echwydd and Catraeth. None of these places, including Rheged itself, is identifiable today. To claim otherwise is to run too far with a tenuous guess by pretending that it becomes a fact if enough people repeat it. The only fact about Rheged is that it is one of several lost kingdoms – if indeed it was a kingdom at all and not merely a single settlement or lordly estate.[25] Sadly, our complete inability to locate Urien, Gwallawg and Morcant deprives Rhydderch's Bernician wars of a wider context and means that we cannot assess their impact on contemporary political geography. We do not know, for instance, if Rhydderch's forces fought a major war of aggression in Bernicia's heartland. The passage in *HB* might instead be telling us that he defended his lands against Bernician cattle-raids. From Adomnán we learn that Rhydderch was held in high esteem by St Columba, who regarded the king of Alt Clut as a friend. Such acknowledgement by the abbot of Iona, himself an Irish royal prince, suggests that Rhydderch was regarded as a powerful ruler. We might therefore wonder if Rhydderch himself, rather than Urien, was the British king most feared by the Bernicians.

The geographical extent of Rhydderch's kingdom is unknown. Its core was the great fortress of Alt Clut on the northern shore of the Firth of Clyde but this was unlikely to have been the only royal residence. In a twelfth-century Life of St Kentigern commissioned by Bishop Jocelin of Glasgow and written by his namesake, a monk of Furness Abbey, Rhydderch dwelt in a *villa regia* ('royal residence') at Partick. Located on the north bank of the River Clyde, Partick lies directly opposite Govan where burials of fifth- or sixth-century date have been found in the graveyard of the old parish church. Although the Glasgow *vita* of Kentigern may say more about twelfth-century ecclesiastical politics than about the residential choices of sixth-century royalty, an estate and lordly hall at Partick would be consistent with the presumed extent of Rhydderch's kingdom.[26] Partick is only eleven miles south-east of Dumbarton and may have been within the core territory of the kings of Alt Clut. Like most early medieval kings, Rhydderch and his family would have been peripatetic, travelling around their domains to make use of a number of residences. Such tours or 'circuits' helped a king to renew bonds of friendship with local elites in different parts of his realm. If Rhydderch was a mighty king to whom many lords owed allegiance, his royal circuit may have taken him far from Dumbarton, perhaps to volatile borderlands where his authority was fragile or contested. His conflict with the Bernicians might have arisen in a frontier zone menaced by English raids, perhaps near the high watershed where the great rivers of Clyde and Tweed begin.

Picts and Scots

Adomnán relates a story in which Rhydderch sent a letter to Columba, seeking an answer to the question of whether he would perish in battle or die peacefully in his own bed. Columba's God-given powers of prophecy allowed him to reassure the anxious king that a non-violent end awaited him. Behind this tale of miraculous foresight lies something else: a fleeting glimpse of diplomatic exchanges between two sixth-century kingdoms. Columba was certainly no stranger to high-level political discourse, having been born into a branch of the Northern Ui Néill, a powerful Irish dynasty whose power-base lay in Donegal. In Britain, as founder and first abbot of the monastery on Iona, he forged close links with neighbouring rulers on the coastlands and islands of Argyll. The nearest of these were the elites of Dál Riata, an area encompassing southern Argyll and parts of north-east Ireland. The inhabitants of Dál Riata spoke Gaelic, like the Irish, and were known among themselves and others as 'Scots'. In Roman times, the Latin term *Scotti* had seemingly been applied to any Gaelic-speaking group with which the Empire came into contact and it continued to be used interchangeably with 'Irish' by writers of the early medieval period. By c.500, Dál Riata comprised a number of small kingdoms, each ruled by one or more *cenéla* or kindreds who competed with one another for regional supremacy.[27] Two of the most powerful kindreds were Cenél Comgaill, 'Comgall's Descendants', and Cenél nGabráin, 'Gabran's Descendants', who respectively ruled the peninsulas of Cowal and Kintyre. Adomnán believed that Columba had received Iona from a Cenél Comgaill king called Conall who appears to have gained the overlordship of Dál Riata in the 560s. After Conall's death, a new overking emerged in the shape of Áedán mac Gabráin of Kintyre whom Adomnán portrayed as Columba's royal patron and friend. Áedán was an ambitious warlord whose military campaigns took him far from his Argyll heartlands.

It is possible that Rhydderch's letter to Columba was less concerned with testing the saint's prophetic powers than with asking the chief cleric of Dál Riata if Áedán was planning to attack Alt Clut.[28]

The prospect of war between Áedán and Rhydderch was no doubt very real, given the proximity of their kingdoms. One or more of several named but unidentified battles credited to Áedán may have been fought against Alt Clut. Other battles seem to have been fought against the Picts, a people whose earlier raids had played a role in the collapse of Roman Britain. Pictish territory in the time of Áedán and Rhydderch included much of what is now north-east Scotland from Fife to Caithness and further north in Orkney and Shetland. Like the Scots of Dál Riata, the Picts were not a homogeneous nation but a number of groups sharing certain cultural traits. Unlike the Scots, the Picts of the sixth century spoke a Brittonic language like the Britons further south, although Gaelic was probably starting to influence the speech of their western-most communities.[29] Áedán's campaigns in Pictish territory seem to have brought him as far east as Circinn, now the district of Angus in Perthshire. Another eastward foray, against a people called Miathi, may have taken place in Stirlingshire. The Miathi were almost certainly the Maeatae, a belligerent group of northern barbarians whom Roman troops had encountered in the second and third centuries. Place-names associate the Maeatae with Stirlingshire and Clackmannanshire, areas that in early medieval times were part of a large district called Manau. Áedán is said to have fought a battle in Manau, and this may have been the *bellum Miathorum*, 'battle against the Miathi', to which Adomnán refers in the Life of Columba. Whether the Miathi/Maeatae considered themselves Picts or Britons is a matter of debate and, in a sixth-century context, might not be a significant question.[30]

Northumbria

Adomnán noted that Rhydderch Hael died at home, peacefully, rather than in the carnage of battle, thus fulfilling Columba's prophecy. The identity of Rhydderch's successor is unknown, but the next king whose reign is firmly attested is Owain, son of Beli, who was active in the early 640s. Owain's father appears in the main Welsh pedigree of Alt Clut as Beli, son of a Neithon whose own father and grandfather are named there as Guipno and Dyfnwal respectively. A rough chronological deduction might lead us to suppose that either Neithon or Guipno was in his prime during Rhydderch's reign, yet there is no independent record of either of them ruling as king. According to *VK*, Kentigern and Rhydderch died in the same year, and the Welsh Annals put the saint's death in 612 or 614. Taking the two sources together, Rhydderch's reign seems to extend into the second decade of the seventh century. Perhaps his immediate successor was Beli's father Neithon, a figure of sufficient fame to be mentioned in a stray fragment of heroic verse referring to a victory won by his grandson Owain. Alternatively, Rhydderch may have been succeeded by Beli, who is probably the unnamed king of Alt Clut mentioned in a poem attributed to the seventh-century Irish monk Riagail of Bangor.[31]

If Rhydderch was still alive at the beginning of the seventh century, his contemporary as king of Bernicia was Aethelfrith, a grandson of Ida. Aethelfrith was the most powerful English ruler of his day, a man praised by Bede for seizing large swathes of land from the Britons. Although the precise geography and chronology of his conquests are unknown, it is likely that he pushed Bernicia's frontier westward through Tweeddale and northward to the Lammermuir Hills. While it is possible that he came into conflict with Rhydderch Hael, or with Rhydderch's successors, there is no indication that he took territory from them, or that his overlordship was ever acknowledged in Alt Clut.[32]

Marriage to a Deiran princess enabled Aethelfrith to bring his neighbours south of the River Tees under his sway, thus creating a single kingdom of the northern English, a precursor of the great realm of Northumbria. After Aethelfrith's death in battle against the East Angles in 616 or 617, his Deiran rival Edwin took over the combined kingship and gained the allegiance of the Bernician aristocracy. If Edwin launched military campaigns against the North Britons, these are not recorded in any surviving source. His relations with the rulers of Alt Clut are likewise unknown but were not necessarily hostile. A number of other North British kingdoms, including Gododdin and the mysterious 'Rheged', had also escaped Aethelfrith's onslaught and seemingly survived Edwin's reign too. The rest, however, had been absorbed into Bernicia before Edwin came to power.

During Edwin's reign, Aethelfrith's children lived in exile among the Picts and Scots. Under the guidance of Irish monks on Iona they received Christian baptism. One son, Eanfrith, fathered a future Pictish king. Others rode to war alongside the military forces of Cenél nGabráin, one of the royal kindreds of Dál Riata, from whom they had received sanctuary and hospitality. In 633, Edwin was slain in battle against the Welsh king Cadwallon, ruler of Gwynedd, on the southern frontier of Deira, Eanfrith returned from exile to claim the Bernician kingship but was killed on Cadwallon's orders while attempting to negotiate a truce. In the following year, Eanfrith's younger brother Oswald came from Dál Riata to challenge Cadwallon, who was still occupying and plundering the lands of the northern English. Cadwallon was destroyed in the ensuing battle, leaving Oswald free to take the Bernician kingship.[33]

Oswald's eight-year reign saw a resurgence of Bernician power. Like his father, he imposed his authority on Deira. His relations with his North British neighbours are less clear. An entry in the *Annals of Ulster* mentions a siege of *Etin* in 638. If, as many scholars believe, this was the stronghold known to the Britons as *Eitin* or *Din Eiddyn* situated on Edinburgh's Castle Rock, the annal might refer to a Bernician assault on the heartland of Gododdin. Some historians go further by suggesting that the event marked the end of the Gododdin kingdom and its subjugation by Oswald.[34] Although this is no more than inference, it would be consistent with the idea that Bernician expansion continued through the 630s and 640s. In any case, there is little doubt that English territory had reached the southern shore of the Firth of Forth by c.650.

Oswald's eventual nemesis lay not in the north but in the English midlands, in Mercia, where a number of older Anglo-Saxon territories had been brought under the overkingship of Penda, a former ally of Cadwallon. Penda destroyed Oswald in 642 at *Maserfelth*, an unidentified battlefield in the midlands, perhaps in the borderlands between southern Deira and north-east Mercia where both Aethelfrith and Edwin had also perished.[35] After Oswald's death, his extensive realm unravelled, leaving his younger brother Oswiu as king of Bernicia while Deira re-emerged as an independent kingdom ruled by Oswine, son of Edwin's cousin Osric. Both kings initially acknowledged Penda's authority, but Oswiu resented the Mercian yoke and sought to cast it off. His unruliness provoked a response from Penda, who launched punitive raids on Bernicia, one of which involved an attempt to burn the royal stronghold at Bamburgh. Penda demanded a hefty tribute-payment which Oswiu may or may not have paid. Bede asserts that the payment was withheld, but the *Historia Brittonum* claims that it was handed over to the Mercian king at 'the city called Iudeu'. *HB* adds that Penda distributed the tribute among 'the kings of the Britons', presumably a group of subordinate rulers, this event being known in later Welsh tradition as the 'Distribution of Iudeu'.[36] The place might be *urbs Giudi*, 'the city of Giudi', a British fortress either on Stirling's Castle Rock or at some other site near the head of the Firth of Forth. The British kings who shared the loot of Bernicia most likely included Penda's subordinates from Wales. Given Penda's military reputation and the scale of his territorial ambitions, it is possible that his overlordship was also acknowledged among the North Britons. If the king of Alt Clut was one of Penda's vassals at the Distribution of Iudeu, a part of Oswiu's tribute-payment may have come to Dumbarton Rock.

Neither the chronology of Penda's attacks on Bernicia nor the date of the Distribution of Iudeu is known, but they must have happened between Oswald's demise in 642 and Oswiu's eventual overthrow of Penda in 655. There is considerable uncertainty about the identity of the king of Alt Clut in this period. Owain, son of Beli, defeated the Scots at Strathcarron near Falkirk in 642 or 643 but this is the only chronological marker for his reign.[37] His son, according to the Welsh pedigree of Alt Clut, was Elffin, who is not mentioned in any other source. A certain Guriat, identified in the Irish annals as king of Alt Clut, died in 654 but is absent from the pedigree. He may have been another son of Owain, or perhaps a brother, unless – like Rhydderch Hael – he sprang from a different branch of the royal kindred. He might even have been a usurper from an unrelated family. Either Owain or his immediate successor was presumably ruling at Dumbarton in 643, when Oswiu of Bernicia fought a battle against unspecified Britons. This may have been a border skirmish between Oswiu and a still-independent British group in Tweeddale or Lothian who hoped to exploit the collapse of Oswald's hegemony. It could equally have been a clash with Alt Clut, especially if Owain – flushed with pride and power after his victory at Strathcarron – sought to extend his eastern frontier at Bernicia's expense. Whatever the circumstances, the result was probably an English victory, for the Irish annalists described the encounter as 'Oswiu's battle'.[38]

Oswiu achieved the supremacy enjoyed by his brother and father after defeating Penda on the banks of the River Winwaed in 655. What followed was a long period of Bernician overlordship in northern Britain, imposed first by Oswiu, then by his son Ecgfrith. During this period, English rule was consolidated in what had been the British kingdom of Gododdin before pushing across the Firth of Forth into southern Pictish territory. Further north, in Perthshire and beyond, at least one major Pictish realm was placed under tribute by Oswiu or by Ecgfrith. Some portion of Dál Riata, too, seems to have recognised these Bernician kings as overlords. In such a climate of English supremacy, it is likely that the kings of Alt Clut made similar pledges of allegiance.[39] Their kingdom was almost certainly the last-remaining North British realm at that time, having outlasted the demise of Gododdin, Rheged and the rest. Their compatriots in North Wales, whose rulers had been allies or vassals of Penda, were probably part of Bernicia's southern hegemony, together with the Mercians themselves. After the murder of Edwin's kinsman Oswine, apparently at Oswiu's instigation, the Deirans were again joined to Bernicia in a unified realm that Bede called

Northumbria, a name meaning 'lands north of the Humber'. The Deiran kingship became, for a short time until its extinction, a cadet role reserved for Bernician princes.

English hegemony in the north lasted for thirty years, surviving even Oswiu's death in 670. It ended, decisively, at *Nechtanesmere*, 'Nechtan's Mire', a marshy site probably near Dunnichen Hill in Angus. There, in May 685, Ecgfrith and most of his troops were slain by a Pictish army led by King Bridei (Gaelic: *Brude*), son of Beli. In one Irish text, Bridei is described as 'son of the king of Alt Clut', a statement that allows us to identify his father as the same Beli who appears in the Alt Clut pedigree as father of Owain, the victor of Strathcarron.[40] The forty-year gap between Strathcarron and Nechtanesmere might be explained by imagining Owain as a young man in 642 or 643, and his brother Bridei as middle-aged or elderly in 685. They may have had different mothers, one of whom was no doubt a Pictish princess through whom Bridei gained a legitimate claim to kingship. Bridei's victory at Nechtanesmere hurled English ambitions back across the Forth and ended the subjection endured by the Picts, Scots and Britons. If the kings of Alt Clut had hitherto languished as tribute-paying vassals of Bernician neighbours, their independence was now restored. They may, for a time, have been obliged to recognise Bridei as the new power in northern Britain, but his death in 693 ended Pictish supremacy for a generation.

The Anglo-Pictish alliance

Ecgfrith was succeeded as king of the unified realm of Northumbria by his half-brother Aldfrith, formerly a cleric, whose ambitions were rather more modest. Bede observed that Aldfrith 'ably restored the shattered state of the kingdom, athough within narrower bounds'. Sporadic clashes between Picts and Northumbrians resumed in the 690s and continued into the second decade of the next century until a peace treaty was agreed sometime around the year 712.[41] It was still in place in 731, when Bede finished his *Ecclesiastical History*, and it lasted until 740. Anglo-Pictish relations in this period seem to have been relatively amicable. The frontier between Northumbria and her North British neighbours seems also to have been quite stable in the first half of the eighth century, with no major hostilities being mentioned in the sources. In the 720s and 730s, Northumbria was plagued by internal conflict between rival royal factions and was hardly in a good position to make war against other powers. In any case, the military policies of Alt Clut in the late seventh and early eighth centuries seem to have been directed westward rather than eastward. The Irish annals mention four battles in Ireland between the years 681 and 709, each involving a force of unidentified Britons. Given that the relevant annal entries were probably written on Iona, and the northern Irish location of three of the battles, it seems likely that the Britons in question were also northern rather than Welsh or Cornish. There is no indication that they were a band of free-booting mercenaries or exiles rather than a royal army led by its own king. We may cautiously identify them as warriors from Alt Clut who fought in Ireland because their king had become embroiled in Irish politics.[42]

In 737, the kingship of Northumbria passed to Eadberht, son of Eata. He was not of the house of Aethelfrith but from another Bernician family who also claimed descent from Ida. Eadberht became king at a time of dynastic strife and his reign was punctuated by outbreaks of internal rivalry. Nevertheless, he appears to have been a strong and ambitious ruler in the mould of his seventh-century predecessors. Like them, he faced powerful neighbours on more than one front. To the south lay the Mercians, so often the bane of Northumbrian kings, led now by Aethelbald, a great-nephew of the fearsome Penda. To the north lay the realm of the Pictish over-king Onuist, a warlord whose achievements already included the defeat and subjugation of Dál Riata. Eadberht proved himself an equal to both Onuist and Aethelbald. In 740, he was engaged in a northern war with the Picts when the Mercians invaded his lands from the south, yet he emerged from this perilous situation with his kingdom and reputation intact. He then began a new expansion of English territory in the north-west, pushing into Ayrshire from Northumbrian lands in Galloway. In 750, he conquered Kyle, ousting its native British landholders.[43] This brought him to the River Irvine and to the coastlands of the Firth of Clyde where, we may assume, his territorial ambitions threatened the heartland of Alt Clut. The reigning king at Dumbarton was Teudubr, himself a proven warlord who had routed a Pictish army in the same year as Eadberht's conquest of Kyle. Teudubr's victory took place at *Mocetauc*, probably Mugdock in Strathblane, where the Pictish casualties included a brother of the mighty Onuist.[44] It may have been partly to avenge this slaying that Onuist agreed to join Eadberht in a combined offensive against Alt Clut. Such an alliance between Pictish and Northumbrian forces was unprecedented. It suggests that both parties regarded the kingdom of the Clyde Britons as a significant obstacle to their respective ambitions and territorial interests. It also suggests that they regarded the dynasty on Dumbarton Rock as a match for either of them campaigning alone.

The Anglo-Pictish onslaught came in 756, four years after the death of Teudubr. The task of defending Dumbarton and its hinterland fell to Dyfnwal,

Teudubr's son, who may have been no stranger to conflict with the Picts. It is likely that Dyfnwal had stood alongside his father in the great victory at *Mocetauc* in 750. Both father and son may have been present six years earlier in a battle between Picts and Britons, an encounter noted in the Irish annals without a location or outcome.[45] Although there is no record of conflict between Alt Clut and Northumbria during Eadberht's reign until the Anglo-Pictish campaign of 756, the Northumbrian king's conquest of Kyle in 750 may have led to raids and skirmishes in frontier areas, perhaps in northern Ayrshire and southern Renfrewshire. Further east, tensions might have been high along the border between British and English lordships in Lothian and Upper Tweeddale.

Our only record of the Anglo-Pictish assault on Alt Clut appears in the twelfth-century Northumbrian chronicle *Historia Regum Anglorum et Dacorum* (*HRA*). This text was discussed in Chapter 1 where we noted that its compiler used a set of older Northumbrian annals. One section of these annals covered the years 732 to 802 and provided the compiler of *HRA* with the following information:

> In the year from the Lord's Incarnation 756, King Eadberht in the eighteenth year of his reign, and Onuist, king of Picts, led an army to the town of Alcwith. And hence the Britons accepted terms there, on the first day of the month of August. But on the tenth day of the same month perished almost the whole army which he led from Ovania to Niwanbirig, that is, to *novam civitatem*.[46]

Two of the three places mentioned in this passage are identifiable. *Alcwith* is Alt Clut, Dumbarton Rock, named here in an English form similar to the one used by Bede when he described the site as a major stronghold of the North Britons: 'the town of *Alcluith*, a name which in their language means Clyde Rock because it stands near the river of that name'.[47] *Ovania*, although less immediately recognisable, is almost certainly the Latinised form of a place-name underlying the modern name *Govan*.[48] A rich collection of early medieval sculpture testifies to Govan's importance as a secular and religious centre of the highest status in the ninth, tenth and eleventh centuries. Moreover, archaeological evidence for Early Christian burials at the site of the old parish church ('Govan Old') suggests continuity of an elite presence through the second half of the first millennium AD. It is therefore likely that the site now occupied by Govan Old was a place of spiritual significance at the time of the Anglo-Pictish campaign of 756. Another important feature lay nearby, within a stone's throw of the church, beyond the further side of an ancient routeway leading to a tidal ford on the River Clyde. This was a massive artificial mound known in later times as the Doomster Hill. Although demolished in the nineteenth century to make way for industrial development, the mound is shown on earlier illustrations with a stepped profile and a flattened summit. Such a shape is reminiscent of the ceremonial mounds found in areas of Viking settlement around the coasts of Britain and Ireland, most notably in the Scandinavian kingdoms of Dublin and Man.[49] The possibility that the Doomster Hill acquired its distinctive shape in the Viking period is briefly discussed in the next chapter. For the moment, we may make the suggestion that the mound did not have this shape prior to the ninth century and that it originally had a round or conical profile. A plausible theory is that it was constructed in prehistoric times as a venue for pagan rituals or as a barrow containing a grave. Archaeological excavations in the 1990s unearthed what appears to have been a ceremonial path linking the Doomster Hill to Govan Old, but whether this feature existed in the eighth century is unknown.[50] There can, however, be little doubt that the mound and church were there when the Northumbrian army departed from *Ovania* in August 756.

The name Govan

Although popular etymology sees Govan as a name of Gaelic origin derived from *Baile a Ghobainn*, 'Place of the Smith', this part of Clydesdale did not become Gaelic-speaking until the twelfth century. In the period when the 'Govan Stones' were carved (c.870 to c.1100) the main language of the area was Cumbric, a northern Brittonic tongue related to Old Welsh. Since the entry for 756 in *HRA* derives from an older Northumbrian chronicle compiled at the beginning of the ninth century, long before the arrival of Gaelic speech on the Clyde, *Ovania* must represent an original Cumbric name. The place in question is almost certainly Govan, but the original form of the modern name is still a matter of debate. Of several theories the most convincing proposes a derivation from a Cumbric equivalent of Welsh *go* 'little' + *ban* 'hill'. *Goban*, 'the little hill', is an appropriate description of the man-made mound known in later times as Doomster Hill. It would also be consistent with 'Hillock', the name given by local people to this feature before its destruction in the mid-nineteenth century. Additional study has suggested the existence of an eighth-century Cumbric form *Gwovan* to account for the Latinised *Ovania* of the Northumbrian chronicles.[51]

In the absence of other references to the Anglo-Pictish campaign of 756, we are wholly reliant on the testimony of *HRA*. The emphasis of the chronicler is clearly on the fate of the Northumbrian army as it marched homeward. Indeed, the campaign itself seems to be of secondary concern, being little more than a sequence of events leading up to a shocking incident: an ambush that caused a near-massacre. The Northumbrian focus suggests that 'the whole army which he led' is a reference to Eadberht's forces rather than to Onuist's, and that the slaughtered troops were Englishmen returning home with loot from the Clyde.[52] The identity of the attackers is more puzzling. Did the Picts treacherously ambush their Northumbrian allies soon after their joint triumph over the Britons? Such an act of betrayal might explain an eighth-century Northumbrian epitaph on Onuist which declared that 'from the beginning of his reign right to the end he perpetrated bloody crimes, like a tyrannical slaughterer'.[53] This hostile description may, however, have originated outside Northumbria, among the Gaelic-speaking Scots of Dál Riata, upon whom Onuist had inflicted *percutio*, 'a smiting', in 741. The *percutio* was a devastating climax to a decade of Pictish aggression and would not have been swiftly forgotten in the west. Perhaps, then, *HRA*'s disparaging description of Onuist as a 'tyrannical slaughterer' came ultimately from a Dál Riatan source?[54] A Northumbrian provenance for such an assessment of his achievements does appear less likely, given the positive outcome of his alliance with Eadberht. Although the two kings had formerly clashed in battle, their combined operation against the Clyde Britons was initially successful. A significant joint victory by the allies on 1 August 756 seems incompatible with the notion of a treacherous Pictish attack on the homecoming Northumbrians nine days later. It has been suggested that Onuist may have secretly negotiated with Dyfnwal of Alt Clut to arrange a British or combined Pictish-British assault on Eadberht's army.[55] Alternative interpretations see Eadberht's force being assailed by English rivals seeking to relieve him of plunder, or by Britons acting independently of the recently defeated Dyfnwal. A British counter-attack might indeed offer the simplest scenario. Having agreed the terms of surrender on 1 August, sealed by an oath of homage to the victors, Dyfnwal may have lost the allegiance of one or more powerful lords within his kingdom. Military forces commanded by such figures would not thereafter have been restrained by royal pledges. It is thus plausible that the homecoming Northumbrians were ambushed by Britons whose leaders no longer recognised Dyfnwal's authority.[56]

The place-name *Niwanbirig* defies identification. It is an Old English name meaning 'new fort' and was probably bestowed on numerous places in

Anglo-Saxon England. The chronicler's *novam civitatem*, 'new settlement', is an approximate Latin translation. The name survives today in modern forms such as Newbury, Newbrough, Newburgh and Newborough. In Scotland, its best-known representative is Newburgh in Fife, two miles north-east of the Pictish royal and ecclesiastical centre at Abernethy. This Newburgh only becomes a plausible candidate for the *Niwanbirig* of 756 if we imagine that the ambushed troops were not Eadberht's Northumbrians but Onuist's Picts, or even that the former were attacked while venturing into the latter's heartland.[57] A second candidate is Newbrough near Hexham, a place deep inside Eadberht's territory, where his soldiers could have been attacked on the last stage of their homeward march from Govan. Whether a settlement of any kind existed at Newbrough in the eighth century is rather more doubtful, given that the place-name is not attested before the early 1200s.[58] A third alternative, perhaps the least plausible, proposes that Onuist and Eadberht immediately followed their triumph over the Britons with a joint campaign against the Mercians and that the subsequent disaster on the way to *Niwanbirig* occurred in the English midlands near Newborough in Staffordshire.[59] All three possibilities come back to the fundamental question: who slew whom on the journey between *Ovania* and *Niwanbirig*?

If, as suggested above, the victims of the ambush were Eadberht's soldiers and the attackers were Britons, the setting is unlikely to have been Newbrough near Hexham. A location so deep within the Northumbrian kingdom is an improbable fit. Indeed, one possible inference from *HRA* is that *Niwanbirig* lay at no great distance from *Ovania* (Govan), just as the latter lay no great distance from *Alcwith* (Dumbarton). Viewed through the eyes of an English chronicler, all three places defined the geographical context of the events of August 756. Two were major centres of power and ritual within the kingdom of Alt Clut, their appearance together being unremarkable. The third, *Niwanbirig*, may have been a place of a different sort, its importance in the narrative being due to its position relative to *Ovania* rather than to its own value or status. In other words, although *Niwanbirig* lay on a route leading away from the ancient religious site at Govan, it was not necessarily a place of equal status. That the route in question was a major highway, suitable for the passage of large numbers of troops, seems likely nonetheless. This observation can be made with confidence, regardless of whether we count eighth-century armies in hundreds or in thousands.[60] Any major road running south from *Ovania* would have been an important link between Lower Clydesdale and other districts along the valley, and thus between Dyfnwal's kingdom and neighbouring realms. In seeking to trace the course of

Eadberht's homeward route on a modern map we find ourselves back among the various *Niwanbirig* theories. As we have seen, *Ovania* can be pinpointed with confidence, but can we locate *Niwanbirig*, the 'new settlement' to which Eadberht's soldiers were travelling when they were assailed?

The name *Niwanbirig* appears, at first glance, to belong to an English settlement. To be more precise, we might feel tempted to think of it as a place under English rule in 756, or as a place known in Northumbria by an English name. Looking again at the events of 756, we can infer from *HRA* that Dyfnwal surrendered to the Anglo-Pictish alliance at Dumbarton Rock on 1 August. At some point thereafter, 'the whole army' – presumably Eadberht's – was at Govan, a site eleven miles upstream on the south bank of the Clyde. On 10 August, this force was travelling away from Govan when it was attacked on the road to *Niwanbirig*.[61] *HRA* does not imply that the Anglo-Pictish forces made a swift departure from Dumbarton after receiving the surrender of the Britons. The capitulation of a major power like Alt Clut was a political milestone which the victors no doubt exploited for every ounce of propaganda. At Dumbarton on 1 August they received Dyfnwal's submission, almost certainly in a formal ceremony, with the terms no doubt including a hefty tribute-payment. Gathering this tribute from the leading families of the British kingdom probably took several days and another ceremony would have been arranged for its presentation to Onuist and Eadberht. If, as *HRA* implies, the surrender took place at *Alcwith*, then the tribute-payment may have been presented at *Ovania*. With its important ford, imposing mound and ancient church, Govan would have been an entirely suitable venue for such rituals. The full process of submission and restitution may have lasted a week or more, with the Northumbrian army not embarking on its homeward march until the eighth or ninth day of August. By the tenth day of the month, the English soldiers might not have gone far along the road to *Niwanbirig* when they were ambushed.

Eadberht's homeward journey from Govan would have taken him east into Northumbrian-held Lothian, or south-east towards Upper Tweeddale, or perhaps due south in the direction of Carlisle. Of the various routes, the most direct pointed towards the Tweed. Along this line ran a Roman road linking Tweeddale to the western end of the Antonine Wall, via Peebles, Carstairs and Motherwell.[62] It may have been somewhere along this road that Eadberht was attacked on 10 August. *Niwanbirig* might at that time have been a 'new settlement' established in the wake of Northumbria's recent expansion, perhaps a frontier fort in former British territory near the headwaters of Clyde and Tweed. If so, its location cannot be identified more precisely.

The fortunes of Alt Clut in the decades following the Anglo-Pictish assault are unrecorded. Whether Eadberht and Onuist secured a prolonged dominance over the kingdom does, however, seem unlikely. Within five years of their victory, both kings had disappeared from the political stage, Eadberht retiring to monastic life in 758 and Onuist dying in 761. The departure of these belligerent neighbours perhaps allowed the Dumbarton dynasty to cast off the yoke of subjection. There is, nonetheless, a hint that the events of 756 paved the way for some measure of Northumbrian influence on the elites of Clydesdale. The hint comes from Cathcart, on the south side of the river, where the old parish church is dedicated to the Bernician royal saint Oswald. Although the date of this dedication is unknown, it may have originated during a period of Northumbrian supremacy in the years after 756.[63] If so, it survived the dynastic upheavals that convulsed Northumbria in the eighth century's final decades.

3

RAIDERS AND SETTLERS

Early Scandinavian raids

The Viking Age in Britain began in 789 when three shiploads of Danes appeared at Portland in Dorset. Their motives and objectives are unclear, but they slew a royal official after he demanded that they present themselves to the king of the West Saxons. Whether this incident counts as a raid is debatable, and many historians prefer to regard an attack on Northumbria four years later as the first documented Viking assault on the British Isles. The latter event was noted with profound dismay in the *Anglo-Saxon Chronicle*, for the great monastery of Lindisfarne was ravaged by 'heathen men'. In the following year, the dual monastery of Monkwearmouth-Jarrow suffered a similar fate.[1] After these horrifying attacks, no further raids on English territory were recorded until the 830s, for the Vikings turned their attention to the coasts and islands of the Gaelic West. The monastery on Iona was attacked in 795 and twice again in the first decade of the ninth century. Raids on Ireland also began in 795 and continued through the 800s, becoming a frequent theme in contemporary Irish annals.[2]

The Vikings were seafarers of Scandinavian origin whose homelands lay in Norway, Denmark and Sweden. They were pagans who worshipped Germanic gods, hence their unashamed plundering of churches and monasteries. Their attacks on the British Isles formed part of a wider sequence of raiding, trading and colonising that took them to various parts of mainland Europe. In the east, they ranged far across Slavic lands and moved through what is now Russia to make contact with the Byzantine Empire. Journeying far across the northern seas they established permanent settlements in Iceland and Greenland, even reaching North America. Those who came to Britain and Ireland were mostly of Danish or Norse (Norwegian) origin, although these ethnic distinctions often become blurred in the sources. By the middle of the ninth century, the character of the raids had changed from swift plundering expeditions to longer military campaigns in which extensive territories were occupied and despoiled. Around this time, a large group of Danes, known to contemporary English chroniclers as *mycel here*, 'The Great Army', first made its presence known. This force arrived in East Anglia in 865, probably from Ireland where it may have had a stronghold.[3] In the spring of 866 the army moved north, invading Northumbria and capturing York. Although the city was retaken by the English it was again seized by the Danes in early 867. An English puppet-king was installed, answerable to the leaders of the Great Army, but they themselves moved south of the Humber to ravage Mercia. In 870, they again plundered East Anglia before coming back through Mercia to attack Wessex, the kingdom of the West Saxons. After a year of fierce fighting, the Danes returned once again to Mercia. There, in 875, they divided their force. One part, led by a king called Halfdan, returned to Northumbria, establishing a headquarters at the mouth of the River Tyne. From this stronghold, Halfdan raided the lands further north until, in 878, his warriors ejected him. In the following year, the English of Northumbria were left leaderless after their own king died. A suitable replacement was found in the person of Guthfrith, a young man of Danish royal blood, who thus became the first Viking ruler of Northumbria.[4] His accession to the kingship was acknowledged by English and Danes alike and heralded a new era for the peoples of northern Britain.

Alt Clut and the Vikings

References to raids on Iona and other Hebridean islands show the presence of Scandinavian pirates in the western seaways from the 790s onwards. Although there are no records of incursions into the Firth of Clyde in the first half of the ninth century, it is unlikely that none occurred. Indeed, the inhabited islands of the Firth were vulnerable and would surely have suffered frequent depredations. Farmers on Arran, Bute and the Cumbraes may have become grimly accustomed to the sight of longships on the horizon. Bute, in particular, must have seemed attractive to heathen warriors, with important monastic sites at Kingarth and on nearby Inchmarnock presenting soft targets and rich pickings. Both monasteries seem to have lain within territory ruled by Cenél Comgaill, a royal kindred of Dál Riata whose heartlands comprised Bute and the Cowal peninsula.[5] In the early 800s, the leaders of Cenél Comgaill probably acknowledged a continuing Pictish overlordship imposed on the Scots in the previous century by Onuist, son of Urguist, who died in 761. This hegemony seems to have remained intact during the reigns of the Pictish kings Constantin (died 820) and his brother Onuist (died 834). It was still evidently in place in 839 when a combined force of Picts and Scots was destroyed in a battle against Vikings. Among the casualties were the Pictish overking and a Dál Riatan ally or vassal, their deaths ushering in a period of dynastic instability in their respective domains. In the ensuing rivalry a new overking emerged in the shape of Cináed mac Ailpín, a Gaelic-speaking Pict whose descendants claimed kinship with Cenél nGabráin, the ancient royal dynasty of Kintyre.[6]

Cenél Comgaill had long been a major power in the Firth of Clyde. Its lands bordered those of the kings of Alt Clut with whom it shared a linguistic and cultural frontier running through the hills and glens on the west side of Loch Lomond. At the dawn of the ninth century, these two groups had been neighbours for hundreds of years. Any Viking incursions into the waters of the Firth would have been a source of mutual anxiety for both, regardless of whether their relationship with one another was friendly or hostile at the time. As we have already noted, there is no record of an early phase of Viking raids in the Clyde firthlands, even if such activity did occur. The first documented attack comes later in the century, in 870, and was not so much a raid as a major assault with far-reaching political consequences. It was reported by chroniclers on both sides of the Irish Sea, with the Ulster annalists noting it in the following entry: 'The siege of Alt Clut by the Norsemen. Anlaf and Ivar, two kings of the Norsemen, laid siege to the fortress and at the end of four months they destroyed and plundered it.'[7]

To understand the context of this momentous event we need to go back nearly thirty years. In 841, a Norwegian force established a colony at Dublin, which soon developed into a major trading emporium and pirate base. Its rulers styled themselves kings and began to extend their influence around the shorelands of the Irish Sea. In 851, Dublin was attacked by another group of Scandinavians whom the Irish called Dubgaill ('Dark Foreigners'). If the traditional identification of these newcomers as Danes is correct, they may have originated among the leadership of the Great Army in Britain. The warlord who brought the Dubgaill to Dublin was a certain Anlaf, probably the same person as Anlaf Conung ('Anlaf the king') who appears in Irish records around this time. Anlaf set himself up as ruler of the Norse colony at Dublin and used the city as a base for raids on Ireland and North Britain. He was eventually joined by his brother Audgisl, with whom he campaigned in Pictish territory in 866, and also by Ivar, usually identified as another brother.[8] In 870, Anlaf and Ivar launched their assault on Alt Clut. Unable to overwhelm the ancient fortress and its impregnable natural defences they besieged it for four months, a sustained assault unprecedented in the history of Viking warfare in Britain and Ireland. The long duration of the siege suggests that

Anlaf and Ivar were not just seeking plunder from the adjacent lands but were determined to capture the Rock itself. They may have had a political motive: the destruction of the royal dynasty of Alt Clut and the neutralising of the North Britons as an effective power. It seems remarkable that the defenders managed to hold out for so long, capitulating only when they ran out of water. The triumphant Vikings then stormed inside, looting and slaying and taking captives. Large numbers of Britons from the Rock and its hinterland were herded onto the waiting longships. Together with Picts, Scots and English captured in other raids, these unfortunates were taken to Dublin to be sold as slaves. Artgal, the king of Alt Clut, together with members of his family, may have been among the prisoners.[9]

Strathclyde

So ended the kingdom of Alt Clut. Its mighty stronghold lay plundered and broken; many of its people were either slain or enslaved; its rulers had suffered a catastrophic defeat. But a new kingdom arose from the wreckage. The royal dynasty survived and the line of kings continued. Artgal died in 872, perhaps in captivity, but his son Rhun succeeded him.[10] A new centre of power was established, not on the heights of Dumbarton Rock but further upstream, at Govan, where the Clyde could be crossed at low tide. Here lay a ritual landscape comprising a mound of probable prehistoric origin, an Early Christian cemetery and an ancient church. Across the ford, at Partick on the north bank of the river, the king and his family seem to have established their main residence on an estate that may have been used by Rhydderch Hael three centuries earlier. They were now no longer the rulers of Alt Clut, the Rock of Clyde, but of Strat Clut, the *strath* or lower valley of the river. It is only from this period onwards, in the years following the great siege of 870, that we can accurately use 'Strathclyde' as the name of a kingdom.[11] The first reference to this name in relation to a political entity is an entry in the *Annals of Ulster* reporting King Artgal's death in 872. Thereafter the name appears in contemporary chronicles from Ireland, Wales and England until the fall of the kingdom in the eleventh century. If a source refers to 'Strathclyde' as a political entity in relation to any period before 870, the information was probably written retrospectively and should be corrected to 'Alt Clut'. The change in terminology appears to coincide with the use of 'Cumberland' and 'Cumbrians' in English chronicles, in relation to the kingdom and its inhabitants. Indeed, it is appropriate and correct for present-day historians to refer to the post-870 rulers of Strathclyde as 'Cumbrian' kings without any hint of ambiguity.

The royal family, having abandoned Dumbarton, would have settled near the ford at Govan with ease. They were no doubt already familiar with the place. In the previous chapter we noted the likelihood that Govan had played a role in the Anglo-Pictish victory celebrations of 756. A near-contemporary Northumbrian record of the place-name, rendered into Latin as *Ovania*, allows us to infer that it was an important site within the kingdom of Alt Clut. This is not only Govan's first appearance in recorded history but its only mention in any source before the twelfth century. A fundamental question thus arises: with only one historical reference to early medieval Govan, how can we feel confident that this was a major royal site in the new kingdom of Strathclyde? The answer lies in a group of thirty-one carved stones, one of the largest collections of early medieval sculpture in Scotland, now housed in the old parish church. These monuments, together with sixteen more that no longer survive, formerly stood in the churchyard among the tombstones of later times. Their ornate carvings suggest that they were commissioned by a wealthy elite keen to display wealth and status through the medium of sculpture. Although the carved motifs include crosses and other Christian imagery some are undoubtedly secular rather than ecclesiastical: images of spear-armed horsemen on several stones suggest that the people they commemorated were members of a warrior aristocracy rather than of a religious community. On art-historical grounds, the Govan sculpture has been dated to the Viking Age of the ninth to eleventh centuries.[12] It is significant to note that the earliest monuments were probably carved between 850 and 900, around the time when the fortress of Alt Clut was destroyed. Sculptured stones similar in style and date to those at Govan are found elsewhere along the Clyde and as far afield as North Ayrshire, but these outlying examples are grouped in ones, twos or threes. Only at Govan is this type of monument found in large numbers. Such a concentration at one site indicates that it was not only a place of considerable importance but also the origin-centre of this particular style of stone-carving. A final point is the presence of a hunting scene on the sarcophagus, the oldest of the stones at Govan Old. Similar scenes are found in other sculptural traditions, such as those of Pictland, and are strongly associated with royalty.[13] Taken together, the archaeological and sculptural evidence from Govan identifies it as the premier centre of royal power in the kingdom of Strathclyde.

A detached portion of the old parish of Govan lay in Partick on the opposite bank of the River Clyde. Here, as already noted, the surviving members of King

Artgal's family probably set up their primary residence after 870. The site in question would later be occupied by Partick Castle, a structure no longer in existence today. Whereas our picture of early medieval Govan owes much to the weighty evidence of the carved stones, at Partick we have little or no archaeological information. We rely instead on a single textual source, a hagiographical *vita* or 'Life' of St Kentigern commissioned by the bishop of Glasgow in the 1100s. The hagiographer, Jocelin of Furness, tells us that King Rhydderch Hael of Alt Clut had a residence at Partick. Although nearly six hundred years separated Jocelin from the era of Rhydderch and Kentigern, the reference to Partick might preserve a kernel of historical accuracy. In the twelfth century, the bishops of Glasgow certainly had an estate there, the precursor of the later castle. It is possible, or perhaps even likely, that they took over a high-status site formerly used by the royal family of Strathclyde.[14] Whether this site reached back to Rhydderch's time in the late sixth century is unknown, but its use by his successors in the Viking Age would fit with the sculptural evidence from Govan. Partick, then, may have been selected as a key residence of the Cumbrian kings after the fall of Dumbarton Rock, with Govan serving as a venue for religious rites and ceremonial gatherings. The mound of Govan, a massive feature overlooking the ancient ford, may have played a key role in these ritual activities. Known as the Hillock or Doomster Hill before its destruction in the mid-nineteenth century, the mound dominated the local landscape.[15] A sketch by the artist Robert Paul in 1758 shows it as a massive, flat-topped mound with two levels and a substantial encircling ditch. Paul's viewpoint was Yorkhill in Partick, directly opposite the mound, but the perspective of his sketch seems to be skewed. In the extract shown as a plate in this book, the trees on the right hide the parish church of Govan Old. In the foreground stands a group of cottages on one side of a lane running alongside the Govan Water, the stream that gave the lane its name: Water Row. The lane ends at the ancient ford where the Clyde could be traversed on foot at low tide or – as in Paul's sketch – by a small ferryboat. To the left stands the Doomster Hill, dwarfing the nearby buildings. Even from the sketch it is obvious that the hill was artificial rather than natural, for this part of Clydesdale is otherwise devoid of such features. Its distinctive 'stepped' profile is reminiscent of similar mounds in other parts of the British Isles and in Scandinavia. The shape has strong associations with early medieval kingship and with large public ceremonies where royal power was displayed. In Scotland, the best-known example is the Moot Hill at Scone, a site whose royal connections span many centuries. Elsewhere in the British Isles, other stepped mounds were sited in areas colonised by Vikings. Some, such as Tynwald Hill on the Isle of Man and the now-vanished Thingmote at Dublin, incorporate the Old Norse word *thing* ('assembly') in their names.[16] The Doomster Hill is plainly a site of similar sort. Its name connects it with local 'doomsters' who dispensed justice at open-air courts in the pre-modern era but it undoubtedly served as a venue for royal rituals in Viking times. It provides additional confirmation of Govan's status as the 'capital' of Strathclyde.

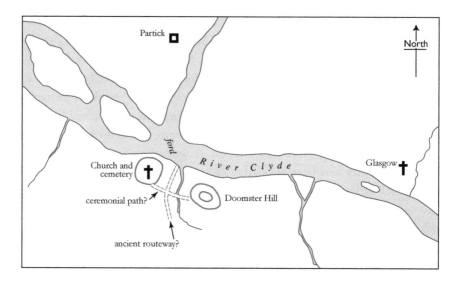

MAP 4 Govan in AD 900

Alba

When the Irish annalists noted the death of King Artgal in 872 they associated him not with the old fortress of Alt Clut but with the successor realm of Strathclyde. They also noted that a neighbouring ruler played a part in his demise: 'Artgal, king of the Strathclyde Britons, was killed at the instigation of Constantin son of Cináed.'

This annal suggests that Artgal was not only the last ruler of Dumbarton Rock but also the first of the new kingdom established further upstream around the ford at Govan. Whether this is the correct interpretation is, however, uncertain. A more secure inference is that Artgal's slaying at the 'instigation' (or 'wisdom') of Constantin, king of the Picts, was a political assassination.[17] The deed was plainly not undertaken by Constantin himself but by an unnamed third party. We can only guess at the context, especially as the Pictish king's sister was the wife of Artgal's son Rhun. Such marriages did not necessarily make friendship between royal houses inevitable. Rhun might have been expelled from his father's kingdom during a period of kin-strife and could have been living in exile at Constantin's court when the Vikings sacked Dumbarton in 870. In such circumstances, Constantin may have sought to install Rhun as the new king of the Britons.[18] Artgal could have had another heir in mind, perhaps a more favoured son whom Rhun regarded as a rival. A completely different scenario would see Rhun not as a friend of his Pictish brother-in-law but as an enemy, in which case Rhun himself may have been Artgal's preferred successor. The slaying of Artgal might then be nothing more than an act of spite by Constantin against a family who, notwithstanding the bond of a dynastic marriage, maintained a hostile stance towards him. Whatever the true circumstances, the Irish annalists clearly believed that Artgal survived the fall of Dumbarton by a year or more. It is possible that he was taken to Dublin as a prisoner, a high-status trophy among the numerous captives borne away by Anlaf and Ivar after their raids on northern Britain. His assassination could have been carried out by Dublin Vikings complying with a request from Constantin. The most literal interpretation of the Irish annal entry, however, is that Artgal did not die in captivity and that he was indeed the first king of the new realm of Strathclyde.

In Chapter 1 we saw that a royal genealogy or pedigree of the Clyde Britons, preserved in a Welsh manuscript, shows the ancestry of Artgal's son Rhun. Either the pedigree's original compiler or a later copyist regarded it as the pedigree of Dumbarton rather than of Strathclyde, for its header reads 'Alt Clut'. Taking the header literally, and in the absence of other information, we could probably assume that both Rhun and his father ruled from Clyde Rock. Although this is possible, the disappearance of the name 'Alt Clut' from the historical record after the Viking siege of 870 weighs heavily against it. It is clear that the name was replaced in the sources by the new name 'Strathclyde'. The only real uncertainty is whether Artgal was king of both the old political entity and the new. In the case of Rhun, whom the *Chronicle of the Kings of Alba* calls simply 'king of the Britons', we can be fairly sure that he was king of Strathclyde alone and that his centre of power lay not at Dumbarton but at Govan. By 872, when his father was slain, he and his family no longer resided on the towering Rock at the head of the firth.

No source gives the name of Rhun's Pictish wife, but she was almost certainly a Gaelic-speaker. Although her father, Cináed mac Ailpín, had emerged in the 840s as a contender for the overkingship of the southern Picts, later traditions connected him with the Scots of Dál Riata. Justifiably or otherwise, his paternal ancestry was attached to the royal house of Cenél nGabráin whose main power-base lay in Kintyre.[19] The year and place of his birth are unknown but he was born in a period when the Pictish overlordship of Dál Riata, established by Onuist in the eighth century, seems to have remained intact. This long-lasting Pictish domination of the Scots brought a surprising cultural change: the rise of Gaelic as the main language of the Picts. By c.800, it is likely that the old Pictish language, a Brittonic tongue like Cumbric, had lost significant ground to Gaelic. At the end of the ninth century, a Gaelic-speaking kingdom based in the southern Pictish heartlands of Perthshire held sway over Picts and Scots alike. The kingdom's name was *Alba*, a word of uncertain origin that may have been widely used in Dál Riata as a Gaelic term for 'Pictland'.[20] Its ruling dynasty was the family of Cináed mac Ailpín, whose grandson Domnall was the first to be described in the sources as *ri Albain* ('king of Alba') rather than as *rex Pictorum* ('king of the Picts'). Within a few generations of Cináed's death in 858, the inhabitants of Alba began to think of themselves as 'Scots', regardless of whether they dwelt in the Pictish east or in the Gaelic west. For reasons that are barely understood, the Pictish overlordship of Dál Riata and the emergence of Alba ended the notion of a separate Pictish identity.

After Artgal's death in 872, the kingship of the Clyde Britons or Cumbrians seems to have been bequeathed to – or seized by – his son Rhun. Relations between Rhun and his Pictish brother-in-law Constantin are undocumented but may have become hostile at some point. An account of Constantin's battles in the *Prophecy of Berchan* tells of 'the battle of Luaire, against the king of the Britons, of green mantles'.[21] Although mentioned in no other source, this must have been fought in the period 862–76 when Constantin reigned as *rex Pictorum*. If the unnamed king of the Britons was Rhun, the battle took place between 872 and 876. If the battle was fought before the Viking assault on Alt Clut, the king 'of green mantles' may have been Artgal. A period of hostility between Britons and Picts between 862 and 870 could even provide a context for Artgal's subsequent death at the instigation of Constantin. The significance of 'green mantles' is unknown and the place called *Luaire* has not been identified. A suggestion that it is now Carlowrie on the River Almond, five miles west of Edinburgh, seems rather doubtful.[22] A site further north or west, in the traditional borderland between Picts and Britons, would probably make more sense but there are no obvious candidates.

Rhun's relations with Anglo-Saxon Northumbria are unrecorded but some historians propose that his Pictish wife, the daughter of Cináed mac Ailpín, had a connection with the Northumbrian royal fortress of Bamburgh. The information comes from the *Prophecy of Berchan* which, in typically enigmatic style, refers to Rhun's son Eochaid as 'son of the woman from Dun Guaire'. In *Historia Brittonum* we learn that the Britons called Bamburgh *Din Guoaroy*, a name of uncertain meaning. It has been suggested that an early Irish poem renders *Din Guoaroy* as *Dun Guaire*, itself a Gaelic name borne by two places in Ireland as well as by two in the Hebrides. It then becomes only a small leap to suggest that Rhun's wife became known as 'the woman from Dun Guaire' because she had formerly dwelt in the old Northumbrian fortress, perhaps in marriage to an Englishman.[23] Needless to say, the entire theory relies on a sequence of guesses, all of which proceed from an unfounded assumption that the Irish poem refers to Din Guoaroy/Bamburgh rather than to another place called Dun Guaire. The Irish sites seem to commemorate King Guaire, a seventh-century Connacht ruler who figures in a number of later tales. While the two Hebridean places called Dun Guaire might also be named after this figure from Gaelic saga, it seems unlikely that the Britons had him in mind when they gave the name Guoaroy to the fortress at Bamburgh. There is, in fact, no compelling reason to believe that Dun Guaire in the *Prophecy of Berchan* is a Northumbrian site at all. Rather than attempting to give Rhun's wife a connection with Bamburgh through an earlier marriage to an English lord, we should look for it elsewhere. Given Cináed's alleged kinship with the Scots of Dál Riata, his daughter may have been associated with one or other of the Hebridean places called Dun Guaire.[24] In the absence of a secure identification or additional information it would be fruitless to speculate further.

Rhun's reign presumably commenced soon after his father's death in 872. He was probably ruling when the northern portion of the Danish Great Army attacked Strathclyde in the second half of the decade. As mentioned earlier, this force came to Northumbria in 875, making an encampment beside the River Tyne. Under the command of Halfdan, one of the Great Army's original leaders, it launched raids on the Picts and Strathclyde Britons.[25] We can assume that these attacks were met by fierce resistance but nothing further is known of them. They may have ceased after Halfdan's warriors expelled him from their ranks in 878.

No source gives the date of Rhun's death or the name of his successor but his kinsman Constantin, king of the Picts, died in 877 in a battle against Vikings. Some historians think Rhun may have been killed in the same encounter, fighting alongside his brother-in-law as an ally or vassal, but this is no more than a guess.[26] We cannot be sure that Rhun owed allegiance to Constantin at any time, or that relations between them were generally friendly. Constantin was succeeded by his brother Áed who reigned for two years before being slain by his *socii* ('associates'). What happened next is uncertain because no coherent account emerges from the various sources. Some texts identify a mysterious figure called Giric as the next king of the Picts while others assert that Áed was instead succeeded by Eochaid, son of Rhun of Strathclyde, and that Giric was merely Eochaid's *alumnus* ('foster father' or 'guardian').[27] The uncertainty raises a number of possible scenarios. One school of thought proposes that Eochaid did not follow Áed as king of the Picts but instead succeeded his father Rhun in Strathclyde. It sees Giric as Áed's actual successor, with Eochaid ruling the Britons as a subordinate. Another theory imagines Eochaid and Giric holding joint kingship over the Picts, with Giric as the senior partner. As a grandson of Cináed mac Ailpín, Eochaid's eligibility for the Pictish kingship must have seemed secure, whereas Giric's ancestry is less certain. The author of the *Prophecy of Berchan* felt sure that Eochaid did indeed succeed Áed, even though the verse in question does not name him. It comes immediately after a verse dealing with Áed's reign:

> After that the king will take sovereignty whose name will be the usurper; alas, west and east, that a Briton should take lordship over the Gaels. The Briton of the Clyde will take sovereignty, the son of the woman from Dun Guaire. Thirteen years – heights of valour – in the high kingship of Alba.[28]

Here, Eochaid's reign is lamented and his right to rule in Alba is questioned. Later, in a verse on Giric, the *Prophecy* states that 'the Britons will be more lowly during his [Giric's] time' and that 'he [Giric] will have in bondage in his house English, Vikings and Britons'. From this we might infer that Giric's relations with Strathclyde included periods of hostility and dominance. Amid all this uncertainty we learn nothing of the sequence of Cumbrian kings, for no source refers to the history of their realm in the final quarter of the ninth century. Clarity does, however, return to the sequence of Pictish kings with the accession of Domnall, son of Constantin, in 889. In a notice of his death eleven years later, Domnall is described as 'king of Alba' rather than as 'king of the Picts'. The change of terminology suggests that his reign marked a period of transition for the mac Ailpín dynasty after the removal of Eochaid and Giric. Eochaid's fate is unknown but Giric is said to have been killed at the old Pictish fortress of Dundurn in Strathearn. Both men may have died there, perhaps in a battle with Domnall's forces.[29] There is no indication that Domnall subjugated the Cumbrians of Strathclyde, nor that their kingdom ceased to be independent after the disappearance of Eochaid. The erroneous idea that Strathclyde was permanently subjugated by the kings of Alba from c.900 was nevertheless promoted by later Scottish chroniclers such as John of Fordun and has persisted even into our own time.

Migration to Gwynedd?

In 1801, an edition of the thirteenth-century Welsh chronicle *Brut y Tywysogion* was printed in a large collection of texts called *The Myvyrian Archaiology of Wales*. Under the year 890 it referred to a series of events that are said to have occurred during the reign of Anarawd, king of Gwynedd. The original entry is in Welsh, here translated into English:

> The men of Strathclyde, those that refused to unite with the English, had to depart from their country and go to Gwynedd. Anarawd gave them permission to settle in the country that had been taken from him by the English, namely Maelawr and the Vale of Clwyd and Rhyfoniawg and Tegeingl, if they could drive away the English; and this they did energetically. But the English came against Anarawd a second time because of that, and the battle of Cymryd was there, and the Cymry routed the Saxons and drove them from the country completely. Thus Gwynedd was freed from the English, through the might of the Men of the North.

No record of a migration from Strathclyde to Wales appears in any early source. The battle of Cymryd, fought beside the River Conwy in 881, is noted in the Welsh Annals but there is no mention of a North British contingent. It was a historical event, a victory for Anarawd over an army of Mercians led by their lord Aethelred, son-in-law of Alfred the Great. There is likewise no reference to Strathclyde immigrants in the relevant sections of the oldest manuscripts of *Brut y Tywysogion*. The source of the story can, in fact, be traced to a sixteenth-century English translation which claimed to have used a Welsh chronicle supposedly written two hundred years earlier. There is no reason to regard it as anything other than a fictional tale.[30] It may have arisen from confusion between the river names Clwyd and Clyde. In any case, no English king – not even Alfred the Great himself – was in a position to subjugate Strathclyde or any other northern power in the late ninth century. If any migration by the 'Men of the North' really had occurred, it would surely have been because of a threat from Pictish or Viking forces.

STRATHCLYDE AND WESSEX

In 870, the year when Vikings from Dublin sacked the fortress of Alt Clut, the Danish 'Great Army' plundered East Anglia. The following year saw the army move west through Mercia to attack Wessex, the last unconquered English kingdom. There it met stern resistance from the West Saxon king Aethelred and his brother Alfred (later known as 'the Great'). Months of hard fighting ensued, with the tide of war eventually swinging in favour of the Danes. After Aethelred's death, Alfred became king and continued the struggle. By early 878, much of Wessex had been subjugated by the heathens but, in May of that year, Alfred won a decisive victory which finally turned the tide. A subsequent peace treaty saw the Danes withdraw north and east of a new frontier marked approximately by Watling Street, an old Roman highway running diagonally north-westward from London. Behind this line the Vikings ruled East Anglia, eastern Mercia and much of Northumbria. In these areas the English lived alongside their former foes and a hybrid Anglo-Scandinavian culture gradually developed. Because Scandinavian rather than English legal codes prevailed, the entire Danish-controlled area came to be known as the 'Danelaw'. The peace, however, was too fragile to endure and raids continued to be launched from the Danelaw against Alfred's kingdom. Alfred withstood these assaults and responded by campaigning across the midlands, defeating the Vikings on land and sea and eventually restoring the great trading city of London to English rule. When he died in 899, after a reign of almost thirty years, he bequeathed a strong, stable realm that was no longer at the mercy of Scandinavian warlords.

Edward and Aethelflaed

In Wessex, Alfred was succeeded by his son Edward, later known as 'the Elder' to distinguish him from his great-grandson Edward the Martyr. Like his father, Edward was determined to stem the loss of English territory to Viking warlords.[1] However, whereas Alfred had concentrated his efforts on the south and midlands, Edward now took the war to the Danes of Northumbria, fighting them in northern Lincolnshire in 909. In the following year, these same Danes attacked Mercia. They were soundly defeated by Edward's West Saxon and Mercian troops at Tettenhall in Staffordshire. In these and in later campaigns, Edward benefited from the valuable assistance of his elder sister Aethelflaed, wife of the Mercian ruler Aethelred. At that time, the still-English western part of Mercia provided a stern bulwark against the Danes and a source of additional manpower for West Saxon armies. Aethelred ruled it as Edward's subordinate, with the title *ealdorman*, yet he was king in all but name.

Edward undertook a programme of fort-building to deter further Scandinavian attacks, continuing a policy begun by his father. Garrisoned by full-time soldiers and sited in a strategic location, each fort (Old English: *burh*) presented a formidable obstacle to enemy forces. After Aethelred's death in 911 from a long illness, his people acknowledged his widow Aethelflaed as their ruler. She was known thereafter as *Myrcna hlaefdige*, 'The Lady of the Mercians', and was renowned as a competent war-leader. She established new fortresses throughout Mercia and led attacks on Viking strongholds in the Danelaw, her greatest triumph being the capture of Derby in 917. On her north-west frontier in Cheshire she built fortresses at Eddisbury and Runcorn to hinder seaborne raiders arriving via the Mersey estuary.[2] She also perceived an ever-present threat from Northumbria, not only from the Danish leadership at York but also from the western coastlands where folk of Norwegian origin had recently established new settlements. These Norse colonists did not come directly from Scandinavia but from long-established Viking colonies in Ireland. In the early years of the tenth century they came to Britain in large numbers, some as farmers seeking land rather than as raiders hunting for loot. Their arrival on Northumbria's western seaboard was part of a wider series of changes in the balance of power.

Modern historians usually refer to the new settlers as 'Hiberno-Norse'. Some left Ireland after their main centre of power at Dublin was captured by an alliance of Irish kings in 902.[3] The Irish may have allowed a few Scandinavians to remain in the city but others were seemingly forced to leave. Norse colonists in other parts of Ireland also moved to Britain, perhaps for reasons unconnected with the fall of Dublin, so the migration was not so much a single event as a process involving different groups and a long timescale. Some migrants arrived on the shorelands of western Northumbria, settling in what are now Lancashire, Cumbria and Galloway, while others went elsewhere.[4] One large group, led by a certain Ingimund, attempted to settle in Anglesey but faced stern opposition from a local Welsh king. Ingimund and his people sought help from Aethelred and Aethelflaed who gave permission to settle in Mercian territory near Chester.

However, the wealth of the former Roman city proved too much of a temptation for the new arrivals, who tried to seize it by force. After their attempt was
repulsed, Aethelflaed took steps to deter future assaults. She is said to have
'restored' Chester in 907, presumably by strengthening the Roman defences and
turning the city into a *burh*.[5]

Aethelflaed's northern alliance

The waning of Scandinavian power in Ireland proved to be only a brief interlude. In 914, a large Norse fleet sailed from bases in Brittany to ravage South
Wales. After raiding far inland, these Vikings were confronted by Mercian
forces and driven back to their ships. They eventually headed to Ireland,
making landfall on the south-east coast at Waterford where they established a
stronghold. In the same year, a sea-battle between rival Norse forces was
fought near the Isle of Man. Where the two sides originated, and what their
dispute was about, are questions to which the sources provide no clear answers.
The victor was Ragnall, described in Irish sources as a grandson of Ivar.[6] His
grandfather is assumed to have been the same Ivar who, with his brother
Anlaf, led the great raid on Alt Clut in 870. Ragnall was thus a member of the
Viking dynasty of Dublin and had a claim on the paramount leadership of the
Hiberno-Norse. After the Irish captured Dublin in 902, his power-base may
have lain among Norse colonies in western Northumbria or on the Isle of
Man. Following his naval victory in Manx waters in 914 he was probably
acknowledged as king by a majority of Norse settlers on both sides of the Irish
Sea. The victory led to his emergence as a serious threat to neighbouring
powers. In 917, he went to Ireland where he and his brother Sihtric became
embroiled in wars between the Norse of Waterford and various Irish kings.
Before the year was out, Sihtric had recaptured Dublin and taken the kingship
of the city while Ragnall had likewise seized power in Waterford.[7] It may have
been to counter the growing menace posed by these ambitious brothers that
Aethelflaed forged an alliance with the kings of Alba and Strathclyde. Our
sole source for this three-way pact is the *Fragmentary Annals of Ireland* (*FAI*),
a controversial text which also provides us with the story of Ingimund.
Aethelflaed's alliance with the northern powers is noted by *FAI* in an annal for
918 where it immediately follows a detailed account of one of her victories.
The battle in question was allegedly fought 'after the installation of Sihtric,
grandson of Ivar, as king'. If we accept the implied chronology, the Mercian
alliance with Alba and Strathclyde was negotiated at some point between

Sihtric's accession as king of Dublin in 917 and Aethelflaed's death in June of the following year. According to *FAI*,

> Aethelflaed, through her own cleverness, made peace with the men of Alba and with the Britons, so that whenever the same race should come to attack her, they would rise to help her. If it were against them that they came, she would take arms with them. While this continued, the men of Alba and the Britons overcame the settlements of the Norsemen and destroyed and sacked them. The king of the Norsemen came after that and sacked Strathclyde, and plundered the land. But the enemy was ineffectual against Strathclyde.[8]

Since Aethelflaed's main concern was the protection of Mercia's borders, there can be little doubt that the 'settlements of the Norsemen' were those whom she regarded as posing an immediate threat to her territory. The reference is probably to the new colonies established in western Northumbria after the post-902 exodus from Ireland.[9] Strathclyde's participation in the alliance is unsurprising, given the northern focus implied by Alba's involvement. It seems a reasonable inference that the Norse settlements attacked by the Britons lay around the Solway Firth, in areas formerly under Northumbrian rule. The Scots may have been expected to harass colonies in Argyll, the old lands of Dál Riata from where the ancestors of the mac Ailpín dynasty supposedly originated. It is likely, for instance, that the Hebridean seaways had seen an increase in Hiberno-Norse activity since 902. No joint military campaign by Alba and Strathclyde is hinted at by the account in *FAI*, which says simply that the Scots and Britons sealed pledges of mutual support with the Lady of the Mercians.[10] There is likewise no hint that Aethelflaed expected her northern allies to support one another in the same way. The Norse king described as mounting a counter-raid on Strathclyde is unidentified but, given that the annal for 918 begins with Sihtric's installation as king of Dublin, Sihtric himself is an obvious candidate. His brother Ragnall is another. Ragnall, as we have seen, probably held sway over the Norse colonies in western Northumbria from 914. Either of these grandsons of Ivar might be the king who attacked Aethelflaed's allies in Strathclyde. Whoever this Norse ruler was, his raid was deemed to be 'ineffectual', perhaps because it inflicted less damage than might have been expected. Strathclyde, by contrast, seems to have made substantial territorial gains in this period, some at the expense of the Norse. On both sides of the Solway Firth, a scatter of place-names indicates a tenth-century revival of the Cumbric language, a process that can only have happened in the wake of major political change.

The place-names indicate that a new aristocracy of Cumbric-speakers replaced the old Northumbrian landowning elite in positions of prominence. Any prospect of a wholesale takeover of these lands by the Hiberno-Norse moving east from their coastal settlements would have evaporated. The only Cumbric-speaking power at that time was Strathclyde, so what we are undoubtedly seeing is a southward expansion of the kingdom around the time when its kings were in a military alliance with English Mercia.

This expansion of Cumbrian power is explored in more detail below but, in the meantime, we turn back to Aethelflaed's anti-Norse coalition. Can her Strathclyde ally be identified? Her Scottish ally can only have been Constantin mac Áeda whose long reign spanned the first half of the tenth century. Constantin succeeded his cousin Domnall as king of Alba in 900 and ruled for more than forty years until his abdication in 943. His father Áed had briefly held the kingship before being slain by treacherous 'associates' in 878, his death heralding the emergence of Giric and Eochaid. While the succession in Alba soon stabilised with the kings Domnall and Constantin, the sequence in Strathclyde is far less certain. The last identifiable ruler of the Cumbrian kingdom in the ninth century was Rhun, son of Artgal, whose reign-length is given in no source. He may have been succeeded by his half-Pictish son Eochaid but this is only one possibility and we essentially lose sight of the sequence of kings. A measure of clarity reappears in the 920s but, with no source giving the name of Aethelflaed's Strathclyde ally in 918, we are left to hazard a guess as to his identity.

According to a summary of Constantin's reign in the *Chronicle of the Kings of Alba*: 'there died in his time Doneualdus, king of the Britons, and Dunenaldus son of Áed, king of Ailech, and Flann son of Maelsechnaill, and Niall son of Áed who reigned three years after Flann.'[11] *Doneualdus* is a Latinisation of *Dumnagual*, a Brittonic name rendered throughout this book in its later Welsh form *Dyfnwal*. It is clearly not the same name as Gaelic *Domnall*, here rendered by the chronicler as *Dunenaldus*. Dyfnwal's appearance in a Scottish text makes it highly likely that the Britons whom he ruled were those on the Clyde rather than a southerly group in Wales or Brittany. The other kings mentioned alongside him were Irish. Until recently, Dyfnwal was regarded by many historians as the last king of an independent Strathclyde, chiefly because of a misreading of the passage. The confusion arose in the opening words, which the scribe of the oldest manuscript of *CKA* wrote as *Doneualdus rex Britanniorum et Dunenaldus filius Ede elig*. The word *elig* was long assumed to be an abbreviation of Latin *eligitur* ('was elected'), hence the common belief that Domnall, son of Áed, must therefore have been 'elected' to the kingship of the Britons after Dyfnwal's death. A further assumption saw Domnall as a brother of Constantin mac Áeda, even though no sibling of this name is mentioned elsewhere. Historians thus proposed that Constantin must have appointed or 'elected' this same Domnall to the throne of Strathclyde after conquering the kingdom, thereby introducing a custom in which the royal heir of Alba ruled the Clyde Britons while awaiting his own turn on the Scottish throne.[12] As we saw in Chapter 1, the idea of tenth-century Strathclyde as a vassal realm of Alba originated with John of Fordun and reflected his own preferred view of Scottish history. A simpler and more logical interpretation of *elig* sees it not as an abbreviation for *eligitur* but as the Latin genitive form of the Irish place-name *Ailech*.[13] *CKA* is therefore describing Domnall, son of Áed, as being 'of Ailech'. The place in question is an imposing hilltop fortress in Donegal, a stronghold of the powerful Cenél nEogain dynasty. We know from the *Annals of Ulster* that one of Ailech's kings in the early tenth century was indeed a certain Domnall, son of Áed, who died in 915.[14] It is surely this individual whom we find listed in *CKA*. He was not an otherwise unknown Scottish prince but rather an Irish king placed after Dyfnwal of Strathclyde in a list of rulers who died during Constantin's reign.

The royal deaths, battles and other events in *CKA*'s summary run in chronological sequence. Many of them appear with precise dates in other sources. The deaths of the three Irish kings named after Dyfnwal appear also in *AU*, with the following dates: Domnall in 915, Flann in 916, Niall in 919. As the same sequence is mirrored in *CKA*, but without the dates, we might assume that the compiler of *CKA* knew this to be the correct chronological order. If he then added Dyfnwal's death at the correct point in the sequence, Dyfnwal must have died before Domnall and no later than 915. Thus, if Aethelflaed's alliance was forged in 918, her Strathclyde ally was probably not Dyfnwal, who had seemingly died at least three years earlier. We should instead associate the military pact and the Cumbrian raids on Norse settlements with Dyfnwal's successor. In the 920s, a man called Owain appears in the sources as king of Strathclyde. If his father was the Dyfnwal whose death was reported in *CKA*, we might tentatively identify Owain as Dyfnwal's successor and as Aethelflaed's ally. It is interesting to note that *FAI* makes no mention of Mercian military aid for Strathclyde when the kingdom was attacked by the Norse, despite Aethelflaed's pledge of assistance. From this we might infer that the attack came after her death in June 918, in which case any personal guarantees she had given would have died with her. The apparent lack of English intervention also suggests that Edward the Elder had no interest in maintaining his sister's pact with the Cumbrians, or that he was incapable of helping them at that time, or that the Norse raid on Strathclyde was so 'ineffectual' that his help was not needed.

The Cumbrian expansion

Before the Viking Age, the kings of Anglo-Saxon Northumbria had ruled a very large realm stretching across Britain from the North Sea to the Irish Sea. The eastern part of this territory stretched from the Humber estuary to the Firth of Forth; the western part from the River Mersey as far north as Ayrshire. This extensive hegemony began to collapse during the ninth century under pressure from Viking raids. By the 860s, when the leaders of the Danish Great Army became the new power-brokers at York, the old Northumbrian kingdom had already shrunk back to its former heartlands on the eastern and western sides of the Pennines. Long-established English settlements in what is now south-west Scotland were then effectively cast adrift. These had been established during phases of Northumbrian expansion in the seventh and eighth centuries, largely at the expense of the Britons. After the collapse of the old kingdom, the Northumbrian aristocracy remained *in situ* as lords of a population that was predominantly English-speaking. Further east, in the old Bernician lands around Bamburgh, an autonomous English lordship emerged in the wake of the Danish takeover of York, its leaders running their own affairs independently of the rest of Northumbria.

West of the Pennines, the expansion of Northumbrian power in the seventh and eighth centuries is marked today by numerous place-names of Old English origin. There are, however, regional differences in their distribution. They survive as the dominant place-name group in inland areas of Lancashire and in the former county of Westmorland but less so in parts of Cumberland and on the shores of the Irish Sea.[15] In western coastal districts a proliferation of Scandinavian names, occasionally showing Gaelic influence, suggests an influx of Hiberno-Norse settlers in the late ninth and early tenth centuries. In some cases, the Norse established new settlements with new names, while in others an existing English site was simply taken over and its name was replaced by a Norse one. Where replacement of an English name in areas of Norse settlement did not occur, we may be seeing survival of Northumbrian landownership and of English-speaking communities under Norse rule. In such instances, the higher authority in the area may have been a Norse *jarl*. Norse names are certainly numerous in a few areas, such as the Lake District in Cumbria and Amounderness in Lancashire. In these districts, many tenth-century

landowners, if not their tenants as well, may have been Norse-speaking incomers. In some instances, we find hybrid 'Anglo-Scandinavian' place-names
incorporating elements from both languages, although not all of these are from
the ninth and tenth centuries. Some may have been coined as late as the 1100s
when Norse influence was still evident in the speech of north-west England.[16]
The overall distribution of Norse place-names in western Northumbria does,
however, suggest that colonists from Ireland and other Gaelic-speaking regions
arrived in significant numbers in the late 800s and early 900s. Some appear to
have made new settlements in undeveloped 'waste' areas avoided by earlier
populations. These sites are usually found in difficult terrain such as wetlands,
uplands, remote valleys and forest-edges. The colonists would, of course, have
been attracted to better-quality agricultural lands, but these had already been
settled centuries before by Britons, then by Anglo-Saxons. Here, the older
Cumbric or English place-names have often been preserved, even in areas taken
over by the Hiberno-Norse, with survival implying that the incomers chose to
leave them intact.[17] It is worth noting that names of recognisably Danish origin
are rare in the north-west, being found mainly in upland areas on the eastern
fringe. They probably represent a separate, westward movement by elements of
the Great Army seeking new farmlands across the Pennines. There is no hint
that they provide evidence for an extension of political power from York, even
if parts of Westmorland may have recognised the authority of the city's
Scandinavian kings by c.940.[18]

A number of older Cumbric settlement-names west of the Pennines survived
both the expansion of Anglo-Saxon Northumbria and the Hiberno-Norse colonisation. There is no need to see these as evidence for the survival of Cumbric
speech, or of pockets of 'Britishness', in the period between the seventh and tenth
centuries. They were probably fossils that had simply not been replaced after
English became the common tongue by the beginning of the eighth century.
More curious is what happened two hundred years later. In the early tenth
century, when Norse colonies were being established in western Northumbria,
new place-names of Cumbric origin began to appear. Looking at a modern map
of north-west England, we see that these new names are mainly found north of
the River Eamont, in what later became the county of Cumberland. They are also
found on the other side of the Solway Firth, in Dumfriesshire. South of the
Solway, they occur in sufficient numbers to show the emergence of new Cumbric-
speaking communities in areas formerly under English rule. Philologists have
long recognised that these place-names were not there before the Anglo-Saxon
conquest in the seventh century.[19] In some cases, a new Cumbric name was

formed from an English one created in the 600s, or from a Norse name of the early 900s. One example of an existing place-name being adapted by Cumbric-speakers is Carlatton, with stress on the second syllable, which was originally an Anglo-Norse hybrid *Cárlatun* ('churl village') stressed on the first syllable. *Cárlatun* would normally have been expected to develop into a modern English name such as 'Charlton' or 'Carleton' but instead it survives today in a form representing its pronunciation in Cumbric. What appears to have happened is that Cumbric-speakers encountered the name *Cárlatun* and stressed it on the second syllable, as they would have done with a tri-syllabic word in their own language. This form must then have become embedded in the landscape, surviving the eventual disappearance of Cumbric speech. Another example is Cumwhitton, where a Cumbric prefix meaning 'valley' has been added to an older English place-name meaning 'estate of a man called Hwita'.[20] Other names indicate that new communities of Cumbric-speakers sprang up in the kind of marginal or 'waste' terrain ignored by earlier Northumbrian settlers but exploited by the Norse. The historical context behind the process is clear: in the tenth century, parts of north-west Northumbria were colonised by an influx of Cumbric-speaking people.[21] While Norse groups were moving east from landfalls on the coast, penetrating the Lake District valleys, groups of Britons were colonising an area between the Solway Firth and the River Eamont. All of these incomers were taking advantage of a power-vacuum created by the collapse of Anglo-Saxon Northumbria. We know from Gaelic elements in their place-names that many of the Norse colonists came from Ireland, perhaps around the time of the fall of Viking Dublin in 902. The Cumbric speakers can only have originated in Strathclyde, the last remaining kingdom of the Cumbrians or North Britons.[22] It is possible that they began to arrive as early as the final quarter of the ninth century, as Anglo-Saxon power declined. Their migration was presumably preceded by military campaigns in which their forces challenged English landowners and Norse colonists for mastery of the fertile lands of the Solway Plain. These contests, although invisible in the historical record, might have reached a climax in the second decade of the tenth century, when the Strathclyde Britons are said to have attacked the Norse in the days of Lady Aethelflaed. It is even possible that Strathclyde's southward expansion was sanctioned or even encouraged by Aethelflaed and her brother Edward the Elder. In the courts of Mercia and Wessex, it may have seemed preferable to let Britons rather than Hiberno-Norse fill the vacuum in north-west Northumbria. As a familiar power which had a long history of contact with English kings, Strathclyde perhaps seemed more of a known quantity and less of a menace to West Saxon and Mercian interests. The place-name evidence suggests that a Cumbric-speaking aristocracy halted the Norse advance across the Solway Plain by taking control of former English estates and overseeing the creation of new settlements in marginal terrain. Either in this region or nearer their heartlands on the Clyde, according to *FAI*, the Britons withstood attacks from a Norse king who may have been Sihtric or Ragnall, but their own territorial gains remained intact. Their colonies south of the Solway endured and a new layer of Cumbric place-names became part of the landscape.

We should note that the distribution of place-names is rarely neat enough to allow linguistic, cultural or political boundaries to be drawn with certainty. In the case of Cumbric names in north-west Northumbria, the picture is inevitably blurred by the difficulty of distinguishing pre-English examples from those associated with the expansion of Strathclyde in the Viking period.[23] There are, however, strong indications that a boundary between Cumbric-speakers and Hiberno-Norse eventually developed slightly west of the River Derwent, perhaps through agreement after a period of conflict. The exact course of this linguistic divide is unknown and it was unlikely to have been demarcated in any formal sense. Shifting political fortunes in this turbulent era meant that land-ownership and political allegiance were not static, especially in districts where a high risk of confrontation made the situation more fluid. In some areas the two groups must have co-existed peacefully, and the discovery in 2004 of a small Viking cemetery near Cumwhitton may be a case in point. The six graves have been dated to the early tenth century and seem to contain two generations of a Norse family who lived in this part of the Eden Valley during the period of Strathclyde rule.[24] East of the Derwent, the area under Strathclyde's control seems to have extended towards the Eden and the Pennine foothills. To the south it was probably bounded by the River Eamont, later the southern bound-ary of the county of Cumberland.[25] Northwards it extended into Dumfriesshire, which in turn connected it with Upper Clydesdale and the heartlands of the Cumbrian kingdom. South of the Eamont lay the rest of western Northumbria, comprising the later counties of Westmorland and Lancashire. Here, too, zones of Norse settlement are identifiable through place-names but the few Cumbric names appear to be pre-English fossils rather than creations of the Viking Age. The name of Carhullan, in northern Westmorland, belongs to the later period and was formed by adding Cumbric *car* ('fortified settlement') to the name of an Englishman, but it lies barely 6 miles south of the Eamont and need not be regarded as a significant exception. Further eastward, beyond the River Eden, the Pennine uplands marked a political frontier between the Cumbric-speaking colonists and the Danes of York. Within these bounds, in former Northumbrian lands under Strathclyde's control, a large number of English-speaking communities remained *in situ*, their continuing presence evidenced by the survival of their place-names. They were absorbed into a sort of 'Greater Strathclyde', retaining their own language and customs but acknowledging the authority of a new Cumbric-speaking elite. The scale of place-name continuity implies that some English lords were allowed to hold onto their estates, presumably in exchange for oaths of fealty to Clyde-based kings. Such stability would have made the transition to Cumbrian rule easier but, in other instances, the English nobility must have fled or been ejected by force, paving the way for Strathclyders to take ownership of vacated estates. This is what may have happened at the southern limit of Cumbrian expansion on the River Eamont, where the likely estate-centre of Penrith ('chief ford' or 'ford end') may have acquired its Cumbric name after the expulsion of a Northumbrian lord.[26]

The fate of Northumbrian religious settlements in the newly conquered lands is not recorded. In the early eighth century, Bede referred to an Anglo-Saxon monastery at Dacre near the confluence of the Eamont with the Dacre Beck. This lay within the area of later Cumbrian colonisation but we do not know if it was still occupied when the newcomers arrived. Did the Northumbrian clergy flee Dacre in the face of force or threats, to be replaced by Cumbric-speaking monks from monasteries in Clydesdale? In adjoining lands settled by the Hiberno-Norse, flight was the preferred option for Abbot Tilred whose story is related in *Historia de Sancto Cuthberto*, 'History of Saint Cuthbert', a Northumbrian text preserved in an eleventh-century manuscript but probably compiled in the tenth century. The *Historia* is an account of Cuthbert's relics and the religious community that venerated them. This is the same community whose chief bishop was based at Lindisfarne until Viking raids made it an unsafe repository. In 883, after many years of wandering, the bishop established a new headquarters at Chester-le-Street on the River Wear in what is now County Durham. Among the community's satellite monasteries in western Northumbria was Heversham in Westmorland, which was abandoned in the early 900s. Tilred, the last abbot of Heversham, fled across the Pennines to Bishop Cutheard at Chester-le-Street from whom he secured a new abbacy at Norham in Tweeddale. Another Northumbrian refugee was Alfred, a farmer or landowner, who 'fleeing from pirates, came over the mountains in the west and sought the mercy of St Cuthbert and Bishop Cutheard.'[27] The place from where Alfred fled is unnamed but the pirates in question were almost certainly the Hiberno-Norse. Tilred no doubt feared the same people, especially if they were

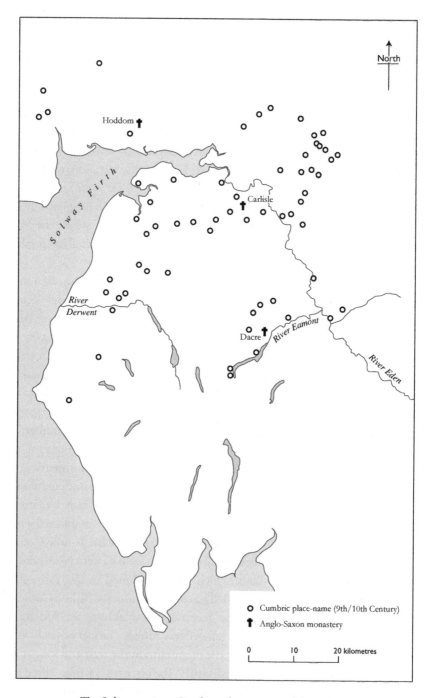

MAP 5 The Solway region: Cumbric place-names of the Viking period
[after Higham 1993, 181]

establishing settlements in the vicinity of his monastery. The likelihood that many of the Norse immigrants were Christians like their former Irish hosts rather than pagans like their Viking ancestors might not have reassured him. Would he have felt similar anxiety if his monastery had lain in territory colonised by Cumbrians from Strathclyde? Perhaps so. While the survival of English place-names north of the Eamont implies that the Northumbrian landowning elite were not completely supplanted, the religious elite may have found their positions less tenable. Northumbrian clerics like Tilred were under the ecclesiastical authority of English bishops at York or Chester-le-Street and would not have abandoned such allegiances willingly. Their brethren in the new Cumbric-speaking areas, faced with the prospect of answering to bishops in faraway Clydesdale, would therefore have faced a stark choice. Many of them probably followed Tilred's example by crossing the Pennines to seek refuge in the east. Large-scale evacuation of Northumbrian clergy and their replacement by Britons has indeed been proposed, partly to explain why church dedications to Kentigern, Glasgow's patron saint, occur in the Solway area. Although these dedications might be dated more accurately to the twelfth century and later, at a time when the cult of Kentigern was spreading far beyond Glasgow, the evacuation scenario may be a fairly close reflection of the truth.[28]

The battle of Corbridge

In 918, the Hiberno-Norse under Ragnall, grandson of Ivar, clashed with the Scots on the River Tyne. The ensuing battle was noted by the Irish annalists: 'The foreigners of Waterford, i.e. Ragnall, king of the dark foreigners, and the two jarls Oitir and Gragabai, forsook Ireland and proceeded afterwards against the men of Alba. The men of Alba, moreover, moved against them and they met on the bank of the Tyne in northern England.'[29] This encounter took place while Constantin mac Áeda held the kingship of the Scots. We find it mentioned in the account of his reign in *CKA*: 'And the battle of Tyne Moor happened in his eighteenth year between Constantin and Ragnall, and the Scots had the victory.'[30]

We seem to find a reference to the same event in *Historia de Sancto Cuthberto*, in the tale of the Northumbrian layman Alfred who fled across the Pennines to escape the Hiberno-Norse. This text gives a more precise location for the battlefield. It tells us that Alfred served Bishop Cutheard at Chester-le-Street

until King Ragnall came with a great multitude of ships and occupied the territory of Ealdred son of Eadwulf, who was a friend of King Edward, just as his father Eadwulf had been a friend of King Alfred. Ealdred, having been driven off, went therefore to Scotland, seeking aid from King Constantin, and brought him to battle against Ragnall at Corbridge.[31]

Ealdred was the English lord of Bamburgh, the former royal stronghold of Bernicia. His family held authority over the northern part of Northumbria between the River Tees and the Firth of Forth. The family's origins are unknown but they may have been descended from earlier Bernician royalty. After the fall of the old Northumbrian kingdom in the late ninth century, the lords of Bamburgh ruled an autonomous territory roughly corresponding to the Bernicia of earlier times.[32] Their relationship to the new Anglo-Danish elite at York is sometimes hard to discern but, as the tenth century progressed, they frequently looked further afield for friends and allies. Ealdred's approach to Constantin is the first recorded contact between the Bamburgh dynasty and its Celtic neighbours. The *Historia de Sancto Cuthberto* goes on to say that the ensuing battle was a resounding victory for the Norse. Although this reverses the outcome given by *CKA*, it is probably more correct. Among the English soldiers was Alfred, the western layman who had travelled across the Pennines to escape the Norse colonists. Having been given land by Bishop Cutheard, probably in Ealdred's domains, Alfred fulfilled his oaths by fighting for his new lord. The *Historia* claims that Ealdred survived the battle, as did his ally Constantin. Although no source refers to the involvement of the Cumbrians of Strathclyde, it is possible that they were among the allied forces defeated by Ragnall. Indeed, it seems unlikely that their king would have stayed on the sidelines in such a contest.

Strathclyde and Edward the Elder

Aethelflaed, the Lady of the Mercians, died in her palace at Tamworth on 12 June 918. Her brother Edward swiftly secured the allegiance of her people, bringing them under direct West Saxon rule.[33] Aethelflaed had already subdued a large part of the southern Danelaw and the remainder was now brought under Edward's control. Within six months of his sister's death Edward was the undisputed king of southern and midland England. Mercia's northern frontier thus became the boundary of his enlarged realm and demanded his immediate attention. His chief source of anxiety was the Viking warlord Ragnall, the victor at the battle of Corbridge in 918. Having seized the kingship of York, Ragnall was now the ruler of Anglo-Danish Northumbria, holding sway over all lands between Humber and Tees.[34] His earlier gains in the Irish Sea zone remained intact, giving him a wide hegemony stretching from the Isle of Man to the

MAP 6 Britain in the time of Edward the Elder, c.920

Yorkshire coast. To counter this looming menace, Edward continued his sister's policy of constructing forts in vulnerable areas of northern Mercia. In 919, he strengthened the defences around the River Mersey by building a *burh* at Thelwall and repairing the Roman fort at Manchester.[35] The programme of fort-building continued in 920, as we learn from the *Anglo-Saxon Chronicle*:

> In this year, before midsummer, King Edward went with troops to Nottingham, and commanded a fortress to be built up on the south side of the river, across from the other, and also the bridge over the Trent between the two forts. He went then into the Peak District, to Bakewell, and commanded a fortress to be built nearby and garrisoned. He was chosen as father and lord by the king of the Scots and all the Scottish people; by Ragnall, and Eadwulf's sons, and all who dwell in Northumbria – English, Danes, Norwegians and others – and by the king of the Strathclyde Welsh, and all the Strathclyde Welsh.[36]

Reading the detail in this passage, historians have been intrigued by the reference to Edward being 'chosen as father and lord' by the northern rulers. Does this mean that they submitted to his authority? Is the chronicler describing a single event, a high-level meeting hosted by Edward and attended by the north-erners, or a series of separate negotiations? The answer to the first question is probably 'No'. Neither *ASC* nor any other source refers to a military campaign in which Edward subjugated the north. It seems very unlikely that the northern rulers would have submitted to him without having witnessed a major demonstration of his power. In 920, they had yet to be convinced that a West Saxon war-leader was willing or able to venture far beyond the Humber–Mersey frontier. Not even the renowned Aethelflaed had done so. Edward himself had ordered Mercian troops to garrison the fort at Manchester, on the north side of the Mersey, but this was hardly more than a foray into Northumbria. When the chronicler described the apparent submission of the northern rulers he was surely exaggerating Edward's authority. In depicting Edward as a mighty king to whom other kings bowed willingly, the entry for 920 is consistent with *ASC*'s role as a propaganda tool for the West Saxon royal house. We should therefore doubt that the northerners actually submitted to Edward. At the most, they may have acknowledged his supremacy in southern and midland Britain.[37] This brings us to the second question, to which we can cautiously answer 'Yes' to the first part. A single gathering, rather than a series of meetings between Edward and individual rulers, is the most likely context. Peeling away the West Saxon propaganda we are left with a tenth-century record of a gathering of equals, an event similar to the *rígdála* or 'royal meetings' described in Irish chronicles.[38] Settling of territorial disputes between kings, rather than displays of homage, seems to have been the primary business at a *rígdál*. Nevertheless, even if the choosing of Edward as 'father and lord' did not entail submission to his authority, his role as host indicates that the meeting took place within his realm. Can the venue be located more precisely? The passage in *ASC* puts the meeting immediately after the fort-building at Bakewell and it is possible that the two events were connected, with the attendees assembling at Edward's new *burh* in the Peak District. While other interpretations and other venues are certainly possible, Bakewell's geographical setting makes it a likely candidate.[39] It lay within fifteen miles of the old Mercian–Northumbrian border, far from the heartland of any particular kingdom, and may have been regarded as suitably neutral ground for a meeting of rulers. Bakewell's importance in the tenth century is implied not only by Edward's *burh* but by a large collection of Anglo-Saxon sculpture now preserved at the parish church. The most notable item is an ornate cross, probably carved in the eighth or ninth century, which now stands in the churchyard. The king of the 'Strathclyde Welsh' who attended the meeting is unnamed but he may have been Owain, Dyfnwal's son, a figure mentioned earlier in this chapter.[40] No mystery surrounds the identity of the other attendees, all of whom had been involved in the battle of Corbridge two years earlier. Although Ragnall is the only one identified by name, the Scottish king was certainly Constantin mac Áeda while the sons of Eadwulf were the lords of Bamburgh.

The main purpose of the meeting is unknown but is likely to have involved some kind of peace accord. Many of the Irish *rígdála* resulted in treaties designed to avert or postpone the threat of war. Similar concerns may have been on the agenda in 920, especially if Ragnall's growing power was making his neighbours nervous. In this context, it is worth observing that Ragnall was the only attendee with whom Edward shared a frontier. If the meeting took place at Bakewell, this frontier lay not far away. Moreover, Edward's *burh* at Manchester may have encroached on territory in western Northumbria that Ragnall regarded as his own and could have been a bone of contention. Ragnall also shared a frontier with the sons of Eadwulf of Bamburgh – Ealdred and Uhtred – from whom he had probably seized territory after the victory at Corbridge. These Northumbrian lords may have come to Edward's meeting in the hope of gaining West Saxon support for the return of lost lands. The presence of Constantin of Alba suggests that he, too, had concerns relating to one or more of the other attendees. In the south, Constantin's kingdom shared borders with Strathclyde and Bamburgh.

Further west, his interests may have been threatened by Hiberno-Norse colonies in Argyll, the southern Hebrides and the Isle of Man, or by Viking warbands answerable to Ragnall. Constantin was no stranger to conflict with the new king of York, having tasted defeat in 918 alongside Ealdred of Bamburgh. The Strathclyde Britons probably shared three borders with Ragnall, one running along the Pennines at the western end of the Stainmore Pass, another on the line of the River Eamont, while the third nudged the Hiberno-Norse colonies in the western coastlands. A fourth frontier may have existed somewhere north of the Solway Firth if, as some historians believe, Ragnall's influence in the seaways had given him a foothold in Galloway. Ragnall's borders with Strathclyde had surely seen much violence during the initial phase of Cumbrian colonisation south of the Solway, in areas where Norse settlers acknowledged him as their king, but relations between the two immigrant groups may have begun to stabilise before 920. Day-to-day contact between Cumbrians and Norse were not necessarily hostile at that time, but relations at the higher level might have remained tense if, as suggested above, Strathclyde forces had fought against Ragnall at Corbridge. Indeed, the fact that three of the northern powers at Edward's meeting had participated in the battle of 918 might prompt us to wonder if the fourth – Strathclyde – had also been involved. *ASC* tells us that the northerners chose Edward as their father and lord. Notwithstanding the likelihood that this statement is a West Saxon embellishment, it is possible that some kind of pledge or acknowledgement was given to the English king. As suggested above, this need not have amounted to much more than recognition of his overlordship south of the Humber and Mersey. The agenda at the meeting may also have included concerns over the ambitions of Ragnall, with his fellow attendees perhaps hoping for promises of peace along their respective frontiers. Perhaps such assurances were indeed given? It was around this time that Edward took control of a large part of south-west Northumbria comprising the region between the rivers Mersey and Ribble. It is possible that he acquired this territory as a result of the royal meeting of 920, as a gesture of faith from Ragnall.[41]

ATHELSTAN

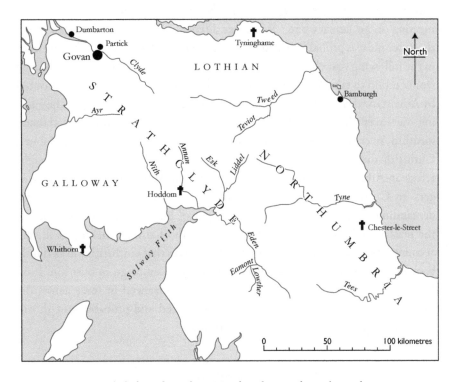

MAP 7 Strathclyde and northern Northumbria in the early tenth century

The mighty Ragnall died in 921. Sihtric took over as king at York, leaving his own power-base at Dublin in the hands of Guthfrith, another of Ivar's grandsons. Guthfrith may have been a cousin of Sihtric and Ragnall, or perhaps their brother. Three years later, at Farndon on the north-west frontier of Mercia, the English king Edward the Elder passed away. He was succeeded in Wessex by Aelfweard, a son by his second wife, but Aelfweard died within four weeks. The West Saxons then turned to Athelstan, Edward's eldest son from his first marriage, proclaiming him as their new king. Athelstan had already been acknowledged as king by the Mercians and thus became the undisputed ruler of all lands south of the Mersey and Humber.[1] He was around thirty years old. His teenage years had been spent at the Mercian court under the wing of his aunt Aethelflaed, from whom he had learned much about kingship, diplomacy and war. Like his father, he began his reign facing the ever-present menace of Scandinavian kings at York and Dublin. At first, Athelstan seems to have adopted a conciliatory approach by giving one of his sisters in marriage to Sihtric of York. The wedding took place at Tamworth in the heart of Mercia where, according to the *Anglo-Saxon Chronicle*, Athelstan and Sihtric had a meeting on 30 January 926.[2] Whatever discussions took place between them, the outcome was probably sealed by the marriage. Unfortunately, Sihtric's death in the following year changed the political situation once again. Guthfrith came from Dublin to take the vacant throne of York but was immediately confronted by Athelstan who invaded Northumbria in force. We know nothing of the ensuing war except its result: Athelstan took direct control of York and claimed lordship over all Northumbria.[3] According to William of Malmesbury, Guthfrith did not immediately return home to Dublin but initially sought refuge in Alba and Strathclyde. William says that Athelstan then sent messengers 'to Constantin, king of Scots, and to Owain, king of the Cumbrians, demanding back the fugitive and declaring war', but Guthfrith escaped before the matter could be resolved.[4] How much truth, if any, lies behind William's account is unclear but we know from other sources that Guthfrith was certainly back in Dublin before the end of 927. Athelstan's campaign to oust him from York was the first time a West Saxon king had advanced in force across the Humber frontier. Such a move was unprecedented and probably sent shockwaves through all the lands of northern Britain.

Eamotum

On 12 July 927, on the banks of the River Eamont near Penrith, Athelstan presided over a high-level meeting similar to the one hosted by his father seven years earlier. Our principal source of information is an entry in the northern 'D' version of the *Anglo-Saxon Chronicle*:

> In this year fiery lights appeared in the northern quarter of the sky, and Sihtric died, and King Athelstan received the kingdom of Northumbria, and all the kings on this island were brought under his rule; first Hywel, king of the West Welsh; and Constantin, king of Scots; and Owain, king of the people of Gwent; and Ealdred, son of Eadwulf, from Bamburgh;

and with pledges and oaths they fastened a peace in the place called Eamont, on 12 July, and renounced all idol-worship, and from there turned away in peace.[5]

The list of attendees was impressive: Constantin, king of Alba; Hywel the Good, a powerful South Welsh king; Ealdred, son of Eadwulf of Bamburgh; and Owain, identified here as a king of Gwent in South Wales. Although the entry makes no mention of Strathclyde this is usually seen as an omission, for the involvement of the Cumbrian kingdom would surely be expected at such a meeting. The venue lay on what is generally presumed to have been the kingdom's southern border. Thus, when William of Malmesbury's later account of the meeting identifies Owain not as a Welsh ruler but as *rex Cumbrorum*, 'king of the Cumbrians', this emendation is accepted by most present-day historians.[6] Moreover, the Welsh kings attended their own meeting with Athelstan later in the year, at Hereford near their border with Mercia, where they submitted to his overlordship.[7] There was little need for them to attend the northern gathering as well. The presence at Eamont of the South Welsh king Hywel probably reflects his special status as a loyal ally of the West Saxon royal house. His presence does, of course, raise the possibility that other Welsh kings were also at the Eamont meeting and one of these could have hailed from Gwent. A certain Morgan, son of Owain, was ruling Gwent from c.930 and his father might be the Owain mentioned in *ASC* 'D'. It is also possible that the chronicler's source placed an Owain at the Eamont in 927 without identifying his kingdom. The chronicler himself may have known of a Gwent ruler called Owain and assumed that this was the Owain at the Eamont. Alternatively, both Owains might have attended the northern meeting, the Cumbrian accompanying his neighbour Constantin while the Welshman travelled north with Hywel and Athelstan.[8]

The 'D' text of *ASC* was written by a Northumbrian scribe and, unlike the southern 'A' text, was not primarily a propagandist text for the rulers of Wessex. When 'D' tells us that Athelstan hosted a meeting at which 'all the kings on this island were brought under his rule' it might not be stretching the truth too far. Some rhetoric is undoubtedly involved but, even allowing for this, we may be seeing a formal acknowledgement of Athelstan's status as the mightiest king in Britain. Unlike his father, he had given the northern peoples a vivid demonstration of military power by expelling Guthfrith from York. After this, no Scottish, Northumbrian or Cumbrian ruler would have doubted his ability or willingness to invade their lands. At the Eamont in 927 a treaty was duly agreed. According to *ASC* 'D', the attendees 'renounced all idol-worship, and

from there turned away in peace'. Renouncing the veneration of idols had little
relevance to kings who were already Christian, so what the chronicler probably
meant was that the attendees vowed not to make common cause with pagan
Viking warlords.[9] To what extent the northerners not only recognised
Athelstan's superiority but also submitted to him as vassals is unclear. The
Welsh kings certainly submitted at Hereford, thereby incurring an obligation
to attend the English court as *subreguli*, 'under-kinglets'. We find them listed as
witnesses in charters issued by Athelstan as he travelled around his domains in
the years after 927.[10] By contrast, the kings of Alba and Strathclyde do not
appear in the witness-lists, their absence suggesting that they had given no
formal oaths of submission at the Eamont.

In *ASC* 'D', the venue of the meeting is called *Eamotum*, an Old English
name meaning 'river junction'. The rivers in question are the Lowther and the
Eamont, the latter taking its name from their confluence. *Eamotum* might refer
to the point of junction itself or to Westmorland Holme, a narrow strip of land
slightly to the west, where the two rivers almost converge while flowing side-by-
side.[11] They eventually merge near Brougham Castle, a medieval stronghold
erected on the site of a Roman fort. William of Malmesbury placed the 927
meeting at *Dacor*, Dacre, a name now borne by a small village beside the Dacre
Beck, a tributary of the River Eamont. The village church stands on the site of
an Anglo-Saxon monastery which may have played a key role in 927, unless
Dacor is actually the original name of the River Eamont.[12] The exact site of the
meeting is unknown. In addition to Westmorland Holme and the river-junction, possible candidates include two prehistoric henges near the village of
Eamont Bridge, the Roman fort at Brougham and the monastery at Dacre.
More than one of these sites may have been used, perhaps at different stages in
the proceedings, or for different purposes. We might wish to exclude Dacre on
the grounds that it lay on the 'Cumbrian' or northern side of the Eamont in
what was arguably Strathclyde territory in 927. A venue on the southern or
'Northumbrian' side seems more plausible for an event presided over by an
English king, and we may note that the henges, the Roman fort and Westmorland
Holme all lie south of the river. Of the two henges, Mayburgh with its steep
encircling bank is reminiscent of an amphitheatre and would have been an
impressive site for a large gathering, but Athelstan may have preferred the more
open setting of King Arthur's Round Table with its wide views of the surrounding landscape. Both henges already belonged to a remote prehistoric past and
would have conveyed an aura of antiquity in the tenth century, just as they do
today. The Roman fort, although long abandoned by 927, would likewise have

retained a sense of ancient authority. Its 'imperial' associations might have seemed particularly appealing to Athelstan, a man of lofty pretensions whose coinage proclaimed him *rex totius Brittaniae*, 'king of all Britain'.[13]

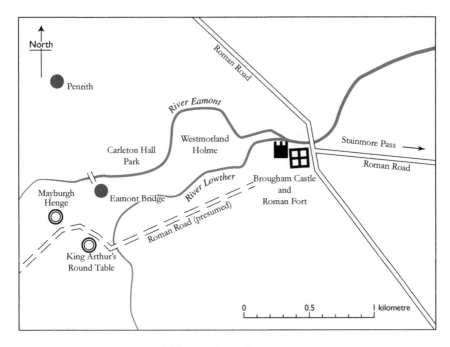

MAP 8 The meeting at Eamotum, 927

The oaths of peace and fealty sworn at *Eamotum* appear to have endured to the end of the decade. No further dealings between Athelstan and the northern kings are recorded for several years after 927. This seems somewhat strange in the light of contemporary events in Northumbria, where the expulsion of Guthfrith had left Athelstan holding the reins of power at York. By analogy with Mercia, the eastern part of which had been restored to English rule by his father and aunt, we might have expected Athelstan to attempt a similar restoration of all ancestral English lands in Northumbria. No such attempt appears to have been made. Even in Northumbrian territory east of the Pennines, which came under his control after the defeat of Guthfrith, there is no real hint that his rule was 'hands-on'. Authority in this area might instead have been delegated to a loyal subordinate who was acceptable to York's Anglo-Danish elite. At the Eamont meeting the only attendee of northern English stock was Ealdred of Bamburgh, and it is possible that it was to him that Athelstan gave the task of ruling the whole of eastern Northumbria.[14] On the other side of the Pennines we have strong indications that Athelstan did exercise direct rule in Lancashire, treating it perhaps as a northern extension of western Mercia. His father had previously taken control of the area between the two great rivers of southern Lancashire, the Mersey and the Ribble, but Athelstan added more territory by purchasing Amounderness. This district, which takes its name from a Scandinavian called Agmund, nestled west of the Pennines between the rivers Ribble and Cocker. Its purchase did not come cheap: Athelstan later observed that he paid for it 'with no little money of my own'.[15] Although unnamed, the vendor was likely to have been a Hiberno-Norse lord, perhaps a kinsman of the eponymous Agmund. Athelstan gave this territory to Archbishop Wulfstan of York, the most powerful churchman in Northumbria and an influential figure among the Anglo-Danish elite. The gift was probably a gesture of goodwill to secure the archbishop's backing for Athelstan's recent takeover of Northumbria.[16] In political terms, the purchase of Amounderness extended West Saxon power beyond the Ribble and gave Athelstan a new north-west frontier near the River Lune. North of the Lune as far as the River Eamont lay old Northumbrian lands that still probably answered to whoever held the kingship of York. Beyond them lay the new Cumbric-speaking settlements in the Solway Plain and the southern frontier of Strathclyde.

The invasion of the north

One or more of the pledges given at *Eamotum* in 927 had been disregarded by 934. In that year, according to the *Anglo-Saxon Chronicle*, 'King Athelstan went into Scotland with a land-army and a naval force, and ravaged much of it.'[17]

Relations with Constantin of Alba had clearly broken down and something had provoked Athelstan to launch a full-scale invasion. We can only speculate as to what the catalyst may have been but it was surely more than a minor transgression of the earlier agreement. One possibility is that Constantin had tried to intervene in Northumbrian affairs, just as he had done twenty years earlier when he had supported the sons of Eadwulf of Bamburgh against Ragnall of York. The *Annals of Clonmacnoise* note the death of a Northumbrian ruler called 'Adulf, son of Etulfe', in 934.[18] This may be the same man mentioned by William of Malmesbury as 'Aldulf', a rebel whom Athelstan expelled from Northumbria. *Adulf* and *Aldulf* look like attempts to render a name like Eadwulf or Ealdwulf, so we might be seeing separate references to an otherwise unknown member of the Bamburgh dynasty. If William of Malmesbury's information is correct, this

Hogback gravestones in Govan Old Parish Church. [© Tom Manley. Reproduced courtesy of http://www.tommanleyphotography.com]

Govan Old Parish Church. [© Barbara Keeling]

Dumbarton Rock. [© Barbara Keeling]

Bamburgh Castle. [© Barbara Keeling]

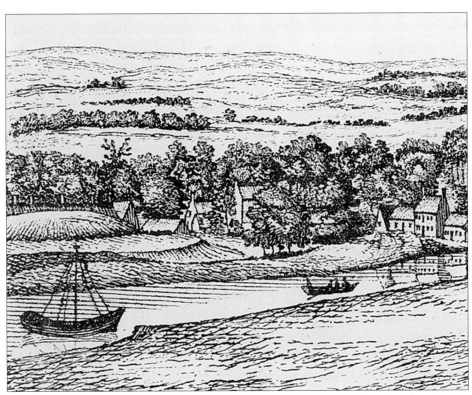

Govan in 1758: from Robert Paul's engraving *A view of the banks of the Clyde taken from York Hill*. The Doomster Hill is on the left. [© Glasgow City Libraries. Licensor www.scran.ac.uk]

Aethelflaed, Lady of the Mercians: commemorative statue erected at Tamworth Castle in 1913, showing Aethelflaed with her nephew Athelstan [© Barbara Keeling]

The Gosforth Cross, Cumbria: a
tenth-century monument displaying
Anglo-Saxon and Norse influence
[© Tim Clarkson]

Anglo-Saxon cross near the east wall
of All Saints Church, Bakewell
[© Barbara Keeling]

Eamotum: the confluence of the rivers Eamont and Lowther near Brougham Castle [© Barbara Keeling]

Lowther Church, Cumbria [© Barbara Keeling]

Dunmail Raise, Cumbria [© Diane McIlmoyle. Reproduced courtesy of
http://esmeraldamac.wordpress.com]

St John the Baptist, Chester: ruins of the medieval church [© Barbara Keeling]

Right. The Giant's Grave, Penrith [© Barbara Keeling]

Below. Carham, 1018: view eastward along the River Tweed near the probable site of the battle [© Barbara Keeling]

individual may have rebelled against Athelstan after 927, scorning whatever trea-
ties had been agreed at *Eamotum*. Moreover, if he really was a member of the
Bamburgh dynasty he might have followed precedent by seeking aid from
Constantin.[19] The Scottish king's support for a Northumbrian renegade would no
doubt have given Athelstan sufficient motive for an invasion of Alba. Further
details of the ensuing campaign are given by the twelfth-century *Historia Regum*
(*HRA*) which tells us that Athelstan 'laid waste Scotland as far as *Dunfoeder*
(Dunnottar near Stonehaven) and *Wertermorum* ('the hills of Fortriu') with a
land army, and ravaged with a naval force as far as *Catenes* (Caithness)'.[20]
Accompanying him on this expedition were the Welsh kings Hywel the Good,
Morgan of Gwent and Idwal of Gwynedd, leading their own forces, together with
Anglo-Scandinavian contingents from the Southern Danelaw. The core of his
army comprised his own West Saxon and Mercian warriors, many of whom would
have been involved in the expulsion of Guthfrith from York seven years earlier.

The northern campaign of 934 was no swift raid for plunder but a sustained
assault on the heartlands of a major kingdom. Dunnottar in Aberdeenshire had
been an important Pictish fortress since at least the seventh century and was
clearly still a place of significance. Never before had it been attacked by an English
king. It lay five hundred miles from Athelstan's palace at Winchester and is
presented in *HRA* as the most northerly site targeted by his land-forces. The hills
of Fortriu were the eastern ranges of the Grampians that in former times had
divided northern and southern Pictland. Beyond them lay Fortriu itself, an
ancient region roughly corresponding to the later Moray, and other erstwhile
Pictish territories further north.[21] Athelstan's fleet attacked Caithness, an area
with long-established Norse colonies, for reasons that are hard to discern, but this
was evidently the northern limit of his campaign. Although the *Annals of
Clonmacnoise* state that the invasion failed to secure 'any great victory', the ravaging of Alba did bring Constantin to heel. By early autumn of the same year, the
Scottish king was in southern England as a member of Athelstan's entourage,
attending the English royal court as an obedient *subregulus* alongside the Welsh.[22]

The Strathclyde Britons were also caught up in the events of 934. Drawing
on older Northumbrian sources, the twelfth-century author of the *History of
the Church of Durham* (*HDE*) stated that Athelstan 'put to flight Owain, king
of the Cumbrians, and Constantin, king of the Scots, and with a land army and
a naval force subdued Scotland, subjugating it to himself'. William of
Malmesbury says that Constantin and Owain had given refuge to Guthfrith
and were threatened with war unless they yielded the fugitive to Athelstan.[23]
Although this offers a plausible context for Athelstan's campaign it does not sit

easily with the Irish tradition that Guthfrith returned to Dublin after his expulsion from Northumbria in 927. Guthfrith was still in Ireland in the early 930s and died there in 934, leaving little room for a period of exile in northern Britain. The story of his exile in Alba and Strathclyde can probably be dismissed, but William of Malmesbury may be on firmer ground when he states that Athelstan invaded Alba because Constantin was 'again in revolt'. This is echoed by John of Worcester's assertion that the Scottish king 'broke the treaty', presumably the agreement forged at *Eamotum*.[24] The reference in *HDE* to Owain of Strathclyde being 'put to flight' suggests that he, too, forsook whatever oaths he had sworn in 927.

Athelstan ravaged the land of the Scots to secure Constantin's submission and to punish him for breaking his pledges. He presumably intended to subdue Owain in the same way, so we should assume that Strathclyde was also invaded and plundered.[25] Owain resisted but was defeated, perhaps during a battle in which he and Constantin stood together against the common foe. Although no such encounter is recorded in the sources, the testimony of *HDE* suggests that Athelstan did indeed meet resistance from the Scots and Britons. The sequence of events may have been a refusal by both Constantin and Owain to submit to his overlordship and their subsequent defeat, either in separate battles or in a single decisive contest against their combined forces. While we cannot hope to pinpoint the location of specific battles in the campaign of 934, we can make a few informed guesses about the route taken by Athelstan's army. The first two hundred and fifty miles of his northward march can be tracked from royal charters he issued along the way. After leaving Winchester at the end of May, he led his army through Mercia, reaching Nottingham in the first week of June. There he issued a charter granting Amounderness to Archbishop Wulfstan of York.[26] He then moved through eastern Northumbria, pausing at Chester-le-Street to bestow a large estate and other gifts on the community of St Cuthbert. It is clear that he was using Dere Street, the old Roman road to the north, which would eventually have brought him to Corbridge on the Tyne. To attack Strathclyde at this point he could have turned east along the south side of Hadrian's Wall, making for Carlisle and the head of the Solway Firth to plunder the lands recently colonised by Cumbric-speakers. Alternatively, he may have continued his northward course as far as the River Tweed, or even further towards Edinburgh. Tweeddale offered a well-trodden route westward into Clydesdale and the heartland of the Britons, while Edinburgh lay just fifty miles from Owain's royal centre at Govan. It is possible, of course, that Athelstan ravaged Strathclyde not on the outward journey but on the homeward trek, when his troops were already laden with Scottish loot.

A king called Owain appears in Athelstan's entourage in 935, witnessing charters in southern England. He is usually identified as the 'king of the Cumbrians' mentioned in the later chronicles, the same Owain who attended the meeting at *Eamotum* and who was evidently 'put to flight' in 934. Alongside Constantin of Alba he turns up at the English court as a *subregulus* obediently fulfilling his obligations.[27] The context is clear: these two northern kings now recognised Athelstan's supremacy and were expected to behave themselves. It is interesting to note the status accorded to the various rulers who witnessed charters as vassals of Athelstan. When Constantin and Owain appear separately, each is first in the list of *subreguli* who witness royal land-grants. When they appear together, Constantin is named first, an indication that he was regarded as Athelstan's most important vassal. After the two northern kings the other *subreguli* are listed in order of status, with Hywel always the first of these. Where neither Constantin nor Owain happen to be present, Hywel moves up to the top of the list, a position that was invariably his own before Athelstan's northern campaign led to a reshuffle.[28] What the witness-lists tell us is that the English court regarded Owain of Strathclyde as the third most powerful king in Britain after Athelstan and Constantin.

Guthfrith, grandson of Ivar, died of a sickness in 934. He was succeeded as king of the Dublin Norse by his son Anlaf who also inherited the family's long-standing claim on the kingship of Northumbria.[29] After Guthfrith's expulsion from York in 927, the Northumbrians had effectively become subjects of Athelstan's realm. His rule over them may have been conducted indirectly if, as suggested above, he delegated authority to a loyal subordinate from Bamburgh or elsewhere. The Northumbrians were not necessarily happy to be part of the empire he was creating. Some of them, perhaps including Archbishop Wulfstan and other members of the York elite, may have resented West Saxon overlordship. The emergence of Anlaf Guthfrithsson therefore posed a very real threat to Athelstan and offered a gleam of hope to those whom he held in subjection. Constantin of Alba began to move out of the English king's shadow in 935 and was a notable absentee when the royal court assembled at Dorchester (Dorset) in December of that year. It may have been shortly afterwards that Constantin made a more overtly rebellious gesture by giving his daughter's hand in marriage to Anlaf, if the report of this union is more than a later fiction.[30] Owain of Strathclyde was present at Dorchester, as the senior *subregulus* in Constantin's absence, but it seems to have been his final appearance at the English court. None of Athelstan's later charters name any *subreguli* among the witnesses, perhaps because of a change of scribe or style, or because the Welsh kings as well as the northerners had ceased to be obedient vassals. The absence of *subreguli* after 935 is indeed striking and might be due to an increase in political tensions.[31] At some point, most probably in 936, Constantin and Owain openly declared the end of their subjection by aligning themselves with Anlaf. With the kings of Dublin, Alba and Strathclyde now ranged against him in a new alliance, Athelstan was soon to face the greatest crisis of his reign. By the autumn of 937, the allies were ready to confront him in a decisive showdown.

The Battle of Brunanburh

In August 937, Anlaf Guthfrithsson won a major victory in Ireland, defeating the Norse of Limerick and capturing their king. At some point thereafter, perhaps in September, he gathered a substantial force and sailed over to Britain, where allies from Alba and Strathclyde came to meet him. The combined armies of the coalition then invaded Athelstan's kingdom, ravaging across the land until the English king marched out to confront them. What followed was a mighty clash of arms, an event described vividly in the *Annals of Ulster*:

> A great, lamentable and horrible battle was cruelly fought between the English and the Norsemen, in which several thousands of Norsemen, who are uncounted, fell, but their king, Anlaf, escaped with a few followers. A large number of English fell on the other side, but Athelstan, king of the English, enjoyed a great victory.[32]

The same battle is mentioned in the *Annals of Clonmacnoise*, which gives additional details about the participants. Although the names are rendered into seventeenth-century English, the people in question are identifiable from other sources. A modern English version is given below:

> Anlaf with all the Danes of Dublin and the north part of Ireland departed and went over the sea. The Danes that departed from Dublin arrived in England, and by the help of the Danes of that kingdom, they gave battle to the Saxons on the plains of Othlyn, where there was a great slaughter of Northmen and Danes, among which these ensuing captains were slain, namely Sihtfrith and Audgisl, two sons of Sihtric, Galey, Anlaf Ffroit, and Máel Muire the son of Cossa Warce, Máel Isa, Gebeachan the king of the Islands, Ceallagh the prince of Scotland, with 30,000 together with 800 captives about Anlaf Guthfrithsson, and the abbot of Arick m'Brith, Iloa, Deck, Imar the king of Denmark's own son with 4000 soldiers in his guard were all slain.[33]

Both *AU* and *AClon* depict the battle as primarily a clash between English and Norse forces, the latter being accompanied by various allies. The Scottish prince listed by *AClon* among the slain captains is presumably an otherwise unknown son of King Constantin. The participation of the Scots themselves is made clear in other sources, an example being the twelfth-century Durham text *HDE* which asserts that the Cumbrians of Strathclyde were also present. *HDE* makes no mention of the 'plains of Othlyn' but gives three additional names for the battlefield:

> Four years later, in the 937th year of the Lord's Nativity, at *Wendun*, which by another name is called *Etbrunnanwerc* or *Brunnanburgh*, he [Athelstan] fought against Anlaf, son of the former king Guthfrith, who came with 615 ships and had the help of the kings of the Scots and Cumbrians. But having trusted in the protection of St. Cuthbert, he laid low an endless host and drove those kings from his kingdom, thus obtaining a glorious victory. [34]

CKA, in its summary of Constantin's reign, refers briefly to 'the battle of Dun Brunde in his 34th year in which the son of Constantin was slain'.[35] Since the first element of *Dun Brunde* and the second element of *Brunnanburgh* can both mean 'fortress' we seem to have, respectively, a Gaelic and an English rendering of the same place-name. The name appears also in a terse entry in the Welsh Annals: *bellum Brune*, 'the battle of Brune'. Drawing together the information from these four sources – one each from Ireland, England, Scotland and Wales – we clearly have a description of a major battle involving the forces of several kingdoms. Casualties were high on both sides but the result was victory for Athelstan and defeat for the alliance that came against him. The battle was fought in late 937 at a place whose name incorporated the element *Brun*.

Unsurprisingly, this triumph for the West Saxon royal house was noted in the 'A' text of *ASC*. Instead of a prose description, however, the chronicler inserted a full-blooded heroic poem. As our oldest account of the battle, this is a source of the highest value, notwithstanding its rhetorical style and propagandist tone. It was almost certainly composed within ten years of the battle, during the reign of Athelstan's half-brother Edmund. Even when rendered into modern English, as in the version below, it remains a stirring example of Anglo-Saxon literature. The poet evidently regarded the main protagonists as West Saxons and Mercians on one side with Norsemen and Scots on the other. His omission of the Cumbrians of Strathclyde does not necessarily mean that he regarded their role as insignificant.[36] He may have chosen to leave them out for technical reasons relating to the structure and metre of his poem. Their absence might also indicate that he regarded the Scots as sufficently representative of Anlaf's allies.

The Brunanburh Poem

In this year King Athelstan, lord of earls,
ring-giver to men, and his brother also,
Prince Edmund, won eternal glory
in battle with sword edges
around Brunanburh. They split the shield-wall,
they hewed battle shields with the remnants of hammers.
The sons of Edward, it was only befitting their noble descent
from their ancestors that they should often
defend their land in battle against each hostile people,
horde and home. The enemy perished,
Scots men and seamen,
fated they fell. The field flowed
with blood of warriors, from sun up
in the morning, when the glorious star
glided over the earth, God's bright candle,
eternal lord, till that noble creation
sank to its seat. There lay many a warrior
by spears destroyed; Northern men
shot over shield, likewise Scottish as well,
weary, war sated.
The West Saxons pushed onward
all day; in troops they pursued the hostile people.
They hewed the fugitive grievously from behind
with swords sharp from the grinding.
The Mercians did not refuse hard hand-play to any warrior
who came with Anlaf over the sea-surge
in the bosom of a ship, those who sought land,
fated to fight. Five lay dead
on the battlefield, young kings,
put to sleep by swords, likewise also seven
of Anlaf's earls, countless of the army,
sailors and Scots. There the Northmen's chief was put
to flight, by need constrained
to the prow of a ship with little company:
he pressed the ship afloat, the king went out
on the dusky flood-tide, he saved his life.

Likewise, there also the old campaigner through flight came
to his own region in the north, Constantin,
the grey-haired warrior. He had no reason to exult
the great meeting; he was of his kinsmen bereft,
friends fell on the battlefield,
killed at strife: even his son, young in battle, he left
in the place of slaughter, ground to pieces with wounds.
That grizzle-haired warrior had no
reason to boast of sword-slaughter,
the old deceitful one, no more did Anlaf;
with their remnant of an army they had no reason to
laugh that they were better in deed of war
in collision of banners,
encounter of spears, encounter of men,
trading of blows, when they played against
Edward's sons on the battlefield.
Departed then the Northmen in nailed ships.
The dreary survivors on the muddy pool
sought Dublin over the deep water,
to return to Ireland, ashamed in spirit.
Likewise the brothers, both together,
king and prince, sought their home,
the West Saxon land, exultant from battle.
They left behind them, to enjoy the corpses,
the dark coated one, the dark horny-beaked raven
and the dusky-coated one,
the eagle white from behind, to partake of carrion,
greedy war-hawk, and that grey beast,
the wolf in the forest.
Never was there more slaughter
on this island, never yet as many
people killed before this
with sword's edge: never, according to those who tell us
from books, old wise men,
since from the East the Angles and Saxons came up
over the broad sea. Britain they sought,
Proud war-smiths who overcame the Welsh,
glorious warriors they took hold of the land.[37]

According to the poem, the battle raged for a whole day from sunrise to sunset. After hard fighting and much slaughter, the English gained the upper hand, driving the enemy from the field and pursuing them as they fled. Among the fugitives was Anlaf himself, who evaded the pursuit to reach the place where his ships were moored. With only a small remnant of his army at his side, he put out to sea and sailed back to Dublin. Constantin likewise escaped, fleeing northward to his kingdom and leaving a dead son on the battlefield. The poem tells us that the main action took place at *Brunanburh*, with the subsequent flight and pursuit spreading further afield as the day wore on. From the description of Anlaf's attempt to evade the pursuit we might infer that he was unable to get back to his ships quickly, or that these were moored at a considerable distance from the battlefield. It seems certain that the mooring-place lay on the shores of the Irish Sea, for the defeated Norsemen are described as heading back to Dublin as soon as they boarded their craft.[38] Brunanburh is the only location certainly named by the poet, but another has been identified by some scholars in the lines *dreorig darotha laf, on dinges mere, ofer deop waeter Dyflin secan*, translated above as 'dreary survivors on the muddy pool, sought Dublin over the deep water'. The words *dinges mere* have been seen as an Old English place-name *Dingesmere* referring to a specific lake or wetland near the moorings of the Norse fleet. Much debate has centred on where this 'mere' might be, with suggestions ranging from inland lakes to estuaries.[39] There is, however, little to be gained from such discussions while the very existence of the place-name is in doubt.

Our next oldest source of information comes from a Latin translation of a (now lost) version of *ASC*. It was written some thirty years after the battle by Aethelweard, a prominent ealdorman with familial connections to the West Saxon royal house. His *Chronicle* contains a brief account of Athelstan's victory:

> In the year in which the very mighty king Athelstan enjoyed the crown of empire, 926 years were passed from the glorious incarnation of our Saviour. After thirteen years a huge battle was fought against the barbarians at *Brunandun,* wherefore it is still called the 'great battle' by the common people. Then the barbarian forces were overcome on all sides, and held the superiority no more. Afterwards he drove them off from the shores of the ocean, and the Scots and Picts both submitted. The fields of Britain were consolidated into one, there was peace everywhere, and abundance of all things, and [since then] no fleet has remained here, having advanced against these shores, except under treaty with the English.[40]

Aethelweard's *Brunandun* combines the familiar element *Brun-* with O
English *dun*, 'hill', a suffix seen also in *Wendun* from the Durham chronicle
HDE. At least two alternative names for the battlefield – Brunandun and
Brunanburh – were seemingly current in tenth-century England. One of these
presumably lies behind the *Dun Brunde* of *CKA*, a name in which Gaelic *dun*,
'fort', is a straightforward translation of Old English *burh*. Aethelweard is
alone in his use of *Brunandun*, but *Brunanburh* was adopted by several later
chroniclers and has become, for modern historians, the standard name for the
battle. Nonetheless, after Aethelweard we are no longer dealing with contemporary sources and must rely on testimony from the eleventh and twelfth
centuries. Some of this later material probably derives from authentic tenth-
century traditions, these being preserved orally or in writing, but not all of it
can be trusted. One piece of misleading information appears in the *Chronicon
ex chronicis* of John of Worcester, a twelfth-century writer who had access to
older data and whose work is usually regarded as valuable. Although John's
sources provided him with good information on the battle of 937, he mistak-
enly believed that Anlaf Guthfrithsson arrived in Northumbria from the east,
via the North Sea and the Humber estuary.[41] The testimony of the Old English
poem, with its reference to Anlaf's flight from the battle and escape over the
sea to Dublin, implies that the Norse fleet was moored on the west coast.
Notwithstanding this, some historians accept John's account and use it in
attempts to place the battle at various sites east of the Pennines. A number of
locations in Yorkshire and elsewhere have thus been proposed as possible
candidates for Brunanburh, each with a meticulously crafted argument to
support its case. Two such examples are Brinsworth in South Yorkshire and
the River Browney at Lanchester in County Durham, both of which are
accompanied by detailed scholarly arguments.[42] The weakness of these and
other eastern candidates is their reliance on the Humber scenario envisaged
by John of Worcester and their incompatibility with the western setting
clearly implied by the tenth-century poem. Their supporters have yet to give
an adequate explanation of why a fleet from Dublin would undertake a very
long sea-journey of eight hundred miles, involving an arduous circumnaviga-
tion of northern Britain, in order to mount a campaign against Athelstan. The
logistical problems of such a lengthy voyage are enough to preclude it from
objective discussion of the battle. It seems abundantly clear that Brunanburh,
wherever it was, should be sought west of the Pennines, in an area within easy
striking distance of the Irish Sea coast.

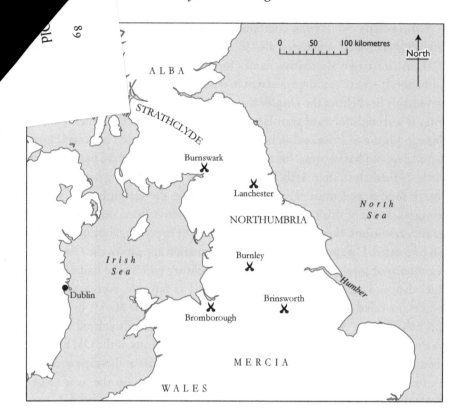

MAP 9 The location of Brunanburh: five popular candidates

Locating the battlefield

Athelstan's victory in 937 was a significant event which was widely reported in chronicles and commemorated in poetry. Modern historians are understandably frustrated that its location is no longer known, hence their continuing quest to find it. The usual starting-point, as with most searches for lost battlefields, is a modern place-name, in this case a name that looks as if it might once have been Brunanburh or Brunandun. This technique, which can be described as 'sounds-like etymology', does have the potential to yield useful results if applied objectively and without bias. Its main drawback is that it encourages a kind of backwards logic which frequently subordinates the primary sources to the needs of a particular theory built around a modern place-name. In other words, the theory becomes the main focus of attention, with data from poetry and chronicles being tested against it and accepted or rejected accordingly. At best, a modern 'sounds-like' toponym ticks enough boxes to be advanced as a plausible candidate. At worst, supporters of a particular location become so convinced by their own argument that they believe the search to be over. None of us, no matter how enthusiastically we lend our support to a particular theory, should lose sight of the simple fact that the site of Athelstan's victory remains elusive. We should also be prepared to acknowledge that it may never be found.

An over-reliance on sounds-like etymology has, to some extent, hindered rather than aided the search for Brunanburh. It has created a dense fog of competing theories. The sheer number of modern place-names containing elements such as Burn, Brom, Brin or some other plausible development from *Brun* has led to a plethora of candidates. There are now more than thirty of these, not all of them worthy of serious consideration. Sifting the wheat from the chaff is no easy task. Some places can be rejected on linguistic grounds, especially when early recorded forms rule out an original *Brun* name. Others seem to pass the linguistic test, and one of these has become the current front-runner in the search for Brunanburh. The place in question is Bromborough, a village on the Wirral Peninsula in Cheshire, overlooking the estuary of the River Mersey. In a twelfth-century document it appears as *Bruneburgh*, a form that could indeed derive from Old English *Brunanburh*. The crucial point here is that *could* is not the same as *did*. Thus, although the etymological argument for Bromborough is convincing, a connection with the battle of 937 remains a possibility rather than a certainty.[43] It is therefore unfortunate that Bromborough's candidacy has been allowed to dominate recent discussion of the topic, to the extent that some of its supporters now regard it not only as a 'best fit' but as the only serious candidate in any search for the battlefield. The danger here is that the Bromborough theory might become a factoid, a fact-shaped object which, despite having the outward appearance of a fact, remains an unproven theory nonetheless. Another aspect of the Brunanburh debate is the failure of many participants to consider the very real possibility that the name of the battle might not have survived in the modern landscape.

A more objective approach considers 'sounds-like etymology' at the end of the search rather than at the beginning. The logical starting-point in the hunt for Brunanburh should then be the primary sources and the geographical information they offer, rather than a modern place-name. A broad geographical context for the campaign of 937 is, in fact, given by the Old English poem, from which we can make the following observations:

1. The battle was fought in territory under Athelstan's rule, for he and his brother Edmund were defending their land.
2. Athelstan's army included West Saxons and Mercians. The enemy forces included Norsemen from Dublin and Scots from Alba.
3. At some point during the battle, the Scots and Vikings withdrew from the field in disarray, with the English harrying them as they fled. The pursuit was long, continuing until the end of the day.
4. The Norse leader Anlaf, with a few survivors, managed to get back to his ship and sail home to Dublin. This must mean that his fleet was moored on the shores of the Irish Sea, within a day's march to (or flight from) the battlefield.
5. Constantín, king of Alba, also escaped with a remnant of his army. No sea-voyage is mentioned, so he presumably returned home on foot.

Additional geographical clues can be gleaned from *HDE*:

1. The place called Brunanburh in the Old English poem was also known as Etbrunnanwerc and Wendun.
2. The English army faced Vikings, Scots and Strathclyde Britons ('Cumbrians').

These are the main geographical clues suggested by the sources. Other texts add little to the overall picture. John of Worcester, for instance, not only imagined the Dublin war-fleet arriving via the Humber estuary but described both Constantín and Anlaf escaping by ship, whereas the tenth-century poet implies that only Anlaf escaped in this way. John may have imagined the Humber as the default point of access for Viking invaders, perhaps because he was aware that the Norwegian king Harald Hardrada had arrived there in 1066.[44] For reasons outlined above, the Humber scenario is a poor fit with the context of 937 and can be rejected. John's description of Constantín escaping by sea is likewise an unwarranted deduction from the poem and should also be set aside. The West Saxon poet seems rather to say that the Scottish king and his surviving troops faced a long homeward march back to their own land. Alongside them, no doubt, trudged whatever remained of the army of Strathclyde.

Where should we place the battle of Brunanburh? The most objective way of finding an answer shuns the temptation to scour a modern map for a soundalike place-name. We should begin by looking instead at a much larger area defined by the primary sources and by tenth-century political geography. Our focus thus moves away from the hunt for a single battlefield to consider a wider 'conflict zone' within which a sequence of military events, rather than one decisive encounter, was played out by the protagonists. The sequence includes the approach of the armies, the main battle, the rout of the invaders and, finally, their exit from the conflict zone. At the outset, we find that the sources give us the following geographical clues:

1. The conflict zone of 937 lay within Athelstan's kingdom.
2. It could be reached without difficulty from Dublin, Alba and Strathclyde.
3. It contained a place called Brunanburh within a day's march of the Irish Sea.

Looking more closely at each of these three points:

1. Athelstan's kingdom in late 937 was based on a large realm bequeathed by his father, Edward the Elder, together with additional territories acquired after 924. After the expulsion of Guthfrith from York in 927, Athelstan's hegemony included the Anglo-Danish kingdom of Northumbria with its heartlands east of the Pennines and its northern boundary on the Tees. In the west, Edward's northern frontier had lain on the Ribble after his acquisition of southern Lancashire but Athelstan's purchase of Amounderness by 934 extended direct West Saxon rule to the River Cocker and perhaps as far as Lancaster on the River Lune. The political status of the area north of Lancaster, roughly coterminous with the later county of Westmorland, is uncertain. It bordered Cumbrian-held territory at the River Eamont and may have been a kind of 'no man's land' in 937, its Norse and English inhabitants caught between conflicting loyalties. The conflict zone of 937 should therefore be sought in lands that we can be fairly sure lay under Athelstan's authority, these being south of the Lune estuary in the west and south of the River Tees in the east. We may note that Athelstan would have been able to mount effective military campaigns west of the Pennines just as easily as on the eastern side. Although many parts of Lancashire were characterised by wetland and other difficult terrain, the region was crossed by two Roman roads connecting the northern and southern margins. On a related point, it has been objected that there are no records of agricultural estates that could have supplied Athelstan's army with food if he had travelled through Lancashire en route to Brunanburh. This can be countered by noting that West Saxon and Mercian campaigning forces most likely drew provisions from food stores stockpiled at fortified sites within the *burh* system. There was certainly a *burh* at Manchester and possibly another at Penwortham on the Ribble, both of which may have been capable of providing logistical support in 937.[45]

2. Military forces from Dublin could strike the coast of Britain with ease,

via a short voyage across the Irish Sea. From western landfalls they could head eastward to York via the Pennine passes or southward into Mercia. Any suggestion that they reached Brunanburh by sailing around the northern tip of Britain, undertaking a wearisome and hazardous sea-voyage of eight hundred miles to strike via the east coast, is completely unrealistic. No competent war-leader would risk such a potentially disastrous venture. This important logistical point deals a fatal blow to the idea of Anlaf's arrival via the Humber. Constantin's forces presumably arrived at the conflict zone after a long trek from Alba – there is no hint that they travelled by ship – and the same can be said of the Strathclyde army. Neither of these powers is likely to have had the naval capability to transport an army by sea. In the case of the Cumbrians, their move away from an ancient citadel in the Firth of Clyde to a site further inland suggests that whatever naval capacity they formerly possesed was much reduced after 870. If a western landfall for the Dublin war-fleet of 937 seems certain, then a Northumbrian setting for the ensuing campaign likewise seems very likely. It is much harder to imagine a Mercian setting, in spite of a belief among some historians that Anlaf's Norsemen ravaged Mercia prior to the decisive encounter with Athelstan. The belief has arisen from William of Malmesbury's statement that Anlaf advanced 'far into England' before being confronted by Athelstan, but it is a big leap to assume that William was thinking of Mercia, especially as his account later refers to 'the northern land' giving support to the invaders. In any case, the huge distances and logistical practicalities involved in bringing the Scots and Cumbrians to a battlefield south of the Mersey should deter us from placing Brunanburh in this region.[46] It is worth noting that there is no recorded instance of these two peoples campaigning anywhere south of a line drawn between the Lune estuary and the Yorkshire Derwent in the early medieval period. The earliest record is to a campaign in 1138 when the Scots advanced as far south as Clitheroe in Lancashire.

3. A day's march is unlikely to cover a distance greater than twenty-five to thirty miles. If the battle began at sunrise and went on for a few hours before the rout and pursuit began, Anlaf's flight to his ships was probably accomplished in the afternoon and evening. His flight need not have taken a straight, direct route to the coast and could have been haphazard and disorganised, with several detours to avoid his pursuers. Brunanburh could therefore lie anywhere within a thirty-mile radius of the place where his ships were moored.

Based on the above observations, we can tentatively draw the conflict zone of 937 on a map. The result is represented on page 96 of this book, which shows the zone to be fairly large, encompassing much of south-west Northumbria. It excludes non-Northumbrian territory, such as the Wirral peninsula and other frontier districts of north-west Mercia, together with Bromborough. Other leading candidates in the search for Brunanburh are also excluded: Burnswark in Dumfriesshire, Lanchester in County Durham and Brinsworth in South Yorkshire. Burnswark's weakness is that it lay deep in Cumbrian territory, in an area ruled by Owain of Strathclyde, and could not have been described as a place where Athelstan was defending his land.[47] Lanchester and Brinsworth lie east of the Pennines and their cases rely on the unlikely scenario of the Dublin fleet arriving via the Humber estuary. The conflict zone does, however, include one fairly popular candidate – the River Brun – together with four that are less well-known: Bruna Hill, Bourne Hill, Bruneberh and Brindle. All five are in the later county of Lancashire and their locations are marked on the map. It should be pointed out that any or none of them might have a connection with the battle of 937. As with Bromborough and other soundalikes, more-or-less credible scenarios can be devised to explain how any of the five Lancashire places *could* be the long-lost Brunanburh. They all share an attribute common to most sites that feature in the etymological debate: a modern place-name that might derive from an original *Brun* form. In common with all other candidates – including Bromborough – the earliest occurrence of the name in each case is too late to enable a tenth-century form to be reconstructed with certainty. Two of the five – the River Brun near Burnley and Bruna Hill near Garstang – are nevertheless highlighted below for further discussion, on the basis that plausible cases can be proposed for them. The other three have also been mentioned in the context of the Brunanburh debate, either in print or online. Bruneberh was the name of a large rock near the harbour at Heysham on the shore of Morecambe Bay. The second element in the name is clearly the Norse word *berg* ('rock') rather than Old English *burh* ('fort') so the name as a whole might simply be descriptive of a prominent 'brown rock' used locally as a boundary-marker or navigational aid. None of the place-names associated with the battle of 937 refers to such a feature so, despite a superficial resemblance between *Bruneberh* and *Brunanburh*, the Heysham site should probably be set aside. Bourne Hill is near Fleetwood in the west of the Fylde peninsula, a part of Amounderness that was dominated by undrained wetland in the Viking period. The main weakness of its case is lack of proximity to a land-route giving easy access or escape for armies from the northern

kingdoms of Strathclyde and Alba. Its isolated position on the coastal edge
of the peninsula, in what would have been difficult terrain in 937, makes it a
poor fit with what we have proposed as the most likely geographical context
for the battle.[48] Brindle is a South Lancashire village between Chorley and
Preston. Its name was recorded in the thirteenth century as *Brumhull* (1203),
Burnhull (1206) and *Brunhull* (1254). This probably means 'hill of the burn',
presumably a reference to the nearby Hough Hill and Lostock Brook.
Although a belief has arisen locally that the older forms of the name suggest
a connection with the battle of Brunanburh, the case for Brindle is not examined in detail here.

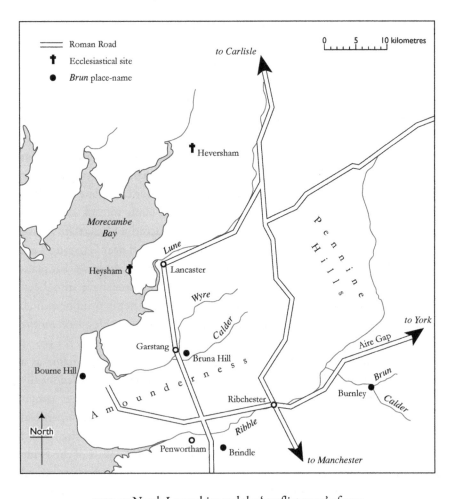

MAP 10 North Lancashire and the 'conflict zone' of 937

The River Brun

This relatively short watercourse, with a length of only four and a half miles, stands roughly midway along the Aire Gap, a major Pennine pass connecting Lancashire and Yorkshire.[49] If Anlaf's objectives in 937 included an attempt to regain his family's hold on the York kingship, a strike through the Gap would be a logical step from a landfall on the Lancashire coast. Interception by Athelstan at some point along this route would seem feasible, especially if the English king brought his forces into Northumbria via the Mersey crossings. Edward the Elder's *burh* at Manchester might then have played a key role in Athelstan's response to the invasion, its nodal position in the Roman road network offering a choice of routes if the invaders moved swiftly east or south. A battle-site near the River Brun seems a possibility if we imagine Anlaf and his allies marching along the Roman highway from Ribchester towards Skipton, their progress being halted near Gisburn by news of Athelstan's approach. Turning southward, following the course of the old Burnley–Gisburn road (now the A682), they would have had to make no more than a ten-mile detour to reach the River Brun. Recalling Anlaf's flight to his ship-moorings, which he reached at nightfall, we may note that a battlefield on the Brun would lie barely thirty miles from the Ribble estuary. The Dublin fleet may have been moored at the mouth of the Ribble or, perhaps, in the Wyre estuary further north where the Norse place-name Skippool ('ship pool' or 'ship river') is suggestive. It should be noted that the idea of a battle on the River Brun works best if the invaders were aiming for York. There is, however, no need to assume that this was their main objective.[50] In any case, although the city may have figured in Anlaf's plans, it is unlikely that Constantin and Owain joined him in 937 merely to support his ambitions. Helping a Dublin Viking to gain the Northumbrian kingship might not have been high on their list of desirable outcomes.

Bruna Hill

Situated one mile south of Garstang and half a mile north of the River Calder, the feature known as Bruna Hill appears quite insignificant when viewed on a map. In fact, it seems not to be much of a feature at all, a mere bump in an otherwise low-lying landscape. This impression swiftly changes when the site is visited, for it then emerges as a well-defined height rising above the surrounding farmland. Today its summit and most of its flanks are hidden beneath buildings and trees but in former times it must have been a prominent feature in the locality. To the north, it faces another low hill on top of which stand the ruins of Garstang Castle. To the west, at a distance of barely two hundred metres from Bruna Hill, runs a section of the Roman road from the Ribble ford at Walton-le-Dale to the fort at Lancaster. This stretch of the ancient highway continued to be the principal route into Garstang from the south during the medieval period until the Preston–Lancaster road was given a new alignment further west. The older road is still well-used by traffic passing through the villages of Bonds, Bowgreave and Catterall. Bruna Hill is close to a place called Howath (or Howarth) which takes its name from a ford on the River Calder. Howath derives from Old Norse *haugr* ('hill') + *vad* ('ford'), the hill in question being Bruna Hill itself.[51] From an archaeological standpoint, if Bruna Hill has any connection with the battle of Brunanburh we should probably expect to find traces of a tenth-century *burh* or some other fortification on the summit. To date, the only archaeological activity at the site has consisted of several small test-pits dug by members of a local society which yielded nothing indicative of medieval occupation.[52] However, the presence of a house and garden on top of the hill meant that the survey-area was restricted. The antiquity of the place-name is likewise unknown, for early forms are lacking, but it appears to have been a single word 'Brunahill' until the twentieth century. A monument known as the Brunahill Cross formerly stood nearby and its base or socket-stone was said to be visible in a field slightly eastward of the hill.[53] The *Bruna* element certainly makes the hill worthy of further study in relation to the battle of 937. One possible meaning of the name *Brunanburh* is 'fort of (a man called) Bruna', while one of the alternative names for the battlefield is *Brunandun*, recorded in Aethelweard's chronicle of c.980, which includes the Old English word *dun* ('hill'). Philologists have suggested that a *dun* was specifically 'a low hill with a fairly level and fairly extensive summit which provided a good settlement-site in open country'.[54] In modern English translation the name *Brunandun* can mean 'Bruna's Hill' or 'hill of Bruna', where the feature in question is seemingly an eminence of no great height in an open landscape. On both onomastic and topographical grounds, then, Bruna Hill near Garstang becomes a plausible candidate in the search for the battlefield. In strategic terms, it lies beside a Roman road running north–south through Lancashire. In the context of tenth-century political geography, it lies within Amounderness, the district purchased by Athelstan which extended his domains beyond the Ribble.

A mystery unsolved

Brunanburh is a lost battle. This incontrovertible fact looms large over the debate and none of the current theories seems likely to escape its shadow. What keeps the debate alive is not just the mystery surrounding the location but the fame of the event in contemporary sources. Brunanburh thus has a special aura that many other battles of the Viking Age simply do not have. To tenth-century observers it was the 'great battle' of their time, a status not even accorded to Alfred's decisive victory over the Danes at *Ethandun* in 878. What Brunanburh lacks is the kind of consensus that has confidently identified *Ethandun* as Edington in Wiltshire. The identification, while not beyond doubt, is secure enough for a modern commemorative stone at Edington to be recognised as an official war memorial. None of the sites currently involved in the Brunanburh debate warrants this sort of recognition. Not even Bromborough, despite the best efforts of its supporters, can claim to be anything more than the most popular candidate of recent years.[55] So the search for Athelstan's victory goes on, with the debate as vigorous as ever and no consensus in sight. Perhaps the time has come for all participants to take a deep breath and a step backwards. The only foreseeable outcome at the moment is that the discussion will continue to go round in circles without getting any closer to the truth. Progress cannot be measured by counting the number of specialist scholars who support a particular theory. Moreover, enthusiastic contributions in print and online might give the impression that the debate is active and vibrant but it is, in fact, recycling the same old theories. It is dominated by the imprecise science of sounds-like etymology which, as any neutral observer can see, has so far failed to locate the battlefield. The debate has become little more than an etymological treasure-hunt, a quest for the soundalike place-name that best fits a gaping hole left by the sources. Few commentators acknowledge the fact that the sources are utterly insufficient for such an exercise, or that etymological guesswork is not the only strategy available. The sources will never yield a place-name that can be pinpointed on a modern map. They could, however, provide a broad geographical context for the Brunanburh campaign, if the right questions are asked of them. One question that is rarely addressed is a twofold query relating to military logistics: how did the armies of Alba and Strathclyde get to Brunanburh, and how did they get home? Finding an answer to this is no less important than locating the battlefield itself, yet the participation of the northern kings is frequently overlooked, to the detriment of the entire debate.[56] The role of the Scots and Cumbrians is not the only aspect of the battle that gets pushed into the shadows when the etymological quest occupies so much of the foreground. However, if a higher value was assigned to factors such as political boundaries, strategic objectives and logistical considerations, participants in the debate might possibly come closer to reaching a consensus. Armed with an understanding of the wider context of the battle they might then be in a better position to recover its elusive location.

Aftermath

The Old English poem tried to portray Brunanburh as a resounding triumph with far-reaching consequences. It therefore seems ironic that the 'great battle' apparently caused no major shift in the balance of power.[57] Athelstan seems to have been unable to build upon his victory in any meaningful way. In the ensuing months he could justifiably claim to be the most powerful king in Britain but this was hardly a big step forward: he had made a similar claim on coins minted before 937.[58] Perhaps more surprising is the absence of any hint that Constantin and Owain submitted to Athelstan's overlordship as they had done after his northern campaign in 934. In the wake of Brunanburh these kings might have expected swift retribution, as punishment for ravaging his lands, but none seems to have been unleashed. There was no counter-invasion of their heartlands, no ravaging of Perthshire or Clydesdale by English soldiers. Why Athelstan apparently failed to consolidate his victory is another puzzling aspect to add to the debate. If he waged any more wars we know nothing of them, for the sources fall silent on the last years of his reign. Even the 'A' text of the *Anglo-Saxon Chronicle*, the mouthpiece of his dynasty, had nothing more to say of him until its year-entry for 939: 'This year King Athelstan died in Gloucester, on

27th October, about forty-one winters, less one night, from the time when King Alfred died. And Edmund Atheling received the kingdom. He was then eighteen years old. King Athelstan reigned fourteen years and ten weeks.'[59]

The death of the 'king of all Britain' at the age of forty-three left a large void on the political stage. Men of ambition were quick to seize their chances and, before the end of the year, Anlaf Guthfrithsson left Dublin and came back to Northumbria. There he gained the kingship of York, having been accepted by the city's Anglo-Danish elite and their leader Archbishop Wulfstan.[60] He eventually turned his attention northward, to lands ruled by the English lords of Bamburgh. While raiding in this region in 941 he plundered the old monastery at Tyninghame, founded by St Baldred in the eighth century. This was the last recorded deed of his career, for he died soon after.[61] In the wake of his passing, his namesake and younger kinsman Anlaf Sihtricsson claimed the Northumbrian kingship, but the York elite instead gave their allegiance to Athelstan's brother Edmund. However, this rejection of the Dublin dynasty turned out to be brief and the Northumbrians soon accepted Anlaf Sihtricsson as their new king.[62] In Irish sources he has the unusual nickname *Cuarán*, meaning 'shoe' or 'sandal', perhaps a reference to royal inauguration rituals involving the symbolic wearing of footwear. His father was none other than the Sihtric, grandson of Ivar, who had held the York kingship in Aethelflaed's time. Anlaf Cuarán soon flexed the military muscle of his new power-base, launching major assaults on English fortresses in Mercia. Together with Archbishop Wulfstan he was besieged by Athelstan's successor Edmund in the former Danelaw stronghold of Leicester. Anlaf and Edmund eventually negotiated a treaty, a term of which was the Norse king's baptism under Edmund's sponsorship.[63]

Meanwhile, in the kingdom of the Scots, Constantin mac Áeda withdrew from secular life to spend his twilight years in monastic retirement. The kingship of Alba then passed to Máel Coluim mac Domnaill, one of Constantin's younger kinsmen, a son of his predecessor Domnall. The Cumbrians, too, had a change of leadership, their king Owain having retired – or died – if indeed he had survived the slaughter at Brunanburh. By c.940, the new king of Strathclyde was Dyfnwal, son of Owain, whose father was presumably the aforementioned *rex Cumbrorum* of the 920s and 930s. Just as Owain had been obliged to steer a path between the competing interests of Athelstan and Constantin, so now Dyfnwal had to deal with the ambitions of Edmund and Máel Coluim. As the middle years of the tenth century approached, the stage was set for a new round of wars, treaties and alliances.

Brunanburh and *Armes Prydein Vawr*

The poem *Armes Prydein Vawr* ('The Great Prophecy of Britain') was composed in Wales in the tenth century, either before or after the battle of Brunanburh. It is preserved in *Llyfr Taliesin* ('The Book of Taliesin'), a Welsh manuscript written in the first half of the fourteenth century, and is the longest, possibly the oldest, of a number of prophetic poems assembled by the compiler. *Armes Prydein* is essentially a call to arms, an emotive plea to all the enemies of the English, urging them to unite in a combined military campaign. The poet envisages a grand anti-English alliance comprising various Celtic and Scandinavian peoples: Welsh, Cornish, Bretons, Irish, Norse, Scots and Strathclyde Britons. The last are referred to as *Cludwys* ('Clyde-folk') and mention is also made of *Alclud*, their former royal stronghold on Dumbarton Rock. In the poem the English are referred to as *Saesson* ('Saxons') and those of Wessex are called *Iwys* or *Iwis*, a Welsh variant of Old English *Gewisse*, which was an archaic name for the West Saxons. The poet describes the Dublin Norse as *gwyr Dulyn* or *gynhon Dulyn* (respectively, the 'men' and 'foreigners' of Dublin) and urges his fellow-Welshmen to form an alliance with them. In spite of these references to the major participants at Brunanburh there is no clear reference to the battle itself. Much scholarship has been devoted to the questions of why and when the poem was composed. If it pre-dated the Brunanburh campaign, is it simply an attempt to solicit wider support for the coalition that was ultimately defeated by Athelstan? If it was composed after 937, to what extent does it fit the political situation of the 940s or 950s? Much scholarship has been devoted to answering these questions but, at the present time, they remain unanswered.[64]

KING DUNMAIL

Dyfnwal, son of Owain, began his reign in what seems to have been a time of relative peace between the Cumbrians and their neighbours. There is no record of warfare involving Strathclyde in the immediate post-Brunanburh period, between 938 and 944, nor any hint that the kingdom lay under the yoke of a foreign power. An entry in the *Annals of the Four Masters*, an Irish chronicle written in the seventeenth century, tells of an English victory over Constantin mac Áeda, Anlaf Cuarán and the Britons in 940, but this is undoubtedly a misplaced record of Brunanburh.[1] During the early 940s, Dyfnwal appears to have maintained fairly stable relations with the kings of Alba, Dublin, York and Wessex. This picture is mirrored in a contemporary account of the travels of a Scottish holy man, St Cathroe, who went on pilgrimage around this time.

Vita Kaddroe, 'Life of Cathroe', is a hagiographical account written within a decade of the saint's death at the Frankish monastery of Metz c.971. Its author was Ousmann (or Reimann) a monk at Metz who had lived there during Cathroe's abbacy.[2] From the *Vita* we learn that the saint was born around the year 900, in the kingdom of Alba, to aristocratic parents whose names were Fochereach and Bania. The names Cathroe and Fochereach suggest that the family was Gaelic-speaking, although their recent ancestry may have been Pictish. There is a hint that they lived in Perthshire: young Cathroe became a teacher at a monastic school overseen by St Bean, his paternal uncle, who may have been based in Strathearn.[3] At around forty years of age, probably in 940 or 941, Cathroe embarked on a pilgrimage to the Continent, following a path taken by many Celtic monks before him. The first stage of his journey brought him to a church dedicated to St Brigit of Kildare, most likely at the monastery of Abernethy in Fife where, according to local tradition, one of Brigit's nuns had founded a mission among pagan Picts in the sixth century. From there, the Scottish king Constantin mac Áeda is said to have personally escorted Cathroe on the next stage of his journey, bringing him to *terra Cumbrorum*, 'the land of the Cumbrians'. A more realistic scenario is that Constantin provided the pilgrim with a company of soldiers to guarantee his safe passage to the

Strathclyde border. Crossing into Cumbrian territory, Cathroe was welcomed by King Dovenald (*Dovenaldus*) whom the *Vita* describes as a relative. Dovenald is undoubtedly Dyfnwal, son of Owain, king of Strathclyde.[4] The name was rendered by the hagiographer in a form similar to its tenth-century pronunciation. It is possible that the original source or informant, who may have been Cathroe himself, had in mind the equivalent Gaelic form *Domnall* (pronounced 'Dovnal') rather than the Cumbric name but this does not challenge the identification with Dyfnwal, despite attempts by some historians to see Dovenald as an otherwise unknown Scottish prince on the throne of Strathclyde.[5] The precise nature of Dyfnwal's kinship with Cathroe is not explained and could have been based on marriage rather than blood. Speculation seems fruitless in the absence of other information and we may note that the number of possible relationships is increased by the existence of Cathroe's half-brothers, the sons of Bania's first husband. Whatever the nature of the kinship, Dyfnwal gave the pilgrim a warm welcome and suitable hospitality, followed by safe passage through his lands, 'to the city of *Loida* which is the boundary of the Northmen [Norse] and the Cumbrians. And there he was received by a certain noble man, Gunderic, by whom he was led to King Erik in the city of York, because this king had as wife a relative of the godly Cathroe'.[6]

The 'city' of *Loida* is here described as a frontier settlement on the border between Dyfnwal's kingdom and a territory under Norse rule. Gunderic, who is otherwise unknown, must have been a lord of this territory, although his name tells us little about him. We cannot even be sure he was of Scandinavian ancestry, although he may have been answerable to a local Norse *jarl*.[7] It seems reasonable to infer from the *Vita* that he was ultimately a subject of the king of Northumbria, to whom he is said to have escorted Cathroe personally. Gunderic is plainly associated in some way with the *civitas* or 'city' of *Loida*, which might even have been part of – or close to – his own place of residence. Previous attempts to identity *Loida* have noted the similarity of the name to *Loidis* in Bede's *Ecclesiastical History* of 731. *Loidis* is an old name for the region around Leeds in West Yorkshire and can be seen in the modern place-name Ledsham as well as in the name of Leeds itself. Although Leeds and its environs lie one hundred miles from the River Eamont, the southern border of Dyfnwal's kingdom, the names *Loida* and *Loidis* are frequently seen as one and the same.[8] This identification sits uneasily with tenth-century political geography and must be rejected, for Leeds cannot have been on the border between Cumbrians and Northumbrians, being too far south. We should look elsewhere for *Loida*, in an area where Dyfnwal was more likely to have had a frontier with the kings of York. Our focus turns to the vicinity of the Eamont itself, where Cumbric place-names at the southern limit of a colonisation by Britons in the Viking period define the southern border of tenth-century Strathclyde. This was surely Dyfnwal's frontier with the Northumbrians in the early 940s, as it had almost certainly been Owain's frontier in Athelstan's time. In 927, Owain had attended a high-level conference with Athelstan beside the River Eamont, probably near its junction with the River Lowther. To the south-west of this confluence lay the valley of the Lowther itself, while to the south-east lay the Roman highway to York, tracing an ancient route across the Pennines via the moorland expanse of the Stainmore Pass. The place where Cathroe crossed from Cumbrian into Northumbrian territory is more likely to have been in this locality rather than in distant Leeds. Why, indeed, would a king of Strathclyde bring Cathroe southward to *Loidis*, just so that an Anglo-Scandinavian lord could take him north-eastward to York? We should probably look for *Loida* near Penrith, where an obvious candidate is the River Lowther and its valley. The oldest recorded form of the river-name is *Loedria* in a charter of the late eleventh century but its origin is unknown and both Celtic and Scandinavian etymologies have been proposed.[9] Might this be the lost *Loida*? The river gave its name to Lowther Castle, formerly Lowther Hall, the ancestral home of the Lowther family until partial demolition in the twentieth century left it a standing ruin. Within the large estate surrounding the castle sits Lowther parish church, housing a small collection of Viking Age sculpture. The church probably occupies the site of a Northumbrian monastery, founded in pre-Viking times, which might in turn have replaced an earlier British foundation.[10] Among the carved stones are three 'hogbacks', probably of tenth-century date, that may have marked the graves of local lords. Ten miles southward lies the source of the River Lowther on Yarlside, 'Jarl's Seat', the highest of the Shap Fells. The name of the hill is suggestive, calling to mind the Norse lords who held lands in western Northumbria in the tenth century.[11] It raises the possibility that a monastery at Lowther served the spiritual needs of a distinct area of lordship ruled by a *jarl* whose residence lay in the vicinity of Lowther Castle. Perhaps Gunderic, the nobleman who guided St Cathroe to York, might have been such a lord? In this period, Latin *civitas* was applied to ecclesiastical as well as to secular sites, so the 'city' of *Loida* might not be Gunderic's lordly residence but a major monastery within his lands.[12] Such a destination would have been appropriate for a travelling cleric and we may tentatively locate it at the site now occupied by Lowther Church.

At York, Cathroe stayed for a while with 'King Erik' whose wife was a kinswoman of the pilgrim. Again, the nature of the kinship is unknown but it may have been linked to that between Cathroe and Dyfnwal, raising the possibility of a family connection between a queen of Northumbria and a king of Strathclyde. Erik's identity is a matter of debate. He is often assumed to be Erik Bloodaxe, a Norwegian warlord of royal blood whose career is described in Norse sagas of the thirteenth century. According to the *Anglo-Saxon Chronicle*, a king called Erik ruled Northumbria sometime between 946 and 948, having been chosen by Archbishop Wulfstan and the Anglo-Danish nobility, but whether he is Erik Bloodaxe of the sagas is uncertain.[13] This same Erik was then expelled by his former backers, before being restored to the kingship in 952 and ruling at York until his violent death two years later. According to the sagas, Erik Bloodaxe emerged in the 930s during a contest between rival claimants for the throne of Norway. He eventually left his homeland and came to Britain where, depending on which saga is consulted, he became a sea-raider in traditional Viking guise or a king of Northumbria.[14] While there is some justification for seeing him as the Erik mentioned in *ASC*, it is also possible that the saga-writers merged the two namesakes together to add an extra dimension to the already colourful career of the Norwegian prince. Neither of these individuals is a chronological match with the Erik of *Vita Kaddroe*, if the date of the saint's pilgrimage has been correctly reported by his hagiographer. In 940 and 941, the years usually associated with Cathroe's journey, the kingship of Northumbria was held by Anlaf Guthfrithsson and his successor Anlaf Cuarán, with the latter ruling until 944.[15] There seems to be no window of opportunity for a king called Erik to take power around the time of Cathroe's arrival in York. We might suspect that the hagiographer knew of a Northumbrian king called Erik and assumed that he was the one who welcomed the saint, especially if the true name of Cathroe's host was unknown or forgotten at the time of writing.[16] If we accept the hagiographer's chronology as broadly accurate, we might feel tempted to substitute his 'Erik' for 'Anlaf' and assign the pilgrimage to 940. If Anlaf Guthfrithsson, the veteran of Brunanburh, was the king who met Cathroe at York, a connection between his wife and Cathroe's family could have been forged during the Norse–Scottish alliance of 937. An alternative scenario is that Cathroe's journey was spread over a number of years, with long sojourns at different places along the way. He might have left Alba c.941, while Constantin was still in power, but may have arrived in York several years later. A second alternative is that the entire pilgrimage took place after 943, when Constantin was in monastic retirement while his kinsman Máel Coluim ruled the Scots, but this requires wholesale rejection of the hagiographer's chronology.

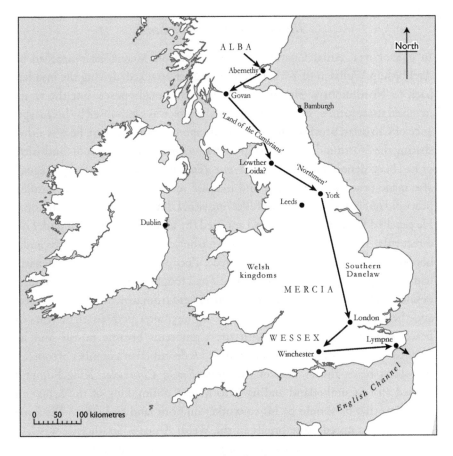

MAP 11 St Cathroe's pilgrimage

After leaving York, Cathroe travelled south into English territory. He came first to London before moving on to Winchester as the guest of King Edmund. Eventually, with the king's blessing, he sailed to the Continent to resume his religious career, finding a position among the Franks. From the account of his journey through northern Britain we may infer that the region was enjoying a period of stability in which a traveller could pass from one kingdom to the next without fear. If the journey took place in 940 or 941, this might mean that the reign of Dyfnwal, son of Owain, began in peace, perhaps in a time when treaties forged in the aftermath of Brunanburh still held firm. Neither the Metz hagiographer nor the tenth-century English chroniclers refer to northern wars in the early 940s, nor do they hint that a new round of hostilities was about to break out. In this period, however, peaceful interludes tended to be fragile and short-lived.

The invasion of Cumberland

In 942 or 943, Anlaf Cuarán launched a raid on Mercia, accompanied by Archbishop Wulfstan of York. Edmund counter-attacked, driving the invaders back to Northumbria. He and Anlaf eventually made peace, but the treaty involved some form of submission by Anlaf which was symbolised by his acceptance of Christian baptism under Edmund's sponsorship. By then, he was either sharing the Northumbrian kingship with his cousin Ragnall, son of Guthfrith, or had been deposed by Ragnall in a *coup d'état*. Before the end of 943, Ragnall also made peace with Edmund and likewise received baptism.[17][18] The ensuing peace did not last long and, in the following year, Edmund invaded Northumbria. He expelled Ragnall and Anlaf and annexed the kingdom, bringing it under his direct rule. This gave him a north-western frontier in the Stainmore Pass and a border with the Cumbrians of Strathclyde, a people against whom his dynasty had not waged war since 937. He himself had fought at Brunanburh, standing beside his elder brother Athelstan on a battlefield from which the Strathclyders and their allies had been utterly routed. By 945, after perhaps eight years of peace, Edmund's relationship with the Cumbrians became hostile and he invaded their territory. What happened next is described in a number of sources, the oldest being the 'A' text of the *Anglo-Saxon Chronicle*: 'King Edmund harried all of Cumberland and let it to Máel Coluim, king of the Scots, on condition that he should be his co-worker on both land and sea.'[18] The same campaign was noted more briefly in the Welsh Annals: 'Strathclyde was laid waste by the Saxons.'[19] Additional information was provided by the later chroniclers. Henry of Huntingdon, writing in the early twelfth century, hinted that Edmund attacked the North Britons because they could not be forced into submission by other means: 'he raided and ravaged the whole of Cumberland, because he was unable wholly to subdue the nation of that province, treacherous and unaccustomed to laws. And he commended it to Máel Coluim king of Scotland, upon this agreement, that he should help him by land and sea.'[20]

Some hundred years after Henry, further details were offered by Roger of Wendover in his *Flowers of History*:

> King Edmund, relying upon the help of Leolin, king of Dyfed, despoiled the whole of Cumbria of all its property, and having deprived the two sons of Dunmail, king of that province, of their sight, he gave the kingdom to Máel Coluim, king of the Scots, to hold of him, that he might defend the northern parts of England against raiders by land and by sea.[21]

The Cumbrian ruler *Dunmail* is none other than Dyfnwal, son of Owain, king of Strathclyde, his name rendered here in an Old English form. *Leolin* is an Anglicised form of Welsh *Llewellyn* but the name is an error by Roger or his source. The king of Dyfed at this time was not Llewellyn but Hywel the Good, formerly a faithful *subregulus* of Athelstan and now seemingly taking the same role under Edmund. Although no other source mentions Edmund's Welsh allies as taking part in the Cumbrian campaign, their participation is probably to be expected. For the anachronistic *Leolin* we should therefore read *Hywel*. Nor need we doubt that the gruesome episode involving Dyfnwal's sons actually happened. The source of Roger's information is unknown, but he may have had access to authentic traditions of a war between Edmund and 'Dunmail', these perhaps including Northumbrian versions of the *ASC* entry or saga material preserved by the community of St Cuthbert at Durham. If we accept Roger's testimony as reliable, we should seek a context for the mutilation of the two princes. They may have been hostages at Edmund's court when the campaign began, their presence in his entourage providing leverage in an attempt to force Dyfnwal's submission.[22] Alternatively, they may have been captured in battle during the invasion of 'Cumbria', before being ritually blinded to deprive Dyfnwal of viable heirs. The cruelty inflicted upon them was, in any case, intended to send a clear message to their father.[23]

The Welsh chronicle *Brut y Tywysogion*, 'Chronicle of the Princes', has already been mentioned. One of its several versions, preserved in a fourteenth-century manuscript, has the following entry for 943, misplaced by a couple of years: 'In the same year Strathclyde was ravaged by the English, who cruelly slew those whom they found in their way, of the Britons and those who belonged to them.'[24] This translation relies on a slight amendment to the final words in the original Welsh text. In unaltered form, the text yields a different translation: 'of the Britons to whom it belonged'. The unaltered version seems an unnecessary statement of an obvious fact: Strathclyde, like Wales, was inhabited by Britons. The sources of *Brut y Tywysogion*, including the Welsh Annals, are unlikely to have offered such information, especially to audiences in Wales who already knew that Strathclyde was British territory. The amended version, suggested by the eminent Welsh scholar Sir John Morris-Jones, makes far more sense. It implies that Edmund's troops ravaged not only the Strathclyders but also non-British communities under their rule.[25] From this we might infer that the victims of Edmund's invasion in 945 included communities of Hiberno-Norse, together with English-speakers, in areas under Cumbrian authority.

Although the Irish sources are silent on the campaign they do mention

Anlaf Cuarán's reappearance in Dublin in the same year.[26] His movements in the preceding months, immediately after his expulsion from Northumbria in 944, are not recorded but it is possible that he spent a brief sojourn in Strathclyde. If his relationship with Ragnall Guthfrithsson was based not on co-operation but on rivalry and mutual hostility, Anlaf may have had few places of refuge. His former power-base at Dublin was ruled by Ragnall's brother, so there is no guarantee that a welcome awaited him there. The Scots were unlikely to have given him sanctuary when their own king was happy to be Edmund's 'co-worker'. Strathclyde was perhaps Anlaf's best or only option at a time when his fortunes were at rock bottom. If he was indeed offered hospitality by Dyfnwal in 944, this might have been enough to provoke Edmund's invasion in the following year.[27]

The only notice of the campaign of 945 in a text produced by St Cuthbert's community comes from *Historia de Sancto Cuthberto*, which offers a slightly confused account. Substituting 'Scotland' for Strathclyde, it tells us that, after Athelstan's death,

> his brother Edmund succeeded to the kingdom, collected again a great army, and hastened to Scotland. Yet in going he turned aside to the oratory of St Cuthbert, bowed his knees before his tomb, and offered prayers, and commended himself and his men to God and the holy confessor.[28]

The oratory visited by Edmund on his way to Strathclyde was at Chester-le-Street, the headquarters of the monks of Cuthbert before their move to Durham. Like his elder half-brother, Edmund sought the support of the Northumbrians by paying his respects to their patron saint. Just as Athelstan had used the Roman highway of Dere Street on his northward march in 934, so Edmund now trod the same route eleven years later. Athelstan's ultimate target had been Alba, the kingdom of the Scots, but Edmund's onslaught was aimed solely at Cumberland, the realm of the Strathclyde Britons. His choice of route is significant, for it suggests that the Cumbric-speaking colonies south of the Solway were bypassed. He may have intended to restore these and other settlements in north-west Northumbria to English rule but, even so, his initial target was the Cumbrian heartland further north, for the Welsh annalists reported that he ravaged *Strat Clut*, the valley of the River Clyde. He perhaps turned aside from Dere Street where it forded the River Tweed, before leading his army west into Clydesdale. The eastern route may, in any case, have been his only viable option, for it seems that his brother's gains in North Lancashire had already been lost.[29]

Unlike his father, Dyfnwal could hope for no help from Alba. As Edmund's 'co-worker', Máel Coluim was hardly likely to defend the Cumbrians against an English invasion. Indeed, things could have got much worse for Dyfnwal if Edmund's English and Welsh soldiers had been reinforced by the Scots. There is, however, no indication that Máel Coluim played an active military role in the campaign. He seems to have stayed on the sidelines while Strathclyde was thoroughly despoiled. No doubt the beleaguered Cumbrians put up a stern defence, fighting hard to protect their land from the onslaught, but eventually they were overcome. At some point Dyfnwal must have surrendered, for we know that he survived the invasion and remained in place as king. Yet his status and authority were thereafter diminished by a heavy yoke of subjection which deprived him of his independence. Not only did he have to recognise Edmund's supremacy, he also had to accept Máel Coluim as an overlord appointed by the English king. The *Anglo-Saxon Chronicle* tells us that Edmund 'let' Strathclyde to Máel Coluim, in return for military co-operation. This 'letting' probably involved some kind of proxy overlordship, with Máel Coluim taking Edmund's place as effective master of the Cumbrian kingdom, perhaps because it was too far away to be overseen from Wessex. Tribute-payments and other benefits of suzerainty would then have accrued to Máel Coluim instead of heading south. In return, the Scottish king was no doubt expected to keep the Cumbrians in check. He was also obliged to give military assistance to Edmund, on land or sea, if called upon to do so. In forging this agreement, Edmund may have been guarding against the possibility of a new eruption of dissent at York, a place where Archbishop Wulfstan and his Anglo-Danish henchmen lurked as uneasy clients of the West Saxon dynasty.

The campaign of 945 would have depleted Dyfnwal's military resources, thereby reducing his effectiveness as a potential ally of Viking warlords. What it did not bring about was a permanent Scottish subjection of Strathclyde. Nor did it put an end to Dyfnwal's dynasty, in spite of his appearance in later legend as the last king of the Cumbrians.[30] If we had no knowledge of Strathclyde's post-945 history we could perhaps be forgiven for thinking that the kingdom was indeed conquered by the English and given to the Scots, but the second half of the tenth century is not a blank page. Reliable sources such as the Irish annals, the *Chronicle of Alba* and the *Anglo-Saxon Chronicle* leave us in no doubt that the Cumbrians regained their independence and maintained it in subsequent decades, eventually emerging into the eleventh century as a still-viable political force. The combined testimony of these early texts is overwhelming and far outweighs the fiction promoted by Fordun.

King Dunmail

An old legend from the English Lake District tells of a king called Dunmail who was killed in battle while fighting 'Saxons'. The battle is said to have taken place in a high pass between the lakes of Thirlmere and Grasmere. After Dunmail's death, his two sons were blinded by the Saxon leader, Edmund. Other captives were ordered to build a cairn of stones over Dunmail's body. A few survivors managed to flee the battle-field, bearing the dead king's crown ('the crown of Cumberland') which they threw into Grisedale Tarn at the foot of the mountain Helvellyn. There the crown lies safely hidden until a time in the future when King Dunmail returns to lead his men to victory. The ghosts of his warriors are said to retrieve the crown each year, on the anniversary of the battle, so that they can take it to the cairn in the pass. After striking the topmost stone with their spears, they always hear a voice from within, telling them to wait until the time is right.

The origins of the legend are shrouded in mystery but it seems to have been known at least as far back as the sixteenth century when the cairn was marked on a map as 'Dumbalrase Stones'. At the end of the following century the cairn was described in a traveller's guidebook as 'a great heap of stones called Dunmail-Raise-Stones, supposed to have been cast up by Dunmail king of Cumberland for the bounds of his kingdom'. From the late 1700s the legend began to appear as a narrative tale, with the cairn being linked to a battle fought in 945.

It is clear that the legend is based on a historical event: the ravaging of Cumberland by Edmund, king of the English. Dunmail is none other than Dyfnwal, king of Strathclyde, who did not die in battle on a high pass but on pilgrimage to Rome. The name Dunmail Raise incorporates the Norse word *hroysi* ('cairn' or 'mound'), a fairly common element in Lakeland place-names, but this is not enough to push the origin of the legend back to the Viking period. The details seem to be part of a tradition reported by Roger of Wendover in the early thirteenth century, for Roger's chronicle is our oldest source for the gruesome detail about the blinding of Dunmail's sons. The legend might even be based on Roger's account, unless both are just versions of an older story preserved in the medieval folklore of Lakeland. The cairn stands on the border between the old counties of Cumberland and Westmorland and was probably erected as a boundary-marker.

Not surprisingly, the legend has attracted the attention of poets, including William Wordsworth whose poem *The Waggoner* (1805) includes the following lines:

> And now have reached that pile of stones,
> Heaped over brave King Dunmail's bones;
> His who had once supreme command,
> Last king of rocky Cumberland.

New alliances: Dyfnwal, Eadred and the campaign of 952

Edmund, king of the English, was slain by a renegade in 946.[31] He was succeeded by his younger brother Eadred, a man of similarly high ambition. In the following year, Eadred travelled to Tanshelf near Pontefract to meet Archbishop Wulfstan and other Northumbrian leaders. With oaths of loyalty the York elite acknowledged Eadred as their king but, within a short time, they had broken their pledges. They chose instead a new ruler, a Scandinavian called Erik, a mysterious figure whose identity is uncertain.[32] He was mentioned earlier in this chapter in the context of St Cathroe's visit to York. According to the *Anglo-Saxon Chronicle*, Erik's reign lasted only until 948 when Eadred marched north to punish the oath-breakers and reassert his authority. The Northumbrian heartlands around York were thoroughly ravaged by West Saxon soldiers who soon pushed Wulfstan and his cronies into a tight corner. At some point, Eadred felt that the campaign had achieved its objectives, for he began the long march home, leaving a portion of his army at Castleford.[33] This garrison was cut to pieces in a sudden Northumbrian assault that Eadred plainly did not expect. In a furious rage he halted his journey and turned around, threatening to wreak a terrible vengeance on Northumbria. The power-brokers at York knew this was no idle threat so they deposed Erik and renewed their pledges to Eadred. However, their fickle loyalty to the West Saxon dynasty evaporated once more and, when Anlaf Cuarán reappeared in Northumbria in 949, he became their new king.[34] Curiously, there is no record of an attempt by Eadred to topple Anlaf, despite his earlier determination to oust Erik and impose direct rule. The impression given by the sources is that Eadred accepted Anlaf's return to the York kingship, however grudgingly, and was either unwilling or unable to dislodge him. It is even possible that Eadred and Anlaf settled their differences by forging a treaty or alliance.[35]

What happened next is unclear, but the political alignments of the early 940s unravelled before the end of the decade. Máel Coluim of Alba, the former 'co-worker' of Eadred's brother, launched a raid on Northumbria in 949 or 950, plundering as far south as the River Tees.[36] The event is described in *CKA* as if Máel Coluim's chief objective was the taking of portable loot – livestock and human captives – with no mention of a political motive. *CKA* adds that Constantin mac Áeda, the previous king, emerged briefly from monastic retirement to urge Máel Coluim to undertake the raid. The English were plainly the victims, especially those dwelling north of the Tees in lands traditionally ruled by the lords of Bamburgh. South of the same river lay territory ruled from Anglo-Scandinavian York but the chronology in *CKA* is too vague to indicate whether the attack came before or after Anlaf Cuarán's return to the city. A couple of years later, in 952, Máel Coluim's warriors were again in action, fighting in a battle against Vikings. In the *Annals of Ulster* this was described as a Viking victory over a combined force of Scots, Britons and English. The annalists referred to the victors as 'Foreigners' (*Gaill*), a common term for Scandinavian raiders and settlers in the Irish texts: 'The Foreigners won a battle against the men of Alba, the Britons and the Saxons.'[37]

The annalists gave no name to the battle but the participation of the Scots suggests a northern location, perhaps in Northumbria. This allows us to identify the Britons as the Cumbrians of Strathclyde rather than as the Welsh of Wales.[38] The identity of the 'Saxons' depends largely on that of the 'Foreigners', who may have been Hiberno-Norse from Dublin, Anglo-Danes from York or another Scandinavian group from elsewhere. It is possible that the 'Saxons' were northerners too, perhaps from Bamburgh, but they could equally have come from another part of Northumbria, or from Wessex and Mercia. Anlaf Cuarán is not mentioned, even though he was at York as king of the Northumbrians in 952, so he perhaps played no part in the battle. The same year saw the appearance of another Viking warlord, a Norwegian prince of high royal blood: Erik Haraldsson, also known as 'Erik Bloodaxe', an individual whom we have previously encountered in the account of St Cathroe's pilgrimage. Some historians think Erik was not only Cathroe's mysterious 'King Erik' of York but also the namesake who held the Northumbrian kingship in the 940s. Other scholars envisage two different Eriks, each ruling Northumbria for short periods in the mid-tenth century.[39] With several puzzles and few certainties, it is reassuring to turn back to the *Anglo-Saxon Chronicle* which states plainly that Erik Bloodaxe became king at York in 952: 'In this year the Northumbrians drove out King Anlaf and received Erik, Harald's son.'[40]

This provides a possible context for the victory of the 'Foreigners' reported in *AU*. The Foreigners may have been led by Erik Bloodaxe himself, with the battle taking place shortly after his installation as Northumbria's new king.[41] His forces would then have comprised not only his Norwegian followers but local Anglo-Danish troops. If this is the correct interpretation of the annal, the unidentifed 'Saxons' might have been rival Northumbrians commanded by Oswulf, the lord of Bamburgh, or another English force sent northward by King Eadred. The most likely scenario is that the 'Saxons' were indeed Oswulf and his warriors, for whom a rendezvous with allied armies from Strathclyde and Alba would have been fairly straightforward. Oswulf regarded Eadred as his liege-lord and was a loyal subordinate, effectively protecting West Saxon interests in the north. If he and Erik Bloodaxe were indeed the respective leaders of the 'Saxons' and 'Foreigners' who fought in 952, we might wonder if the old alliance of Aethelflaed's time had been revived, with a new generation of Englishmen, Cumbrians and Scots confronting forces from Anglo-Danish York. Back in 918, the northern kings and the lords of Bamburgh had probably shared Aethelflaed's anxieties about Ragnall and his use of York as a base for raids. Thirty-four years later, their descendants may have responded to a similar threat from Erik Bloodaxe by aligning their concerns with those of Aethelflaed's nephew Eadred. This is consistent with an idea already mooted above, namely the possibility that Eadred saw Anlaf Cuarán – but not Erik Bloodaxe – as an acceptable ruler of Northumbria. It does, however, require that the kings of Alba and Strathclyde held the same opinion on Anlaf and were happy to be aligned with Eadred.[42] Conversely, the Anglo-Danish nobility at York may have resented any further prospect of West Saxon interference in their affairs. If Anlaf was becoming acceptable to Eadred, this could explain why he was deposed in favour of Erik. Other scenarios are available and should be considered. For instance, neither Anlaf nor Erik may have been connected with the battle of 952 and the 'Foreigners' might simply have been a large band of Vikings from Ireland or Orkney or Scandinavia, led by men with no claim on the Northumbrian kingship.

The likely participation of the Cumbrians in the battle of 952 warrants a closer look. We should not assume that they fought as vassals of Máel Coluim of Alba rather than as members of an independent army under its own leader. Máel Coluim's overlordship of Strathclyde had been bestowed by Edmund in 945 but was conditional on the relationship between one English king and his Scottish ally. There is little doubt that the 'letting' of Strathclyde expired when Edmund died in 946.[43] Moreover, the terms of Dyfnwal's surrender after the devastation of his lands by English and Welsh troops would have been dictated by Edmund, not by Máel Coluim. There was no automatic transfer of oaths and treaties to an overking's successor, nor is there any record of a new campaign by Eadred to enforce renewal of the terms imposed on the Cumbrians in 945. Eadred was too far away to demand Dyfnwal's submission without mounting another full-scale invasion. It seems highly likely, then, that the Cumbrians reasserted their independence in the wake of Edmund's death and rejected the Scottish overlordship that had been imposed in the previous year. With his English 'co-worker' gone, Máel Coluim would have had to maintain his authority in Strathclyde by himself, using his own military resources to enforce it. There is no indication that he did so, no record of a punitive raid to keep the Cumbrians under his heel, so he presumably relinquished overlordship in a mutual face-saving treaty with Dyfnwal. By 952, these two kings had seemingly settled their differences and were standing together against the 'Foreigners', pitching their armies into battle alongside English allies. A growing friendship between Strathclyde and Alba might even lie behind the naming of one of Dyfnwal's sons as Máel Coluim, unless this was a gesture of homage to the Scottish king during his period of overlordship.

One event of 952 that is almost certainly connected with the return of Erik Bloodaxe and the expulsion of Anlaf Cuarán is the arrest and imprisonment of Archbishop Wulfstan. Whether this occurred before or after Anlaf's departure is unknown, but it was certainly ordered by Eadred. Wulfstan had been a key figure in northern politics for twenty years but his policies had rarely coincided with the ambitions of the West Saxon dynasty. The *Anglo-Saxon Chronicle* states that he was arrested 'because accusations of him had often been made to the king'.[44] How the arrest was accomplished we cannot say, but the archbishop's time as kingmaker at York was over. He may have been handed over by Erik or Anlaf or a pro-Wessex faction among the Northumbrian aristocracy. He was released from prison in 953 but remained south of the Humber until the end of his days, serving as bishop of Dorchester and dying at a Mercian monastery in 956. He lived long enough to see the end of the Northumbrian independence that he and his henchmen had striven so hard to maintain. The end came in 954, when the Northumbrians themselves expelled Erik Bloodaxe and recognised Eadred as their king. Erik was eventually slain on Stainmore, the remote borderland between Northumbrian and Cumbrian territory. His death seems to have been an assassination forged in treachery, with Oswulf of Bamburgh implicated in one version of events.[45] The location of Erik's demise, on the old Roman highway from York to Penrith, has led to a suggestion that he was leaving Northumbria to seek sanctuary in Strathclyde. If, however, he was the unnamed victor in the battle of 952, where the Cumbrians fought on the losing side, then Strathclyde might seem an unlikely destination. He may rather have been attempting to reach the Norse colonies on the western coast.[46] Whatever the true circumstances, his departure brought a major change to the political map: Northumbria was now an indivisible part of a large realm ruled by the descendants of Alfred the Great. The old royal city of York became the headquarters of an earl appointed by a southern English king.[47] Another earl, based at Bamburgh, guarded the northern frontier of the newly enlarged kingdom. A political entity recognisable as the 'England' we know today was starting to take shape.

Máel Coluim was slain in the same year as Erik Bloodaxe, by a group of fellow-Scots. His successor was Ildulb, a son of Constantín mac Áeda, whose name seems to be the Gaelicised form of a Germanic name like Ealdwulf or Hildulf. Ealdwulf is an Anglo-Saxon name similar to Eadwulf and Ealdred, both of which were borne by lords of Bamburgh in the tenth century. Perhaps an otherwise unknown Ealdwulf was a member of the same family at a time when Constantín was their ally? If so, this Ealdwulf may have inspired the naming of Ildulb. The name Hildulf is not Anglo-Saxon and, although it might be the name underlying Ildulb, it does seem less likely than a name attested among Alba's southern neighbours.[48] Further south, in Wessex, the death of King Eadred in 955 brought his nephew Eadwig, son of Edmund, to the throne. There is no mention of dealings between Eadwig and Strathclyde, whose king was evidently still Dyfnwal, son of Owain. Ildulb, however, had dealings with English and Britons alike. According to *CKA*, he acquired the old Northumbrian fortress of Edinburgh after it was 'vacated' by its soldiers who, we may assume, were an English garrison answerable to the lords of Bamburgh.[49] This was a significant event, for the acquisition of Edinburgh brought Scottish rule south of the Forth–Clyde isthmus. The English are unlikely to have 'vacated' the fortress voluntarily, so we should probably envisage a Scottish assault on Lothian followed by English withdrawal from the southern shore of the Firth of Forth. If all this took place during Eadwig's short reign (956–9), there was little prospect of a major English counter-offensive, for Eadwig was distracted by internal revolts and other troubles at home.[50] The Mercians and Northumbrians rejected his rule in 957 and this may have given Ildulb an opportunity to capture Edinburgh. It is even possible that the *Prophecy of Berchán* alludes to this campaign in its verse on Ildulb: 'Woe to Britons and English in his time, during the reign of the champion of fine weapons; joy to the Scots with him, both laity and clergy.'[51]

The reference to Britons suggests that Ildulb gained a victory over Strathclyde.[52] If this was associated with his taking of Edinburgh, the 'woe' of the Britons could have been due to loss of land along their eastern border, perhaps in Lothian itself. There is also a slight possibility that the Scots seized Edinburgh not from the English but from the Britons, especially if Strathclyde had expanded into Lothian during the Viking period.[53] Such expansion might have mirrored the movement of Cumbric-speakers into north-west Northumbria and could likewise explain the late Cumbric place-names in Lothian.[54] Both Lothian and the region south of the Solway Firth had been Northumbrian since the seventh century, but the collapse of the Anglo-Saxon kingdom left these outlying areas vulnerable to conquest by other powers. The ancient fortress on Edinburgh's Castle Rock had once been a North British stronghold and it may have briefly reverted to Cumbrian control in the late ninth or early tenth century, with a garrison of Strathclyders, before falling permanently into Scottish hands during Ildulb's reign.[55] The Cumbrians were still ruled by Dyfnwal, son of Owain, when they endured the 'woe' inflicted upon them by Ildulb, and Dyfnwal was still king when Ildulb was slain by Vikings in 962. By then, the English also had a new monarch, having put the crises of Eadwig's reign behind them.

THE LATE TENTH CENTURY

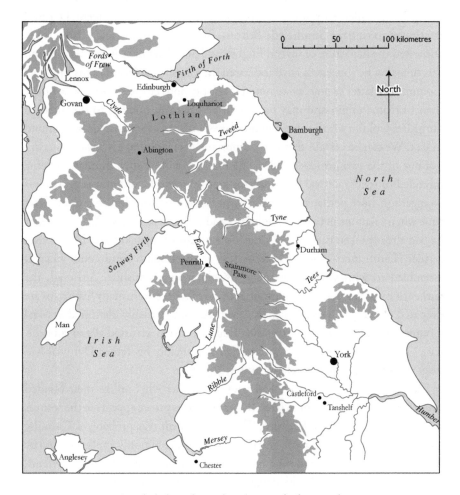

MAP 12 Strathclyde and Northumbria in the late tenth century

When Eadwig died in 959 the kingship of the English passed to his brother Edgar. This was essentially a West Saxon succession, for the Mercians and

Northumbrians had already proclaimed Edgar as king two years earlier.[1] Edgar was only sixteen years old in 959 but was cast in the same mould as the mighty Athelstan. Like his illustrious uncle, Edgar would be remembered by history as a ruler of high ambition who sought overlordship of the whole of Britain. The start of his reign coincided with the last years of Ildulb's reign in Alba. Upon Ildulb's death in 962, the mac Ailpín dynasty was plunged into a bitter kin-strife involving rival claimants for the throne. A king called Dub, a son of Ildulb's predecessor Máel Coluim, ruled from 962 to 966 until his violent death brought Ildulb's son Cuilén to power.[2]. Throughout these years, the resilient Dyfnwal continued to rule the Strathclyde Britons. By 970, Dyfnwal's reign had already witnessed the departure of several English and Scottish kings. It was also around this time that he appears to have abdicated the kingship in favour of his son Máel Coluim. The latter's name, as we noted in the previous chapter, is of Gaelic rather than Brittonic origin and may have been bestowed in homage to the Scottish king Máel Coluim who had been granted overlordship of Strathclyde by Edmund in 945. We can be certain that the Cumbrian Máel Coluim, Dyfnwal's son, was not one of the two princes blinded by Edmund's troops, such mutilation being intended to render a royal heir unfit for kingship. Máel Coluim was probably a younger son, born perhaps during the period of Scottish overlordship or in a later time when relations between Cumbrians and Scots were warmer. It appears that he had already taken the reins of kingship, or some of them, by 970. In that year, a ruler (Latin: *dux*) called 'Malcolm' was at the English royal court when it assembled to witness a land-grant at Woolmer in Hampshire. Although the authenticity of the charter in question is by no means certain, many historians are prepared to accept it as genuine. The *dux* Malcolm is usually identified as Máel Coluim, king of Strathclyde, attending Edgar's court as a trusted ally or subordinate.[3] If he was indeed a *subregulus*, then presumably his father Dyfnwal had been in a similarly unequal relationship with Edgar.

Máel Coluim seems to have had another brother who, unlike their blinded siblings, was a man of vigour in 970. The name of this prince appears in the sources as *Amdarch*, *Radharc* or *Radhard*. The correct form was probably a Cumbric equivalent of Welsh *Rhydderch*, and this is the name commonly applied to him by modern historians.[4] Around the time when Máel Coluim may have been attending Edgar's court, Rhydderch's daughter was violently assaulted by the Scottish king Cuilén. The sources assert that the victim was kidnapped, raped and possibly murdered. This heinous crime was then avenged by her father, by whom the perpetrator was slain in battle or, according to one tradition, in a house that was set on fire.[5] The place of Cuilén's demise lay in *Loinas*, which could be Lothian or the Lennox. One source puts the slaying at *Ybandonia*, which might be a garbled spelling of *Laudonia*, a Latinised name for Lothian. Alternatively, it could be a pseudo-Latinised form of the name now borne by the village of Abington in Lanarkshire. *Abington* is a name of English origin coined in pre-Viking times by Northumbrian settlers. It is possible that one of its early forms was Latinised as *Ybandonia*, in the same way that the old name of Abingdon in Oxfordshire appears in a Latin document of c.1200 as *Abbendonia*.[6] Abington lay on the south-western fringe of Lothian in lands that had formerly been under Northumbrian rule but were possibly within the kingdom of Strathclyde by c.970. The presence of late Cumbric place-names in Lothian implies colonisation by Britons after the ninth century, so the area around Abington might indeed have been in Cumbrian hands at the time of Cuilén's death.[7] Lennox, the valley of the River Leven between Dumbarton and Loch Lomond, was undoubtedly part of the ancient heartland of Strathclyde. If this was where Cuilén met his doom, the violation of Rhydderch's daughter may have been committed while he was a guest of the Cumbrian royal family. Both Lennox and Lothian can justifiably lay claim to be the district where he answered for his deeds.

Cuilén's successor in Alba appears to have been Anlaf, son of Ildulb, whose Norse name suggests that his mother may have been of Viking stock. Anlaf's main rival was Cináed mac Maíl Coluim, a son of the man who had been the 'co-worker' of Edmund after the English king subjugated Strathclyde in 945. Little is known of Anlaf before he was slain by Cináed in 977 but it is possible that they ruled simultanously as competing claimants for the Scottish throne. After 977, Cináed ruled alone. At some point during his reign, according to *CKA*, he plundered 'part of Britannia'. Here, the name *Britannia* means 'a terri-tory of the Britons' rather than the island of Britain as a whole.[8] The target was undoubtedly Strathclyde, but the raid ended in defeat at the Moss of *Uacoruar* (or *Vacornar*) where Cináed's army suffered heavy casualties. The site of the battle is unidentified but it may have lain on the northern frontier of Strathclyde among the mosslands of the Forth Valley. This setting would be consistent with a reference to fortifications being erected by Cináed at 'the fords of Forthin' if, as seems likely, these were the famous Fords of Frew on the River Forth. As a traditional crossing-point offering safe passage through an extensive area of undrained mosses, Frew was much-used by medieval armies and still played an important role in the Jacobite rebellion of 1745. If this was where Cináed built his fortifications, to guard the fords against attack from Strathclyde, the Moss of Uacoruar could have been one of the ancient wetlands of the Forth valley. An alternative possibility is that *Uacoruar*, the spelling given in the manuscript, might be a misprint for *Lacoruar*, a place-name found in a Latin document of the twelfth century. The place in question is Loquhariot in Lothian, eight miles south-east of Edinburgh, near a village called 'Mossend'.[9] *CKA* also states that Cináed plundered English territory as far south as *Stanmoir*, *Cluia* and 'the lakes of *Derann*', at one point capturing 'the son of the king of the English'. *Stanmoir* is undoubtedly the Stainmore Pass through the Pennines, while *Cluia* and *Derann* should likewise be thought of as places in Northumbria.[10] Although described as a king's son, the English captive was presumably a son of Eadwulf, lord of Bamburgh, who bore the curious nickname 'Evil Child'. No source mentions an English counter-attack or says what happened to the hostage. Nor do we hear of any northern campaign by King Edgar, even though his domains bordered those of the Scots and Cumbrians. Our main information on Edgar's relationship with these peoples comes from a reference to a royal meeting attended by Cináed of Alba and Máel Coluim of Strathclyde.

The conference on the Dee

In 973, Edgar mounted a display of pomp and power by sailing with his fleet from the estuary of the River Severn to the estuary of the Dee. Mooring at Chester, he went ashore to preside over a gathering of rulers, an event reminiscent of the royal meetings convened by his grandfather and uncle in 920 and 927 respectively. A brief notice appears in the 'D' text of the *Anglo-Saxon Chronicle* in its entry for 973:

> In this year the atheling Edgar was consecrated king at Bath on the day of Pentecost, on the 11th of May, in the thirteenth year after he succeeded to the kingdom, and he was but one year off thirty. And immediately after that the king took his whole naval force to Chester, and six kings came to meet him, and all gave their pledges that they would be his allies on sea and land.[11]

Although the six kings are not identified in *ASC*, we know that they came from various parts of Wales and northern Britain. Their names are provided by later chroniclers, such as John of Worcester, who had access to texts that no longer survive. John not only identified the attendees but increased their number from six to eight, listing them as follows: 'Cináed, king of the Scots; Máel Coluim, king of the Cumbrians; Maccus, king of very many islands; and five others: Dufnal, Giferth, Hywel, Iago, Iudicael'.[12]

Variants of this list appear in other twelfth-century chronicles but the original source was probably a set of Northumbrian annals that is now lost. To what extent we should regard the list as authentic is a matter of debate, with some historians being more sceptical than others. Nevertheless, there is little doubt that an important royal meeting did take place at Chester in 973, with Edgar presiding and other kings in attendance. It would have been surprising to find Cináed of Alba and Máel Coluim of Strathclyde excluded from such a gathering, so their inclusion in John's list is unremarkable. Twenty years earlier, another likely attendee would have been the king of Anglo-Danish York, but the last of these had been slain in 954. We might have expected Anlaf Cuarán to be on John's list, given that he still held the kingship of Dublin in 973, until we observe that he was no longer pursuing ambitions in Britain. During Edgar's reign, the main Viking menace in the western seaways came not from Anlaf but from Guthfrith and Maccus, the sons of a certain Harald.[13] Their origin is unknown, chiefly because their father is hard to identity among several namesakes who were active around the middle decades of the tenth century. He may have been the Norwegian king Harald Fairhair – the father of Erik Bloodaxe – or the Danish king Harald Bluetooth, or perhaps Harald Sihtricsson, king of the Limerick Vikings and brother of Anlaf Cuarán. Regardless of who this Harald was, his two sons are named in the Welsh chronicle *Brut y Tywysogion* as plunderers of Anglesey.[14] If the *Brut* preserves an authentic tradition of Viking raids at a time when Edgar was king of the English, Edgar may have perceived the Haraldsson brothers as a threat to his interests. The Maccus of John of Worcester's list might then be identifiable as Maccus Haraldsson, his presence at the meeting of 973 testifying to his status as a key figure in contemporary politics.[15] Of the eight kings named by John, we can probably accept Cináed of Alba, Máel Coluim of Strathclyde and Maccus Haraldsson as secure identifications, with the rest being less certain. The name *Dufnal* can be read as *Dyfnwal* rather than as Gaelic *Domnall*, but no Welsh king called Dyfnwal is known from the tenth century, so the Dufnal of 973 should be a Briton of the north. Most historians identify him as Dyfnwal, son of Owain, the former king of Strathclyde, here attending a royal conference with his son and successor Máel Coluim.[16] Why a retired monarch would be present at such an event is uncertain but Dyfnwal's participation would have been approved by Edgar and, no doubt, by the other attendees. With more than thirty years' experience of international politics under his belt, Dyfnwal might even have taken the role of 'elder statesman' in the proceedings, but his primary concern would have been to secure a positive outcome for Strathclyde. John of Worcester next names 'Giferth' who might be Guthfrith Haraldsson, brother of Maccus. William of Malmesbury's version of the list has 'Siferth', not Giferth, which would require us to imagine an otherwise unknown Viking warlord with a name like *Sigfrith*. Of the final three attendees, two are probably identifiable as the Welsh king Iago of Gwynedd and his nephew Hywel. Iago, like Dyfnwal, was a thirty-year veteran whose reign had begun in the early 940s. Age or infirmity may have prompted him to be accompanied to the royal meeting by a younger kinsman. In the following year, he was toppled from power by this same Hywel. Lastly, the identity of Iudicael is uncertain but his name suggests that he was from Wales or Brittany.

After listing the participants, John of Worcester adds that they all went down to the bank of the river. There Edgar boarded a small boat or 'skiff' and, according to a curious tale related by John,

> having set them to the oars and having taken the helm himself, he skilfully steered it through the course of the river Dee, and with a crowd of ealdormen and nobles following in a similar boat, sailed from the palace to the monastery of St John the Baptist where, when he had prayed, he returned with the same pomp to the palace.

To some modern historians, this looks like a fictional story designed to show Edgar's superiority. The image of a powerful English king taking the role of helmsman while other rulers toil at the oars certainly smacks of symbolism. Whether it is entirely an invention is hard to say, for it could be based on a real incident which John or his sources embellished for their own purposes. It is possible, for instance, that the attendees of the meeting really did travel along the river in a boat, their co-operation on the journey symbolising an intention to work together for peace. In such a context, Edgar's taking the helm would have been an appropriate role for the host rather than an acknowledgement of exalted status.[17] We may also note the reference to the monastery of St John the Baptist, an important ecclesiastical site associated with Mercian royalty and a likely venue for religious ceremonies involving Edgar and his guests. The monastery stood next to a Roman amphitheatre which would have offered an impressive setting for an assembly of kings and warlords with their entourages. Aside from the boating episode, most historians now believe that the idea of Edgar receiving oaths of loyalty from the other rulers is little more than propaganda. The English king's chief purpose in hosting the event may have been to protect his north-western border by obtaining assurances from Cináed, Máel Coluim and the Haraldssons that they would not form alliances against him, either with one another or with Anlaf Cuarán of Dublin. In this sense, the meeting can probably be regarded as a peace-summit rather than as a display of supremacy by the host.[18]

Aethelred's raid

Dyfnwal, son of Owain, died in 975 while on pilgrimage to Rome. Whether he reached the city before his death we cannot say, but the Welsh compiler of *Brut y Tywysogion* evidently thought that he did.[19] It would be interesting to know if Dyfnwal was a lay or clerical pilgrim. Did he become a monk after abdicating his kingship? This is what his Scottish contemporary Constantin mac Áeda is said to have done after his own retirement in 942, and other early medieval kings are known to have done the same.[20] Some were forced to make this career-change, while others chose it voluntarily. An alternative possibility is that Dyfnwal merely retired to one of his estates, taking a background role while his son Máel Coluim ruled the kingdom. He might have wished to visit Rome before the end of his days, as a form of repentance, or he may have intended to die there. We may note that Anlaf Cuarán, another veteran of the political scene, travelled to Iona to seek absolution for past sins, so perhaps this was Dyfnwal's motivation in journeying to Rome. The year of Dyfnwal's passing also saw the death of King Edgar, whose successor as king of the English was his son Edward. The latter's murder in 978, after a reign of barely three years, propelled his teenage half-brother Aethelred to the throne.[21] Aethelred is known to posterity as 'the Unready', an epithet in modern English that is actually a mis-translation of Old English *unraed* ('poor counsel'), which in this context means 'badly advised'. The epithet first appears in texts of the twelfth century and was bestowed retrospectively. It reflects a belief that Aethelred's reign had been tainted by a policy of appeasement towards Danish raiders, this policy being seen as the work of his advisers. In reality, Aethelred was a strong king who simply had the misfortune to be on the English throne when a new phase of Danish raids began. These attacks wreaked much havoc in eastern England and culminated in a great Danish victory at Maldon in Essex in 991.[22] Aethelred was not present in the battle but its outcome affected his policy towards the enemy and he began making payments, known to later chroniclers as 'Danegeld', in an attempt to buy peace. This policy obtained a few temporary respites but, by 994, the powerful Danish king Sweyn Forkbeard was emerging as the main thorn in Aethelred's side. In 995, Sweyn was active in the Irish Sea and in the same year plundered the Norse colonies on the Isle of Man.[23] The role of Strathclyde in this period is uncertain. At the time of Sweyn's raid on the Manx settlements, the Cumbrian kingdom was still ruled by Máel Coluim, Dyfnwal's son, who had reached some kind of agreement with Aethelred's father Edgar in 973. Unfortunately, the sources are silent on Strathclyde's affairs in the final quarter of the century. While it is possible to surmise that the absence of any mention of Danish raids on Strathclyde might imply friendly relations between Sweyn and Máel Coluim, the silence of the sources could be due to textual reasons such as non-survival of manuscripts. We likewise know nothing of Máel Coluim's relationship with the English after 973. What we do know is that he died in 997, for the Irish annalists noted his passing in that year.[24] He may have been succeeded by Owain, son of Dyfnwal, an obscure figure whose only appearance in the historical record comes in a notice of his death in 1015.[25] Although this tells us nothing about Owain other than the name of his father, it allows us to assign him to the royal house of Strathclyde. No king named Dyfnwal is known to have reigned in Wales in this period, nor is there any record of a Welsh Owain with the patronym 'Dyfnwal's son'. By contrast, both names appear frequently in the long line of Cumbrian rulers, especially in the eighth to eleventh centuries where they often appear in combination. Owain's patronym further suggests that he was a younger brother of Máel Coluim or, perhaps more likely, a prince of the same family in the next generation. His father Dyfnwal might have been a brother or cousin of Máel Coluim, and hence a son or nephew of the Dyfnwal who died in 975.[26] Further speculation is possible but, in the absence of additional data from the sources, we know too little about what was happening in Strathclyde in the last few years of the tenth century. What we do know, however, is that the next century dawned with a major English raid on the Cumbrian kingdom. It was launched by Aethelred the Unready in the portentous millennial year 1000, three years after the death of Máel Coluim. Our source of information is an entry in the *Anglo-Saxon Chronicle*: 'In this year the king went into *Cumberlande* and ravaged nearly all of it. His fleet went out around Chester, and should have come to meet him, but could not, so it plundered the Isle of Man.'[27]

Here, as with earlier entries in *ASC*, the term *Cumberlande* means 'land of the Cumbrians' rather than the later English county. There is little doubt that the target of Aethelred's raid was the domain of the kings of Strathclyde.[28] However, bad weather seemingly prevented the English fleet from making a rendezvous with the army, forcing the ships to turn back. The diversion towards Norse-controlled Man suggests that the ships were not far from the island when they changed course. The decision to abandon the royal expedition would not have been taken lightly by the English naval captains, for their king was relying on them for military and logistical support. Raiding the Manx Vikings would thus have been an option of last resort, to salvage something positive from a plan that had clearly gone awry. We might infer that the fleet was passing the north-west coast of Man when conditions forced it to change course. If the ships were indeed in this part of the Irish Sea, in the narrow channel between Galloway and Antrim, their original objective was surely the Firth of Clyde.[29] Meanwhile, Aethelred and his army pressed onward, undeterred by the loss of naval support. They invaded the land of the Cumbrians and ravaged 'nearly all' of it. The chronicler's description implies systematic plundering of the heartlands of Strathclyde, with Govan and other key places no doubt falling prey to English marauders. By looting or destroying the resources that sustained the Cumbrian elite, the raiders were removing its capacity to fight back. A political motive for the campaign is therefore a possibility, with Aethelred seeking to neutralise the Cumbrians because of what they had done – or might yet do – to harm his interests. His assault on their kingdom is his only known campaign against one of the major northern powers and therefore warrants an explanation. One possible scenario is that the rulers of Strathclyde had aligned with Aethelred's Scandinavian enemies, perhaps even with his arch-foe Sweyn Forkbeard.[30] According to the twelfth-century chronicler Henry of Huntingdon, Aethelred attacked *Cumberlande* because Danish forces were using it as a base for raids on English territory.[31] Although this might be nothing more than an educated guess on Henry's part, it might equally be not far from the truth. Another possibility is that the Cumbrians had renewed their old alliance with the Scots and were supporting them in attacks on Northumbria. Forces from Strathclyde may have taken part in forays into English territory by Cináed mac Duib who was king of Alba at the time of Aethelred's raid on Cumberland. The bond of friendship between the two northern kingdoms was certainly reaffirmed in the second decade of the new millennium when, as we shall see in the next chapter, their armies stood side-by-side against the English in one of the great battles of the age.

Tenth-century sculpture and its cultural affiliations

Sculpture from the Viking period, much of it carved in the tenth century, survives today in many parts of the former kingdom of Strathclyde. The monuments include free-standing crosses, recumbent slabs and 'hogback' gravestones. Some survive complete, in various stages of weathering, while others are preserved only as fragments. The majority are found as solitary items, either in their original positions or in newer settings, but small groupings of up to six monuments also occur. The largest grouping, by a significant margin, is at Govan, where the old parish church now accommodates thirty-one carved stones. In art-historical terms, a variety of sculptural styles is evident across the entire area of the Cumbrian kingdom, suggesting that a range of cultural influences was at work.[32] Particular local styles have, however, been identified in certain areas, with Govan itself being a prime example of a likely sculptural centre. Monuments showing close affinity with the Govan collection are found within the old heartlands of Renfrewshire, Lanarkshire and the Lennox, with outliers in Ayrshire. All are generally regarded as products of a style or 'school' of stonecarving whose origin-centre lay at Govan.[33] Beyond these core territories, but still within the kingdom's tenth-century borders, monuments of the 'Govan School' give way to others carved in different styles. In Dumfriesshire, for example, cross-shafts decorated in a late Anglo-Saxon style continue a tradition of Northumbrian stonecarving reaching back to the early eighth century, displaying a high level of craftsmanship. Further west, in Galloway, similar continuity has been recognised at the Northumbrian ecclesiastical settlement of Whithorn, the site of a seventh-century English bishopric, where a distinct 'school' of sculpture seems to have arisen in Viking times.[34] It is likely that this area was not part of Strathclyde in the tenth century, and that the patrons of the

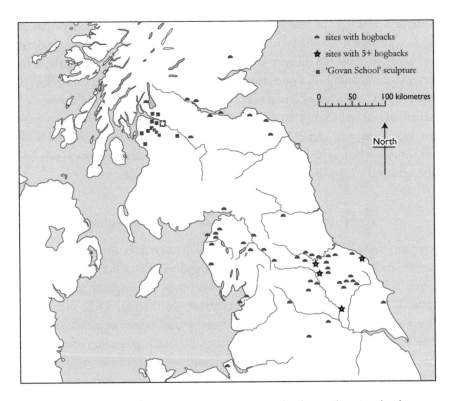

MAP 13 Hogback monuments in southern Scotland / northern England
and sculpture of the 'Govan School'

Whithorn sculptors were Norse aristocrats answerable to their own kings in Dublin, Man or Galloway. South of the Solway Firth, in what were certainly Strathclyde's southernmost domains, Anglo-Saxon styles are again the dominant type. Here, where the lands of the Cumbrian kings bordered those of the Hiberno-Norse, a recognisably Scandinavian influence emerges, most strikingly on free-standing crosses such as the fine example at Gosforth near the Irish Sea coast. On the southern limit of Cumbrian territory near the River Eamont, the crosses and hogbacks comprising the enigmatic 'Giant's Grave' at Penrith are distinctly Anglo-Saxon. South and east of this frontier, in lands not controlled by the kings of Strathclyde, monuments carved in this same style show that it was common throughout tenth-century Northumbria.[35] At Govan, the stone-carvers borrowed ideas from a number of sculptural traditions: Pictish, Irish, Welsh, Scandinavian and Anglo-Saxon. This kind of borrowing or exchange seems to have been common practice across the British Isles, giving a multicultural aspect to many of the monuments that survive today on both sides of the Irish Sea.[36] It is worth noting that the web of cultural interactions displayed by the sculpture seems to mirror the frequently complex political relationships between the peoples of tenth-century Britain.

The Giant's Grave

In the graveyard of St Andrew's Church at Penrith is an enigmatic group of early medieval monuments known as 'The Giant's Grave'.[37] It consists of four hogback tombstones and two free-standing crosses of which only the shafts remain. The hogbacks are arranged in pairs on either side of the Grave while the crosses stand at the eastern and western ends. Prior to the rebuilding of the church in the early 1720s, the Grave stood in a different position but in an almost identical arrangement, the main difference being the placement of the hogbacks which were in a different order. All six stones are decorated with carvings which include interlace patterns, human figures and animals. On art-historical grounds they have been dated to the tenth century, although it is clear that they were not carved at the same time. The western cross appears to be the earliest, having probably been carved between 920 and 950. To this period also belongs a separate monument known as 'The Giant's Thumb', a cross which stands some yards away.[38] It is likely that the Thumb is the oldest monument in the churchyard. The eastern cross of the Giant's Grave seems to be a product of the late tenth century while the hogbacks probably appeared at various times after c.920. In stylistic terms the carvings on all these monuments show affinities with Northumbrian sculpture from both sides of the Pennines. One of the hogbacks displays a serpent similar to the creature carved on a hogback at Gosforth while the interlace on the western cross invites comparison with a tenth-century cross at Leeds. Another of the Giant's Grave hogbacks has a small carving of a robed figure with raised arms who is probably a Christian priest. It seems likely that this stone once marked the resting-place of a senior cleric, perhaps a local bishop or abbot. Given the date, there is little doubt that his secular patrons were Cumbrian lords from Strathclyde. He may have been a Strathclyder himself, for the Anglo-Saxon style of the carvings need not imply that the elite who commissioned the hogbacks, or the people interred beneath them, were of English ancestry. Indeed, the most plausible context is that a 'school' of local Northumbrian stonecarvers was engaged by the newly-arrived Cumbrian aristocracy to create memorials for its deceased members. The six monuments comprising the Giant's Grave were presumably not meant to be arranged in the way we see today. They may nevertheless have originally formed a distinct group in a particular part of the churchyard. At what point the association with a giant was made is unknown but the identity of this figure is no mystery. He appears in local folklore as 'Ewen Caesarius' or 'Sir Owen Caesar' and was said to be a local king who hunted wild boar in Inglewood Forest. When the Grave was excavated in the 1500s a number of objects were unearthed, the most noteworthy being a sword and human bones.[39] In the minds of contemporary observers, these finds no doubt confirmed the tradition that the legendary Ewen was buried there. The tradition was clearly much older and must have been circulating in medieval times. Stories about Ewen associate him with Castle Hewen, an ancient settlement which appears to have been occupied in Roman times and perhaps in later centuries, but whether he himself is based on a historical figure from this period is uncertain.[40] He has sometimes been identified as Owain of Rheged, a warrior of the sixth century whose father Urien ruled one of the kingdoms of the North Britons. This stems from a theory – as yet unproven – that Rheged may have lain in the vicinity of Carlisle or in the Eden valley. Another candidate is one of several Strathclyde kings called Owain, the likeliest being the one who attended the royal meeting at the River Eamont in 927. He was undoubtedly familiar with the churchyard at Penrith and may have seen the Giant's Thumb and other early monuments when they were newly carved. His own grave, however, probably lay at Govan in the heartland of his realm.

BORDERLANDS

The eleventh century was to be the last in which the kingdom of Strathclyde existed as an independent power. Within a few decades of Aethelred's raid on their territory in the millennial year 1000, the Cumbrians would be wiped off the political map. At the dawn of the century, however, they remained unconquered. In the previous chapter, we considered the possibility that the king of Strathclyde at this time was Owain, son of Dyfnwal, whose death in 1015 was noted in the Welsh annals. His contemporary in neighbouring Alba was Máel Coluim mac Cináeda, who took the kingship of the Scots in 1005 after destroying his rival Cináed mac Duib.[1] Máel Coluim's father was the earlier Cináed who had attended King Edgar's royal meeting at Chester in 973. The repetition of names is rather confusing but is chiefly due to the kingship of Alba having been monopolised by one family, the mac Ailpíns or 'Alpinids', who had ruled almost continuously since the 840s. By contrast, the succession in England was now disputed between the descendants of Alfred the Great and the royal house of Denmark. Edgar's son Aethelred the Unready, plunderer of Strathclyde in 1000, spent the first decade of the eleventh century in a fierce contest with the Danish king Sweyn Forkbeard. The latter, after many years of raiding in traditional Viking mode, grew determined to depose Aethelred by force and make himself king of England. In 1013, Aethelred buckled under the pressure and fled to Normandy, a region ruled by descendants of Danish Vikings.[2] He returned to England after the death of Sweyn in 1014 and succeeded in ousting Sweyn's half-Polish son Cnut, but survived for only two more years. His death in 1016 paved the way for Cnut to take the kingship.[3] The rivalry between the two factions had left northern England largely unscathed, with Northumbria continuing to be governed by English earls on behalf of whichever West Saxon or Danish king held power in the south. One Northumbrian earldom was based at York, the former royal capital, while the other was centred on the old fortress of Bamburgh, still held by descendants of its tenth-century lords. At the beginning of the eleventh century, Bamburgh's earl was Waltheof, son of Oswulf, whose father had played a part in the demise of Erik Bloodaxe in 954. Waltheof himself must have been quite old at the beginning of the new millennium and his authority was already passing to his son Uhtred.[4]

In Ireland, meanwhile, the new broker of power was Brian Bóruma ('Brian Boru'), king of Munster. Brian claimed the high-kingship of Ireland in 1002 and held much of the country under his sway.[5] His dealings with the Norse are described in *Cogadh Gaedhel re Gallaibh* ('The Wars of the Gaels against the Foreigners'), a panegyric text of the early twelfth century. Modern historians are sceptical of the reliability of this work, regarding it as little more than a eulogy for Brian and propaganda for his descendants, but it remains a potentially useful source. In one section, it tells of a fleet being sent by Brian to plunder various places in Britain. The ships carried Irish and Norse warriors from many parts of Ireland, 'and they levied royal tribute from the English (*Shaxan*) and the Britons (*Bretan*), and the men of *Lemnaig* in Scotland, and Argyll, and their pledges and hostages along with the chief tribute'.[6]

The context seems to be a raid on northern Britain, so the English are probably those of western Northumbria and the Britons are presumably those of Strathclyde. *Lemnaig* is almost certainly the Lennox, which in modern Scottish Gaelic is *Leamhnachd*. In Brian's time, the Lennox was part of Strathclyde, not Scotland, and its inhabitants were Britons, but a twelfth-century Irish author might not have known this. It is the kind of discrepancy that rightly attracts scepticism to the entire passage, hence the belief among many historians that the raid is probably fictional.[7] With no record in the Irish annals, or indeed in any other source, we might indeed be tempted to assume that it was invented by the author of *Cogadh Gaedhel re Gallaibh* to exaggerate Brian's power. However, the presence of a nobleman from Moray in Brian's army at the famous battle of Clontarf in 1014 shows that he did have dealings with northern Britain, these providing a possible context for a predatory raid across the Irish Sea.[8] The editor of one nineteenth-century edition of *Cogadh Gaedhel re Gallaibh*, while casting doubt on the authenticity of the passage, wondered if it might have 'some foundation in fact' and considered the possibility that Brian may have encouraged his allies to satisfy their desire for loot by rampaging in Britain rather than inside his Irish domains.[9]

The author of *Cogadh Gaedhel re Gallaibh* placed Brian's raid in or shortly after 1006. In that year, King Máel Coluim of Alba launched a raid against his English neighbours, an event described in the twelfth-century Northumbrian text *De Obsessione Dunelmi* ('On the Siege of Durham'). According to this source, the Scots advanced as far south as the monastic settlement at Durham, where St Cuthbert's remains had recently been enshrined, and laid siege to it. *De Obsessione* tells of the subsequent defeat of the besieging force by Uhtred, son of Earl Waltheof of Bamburgh.[10] There is no hint that the Cumbrians of Strathclyde were involved in the campaign. In any case, their ability to assist the Scots in raids on Northumbria may have been reduced by the comprehensive ravaging of their lands by Aethelred six years earlier. Indeed, the devastation wrought in 1000 may have neutralised Strathclyde's military effectiveness for a number of years, until both land and people recovered. We should also keep in mind the possibility that Aethelred's onslaught may have forced the Cumbrian king to acknowledge him as overlord. If such a submission remained in place in 1006, it might explain why Máel Coluim's raid on Northumbria seems to have been undertaken without Cumbrian support. The raid itself was significant enough for Uhtred's victory to be mentioned in the Irish annals.[11] In *De Obsessione* we see a grateful Aethelred rewarding Uhtred with the earldoms of Bamburgh and York. Even if this account embellishes the truth, there is no doubt that Aethelred would have been reassured in the knowledge that his northern frontier was defended by a competent warlord.

Ten years later, in 1016, the pattern of allegiances and alliances changed again when Aethelred's death enabled Cnut to take the English throne. The previous year had seen the passing of Owain, son of Dyfnwal, whom we have cautiously identified as a king of Strathclyde. In noting the death of this mysterious figure, the Welsh annals state that he was killed, presumably in battle. If so, the circumstances of his demise are invisible, but it seems likely that he was succeeded by another Owain, a namesake who appears in the sources with the Latin epithet *Calvus* ('Bald'). Although we have no information on the parentage of Owain the Bald, his name suggests that he belonged to the family that had ruled during the previous century. He may have been a son of Máel Coluim, son of Dyfnwal, who died in 997.[12] The little we know of Owain relates to a single battle in which he led the army of Strathclyde to victory over the English.

The battle of Carham

In the early twelfth century, the author of the *History of the Church of Durham* (*HDE*) looked back on a dark episode in Northumbrian history:

> In the year of our Lord's incarnation 1018, while Cnut ruled the kingdom of the English, a comet appeared for thirty nights to the peoples of Northumbria, and with dread presage foreshowed the province's future disaster. For, shortly afterwards – that is, after thirty days – while they fought at *Carrun* against a countless host of Scots, almost the entire population, from the River Tees to the Tweed, perished with their nobles.[13]

In *Historia Regum Anglorum* (*HRA*), another twelfth-century text, the same battle is likewise entered under the year 1018, with additional information about the protagonists: 'A great battle was fought at *Carrum* between the Scots and the English, between Uhtred, Waltheof's son, the earl of Northumbria, and Máel Coluim, king of Scots, the son of Cináed. And with him in the battle was Owain the Bald, king of the Clyde-folk.'[14]

HRA renders Owain's name and epithet into Latin as *Eugenius Calvus* and calls him *rex Lutinensium*. This is his only appearance in the historical record and, at first glance, he seems to be described as 'king of the Lutinenses'. The term is wholly unfamiliar and, in the context of early medieval Britain, altogether meaningless. It is clearly an error for *Clutinensium*, 'of the Clyde-folk', from a nominative form *Clutinenses*. The latter is similar to *Stratcluttenses* ('Strathclyders'), a word found in the ninth-century *Life of King Alfred* by Asser. Indeed, *Clutinenses* should perhaps be emended to *Clutenses* (or *Clutienses*), this being the most likely form in the older Northumbrian chronicle from which *HRA* obtained its information.[15] The place named as *Carrun* or *Carrum* is now Carham-on-Tweed, a village on the south bank of the river, some three miles south-west of Coldstream. It lies one mile west of Wark Castle, also known as Carham Castle, an Anglo-Norman stronghold erected in the early twelfth century.[16] The compiler of *HRA*, after identifying the main protagonists in 1018 as Uhtred of Bamburgh and Máel Coluim of Alba, gave the Scottish king's patronymic before adding that Owain the Bald was 'with him'. The order in which these pieces of information are presented implies that Owain accompanied Máel Coluim, not Uhtred, to the battlefield. What *HRA* does not explain is whether the northern kings went to war as allies, or as overlord and vassal. Máel Coluim was arguably the more powerful of the two, in terms of the military resources available to him, and as king of a larger realm, but this does not necessarily mean that Owain was his subordinate. In the absence of any hint of Scottish overlordship in Strathclyde in the first quarter of the eleventh century we should probably see Owain and Máel Coluim as allies who had equal roles at Carham. It is unsurprising that Owain appears at the end of the entry for 1018, almost as an afterthought, for the twelfth-century author knew that the main threat to northern England in his own time came from the Scots. By then, of course, the kingdom of the *Clutenses* had ceased to exist.

In *HRA*, the leader of the Northumbrian army at Carham is named as Earl Uhtred of Bamburgh, an identification accepted by many historians. Others, however, are less convinced, chiefly because of an entry in the *Anglo-Saxon Chronicle* which states that Uhtred died in 1016, According to *ASC*, Uhtred was killed on the orders of Cnut, despite having submitted as a vassal.[17] In the same year,

Uhtred had given aid to Edmund Ironside, a son of Cnut's rival Aethelred the Unready, but plainly hoped that an oath of loyalty would be enough to secure Cnut's forgiveness. Having removed Uhtred, Cnut appointed the Norwegian warlord Erik Haakonsson as the new earl of Northumbria. The reporting of this sequence of events in *ASC* implies that it occurred within a single year, 1016, and that Uhtred was already dead when the battle of Carham was fought two years later. *ASC* does not mention the battle, so we are left to wrestle with a chronological problem: if *HRA* is correct, then Uhtred was alive in 1018; if *ASC* is correct, he died two years earlier. Historians have attempted to reconcile the two accounts by proposing that one or the other must be mistaken. One solution is to see Uhtred's brother Eadwulf *Cudel* ('Cuttlefish') as earl of Bamburgh in 1018 and as commander of the English forces at Carham.[18] This is consistent with *ASC* but contradicts *HRA*'s assertion that the commander was Uhtred himself. An alternative suggestion is that the entry for 1016 in *ASC* compressed a longer sequence of events spanning two or more years, and that Cnut ordered Uhtred's death after the Northumbrian army's defeat in 1018. It has even been suggested that the battle itself may have been fought in 1016, and that *HRA* was right about Uhtred's role but wrong on the date. One eminent historian observed that this scenario seemed all the more plausible to him because 'names are better remembered than dates'.[19] As the date of the battle and the identity of the English commander are crucial to an understanding of the historical context, both are examined in more detail below.

1016 or 1018?

From *HDE* we learn that a celestial phenomenon occurred in the year of the battle of Carham, as a grim omen of the impending Northumbrian defeat: 'a comet appeared for thirty nights to the peoples of Northumbria, and with dread presage foreshowed the province's future disaster'.[20] Before the advent of a scientific approach to such phenomena, comets and other astronomical objects were commonly regarded with superstitious foreboding. Comets are rare, and rarely visible to the naked eye, so they were regarded in ancient times as supernatural phenomena of special significance, their sudden appearance in the sky being attributed to gods. Modern science has long since provided a more rational explanation and, by looking at records from the past, astronomers have been able to chart the arrival of particular comets across hundreds of years of human history and in many different parts of the world. They have identified the years in which one or more comets have passed close enough to Earth to be visible without help from technology.

We have no reason to doubt that a comet appeared in the skies above Northumbria in the year of the disaster at Carham. The compiler of *HDE*, writing a hundred years later, believed that both events occurred in 1018, not 1016. His dating is supported by contemporary records from China, Korea, Japan, Germany, Italy and Ireland, all of which note the arrival of a comet in late summer or early autumn of 1018.[21] Its distinguishing feature was a long, bright tail: Chinese and Korean observers described it as a 'broom star', while to the Irish it was a 'hairy star'. Modern astronomers have established that it was a 'non-periodic' comet whose journey through the cosmos brought it close to Earth on only one occasion.[22] Detailed collation of contemporary observations and descriptions indicates that the phenomenon was first seen on 3 August 1018, when it was noticed by Chinese observers. It remained visible in the skies over China for thirty-seven days before passing out of view on 8 September. This period of visibility is consistent with the 'thirty nights' of *HDE*, but to other European observers the comet was only visible for a fortnight. In the context of the date of the battle, it is worth noting that no comet was recorded anywhere in the world in 1016. The astronomical data therefore supports the belief that the battle of Carham was fought in 1018. This date finds further support in the sequence of royal succession in England, for *HDE* states that the battle occurred 'while Cnut ruled the kingdom of the English'. This is unlikely to refer to 1016, for Cnut was not crowned king of England until December of that year.[23]

Uhtred or Eadwulf?

The question of who led the Northumbrian forces continues to divide scholarly opinion. Here, it will be suggested that the commander was Eadwulf Cudel, not Uhtred, and that the confusion lies with *HRA* rather than with *ASC*. While it is possible that *ASC* wrongly assigned Uhtred's death to 1016, other information suggests that he did indeed die in that year. Looking back to 1006, we recall that Uhtred's reward for defeating the Scots at Durham was a royal gift, bestowed by a grateful King Aethelred, of the earldoms of Bamburgh and York. After Uhtred's murder, which *ASC* placed ten years later, the York earldom was granted to Erik Haakonsson. In the following year, 1017, Erik was still the earl of York, so we have good reason to assume that Uhtred was no longer part of the Northumbrian political scene. The most obvious deduction is that he was dead. An alternative scenario, in which Cnut deprived Uhtred of York in 1016 but let him keep Bamburgh, before slaying him in 1018, has been suggested, but it over-complicates the picture.[24] From the little we can glean of Uhtred's character, he does not seem the kind of man to accept demotion and loss of status meekly. If the York earldom had been given to someone else while he was still alive, leaving him with Bamburgh alone, he would probably have rebelled against Cnut. Conversely, if he was out of the picture, the earldom of York could be given to a less troublesome individual. The sequence of events probably unfolded in the way described in *ASC*: Uhtred, earl of Northumbria, pledged allegiance to Cnut in 1016 but was killed before the year was out, the southern part of his earldom being granted to Erik Haakonsson. This would mean that *ASC* preserves a more accurate account than *HRA* and shows greater knowledge of the sequence of earls in eleventh-century Northumbria. The compiler of *HRA*, although he had a list of earls, seems to have had no dates for them.[25] Thus, although the compiler knew that Eadwulf Cudel succeeded Uhtred as earl of northern Northumbria, he may not have known when this took place, but assumed that Uhtred was still earl in 1018. We might thus wish to reject the idea that the *ASC* entry for 1016 indicates West Saxon ignorance of northern affairs and choose instead a logical alternative, namely that the compiler of *HRA* was unaware that Uhtred was dead by 1018 and that it was Eadwulf Cudel who led the Northumbrians to defeat in that year.[26]

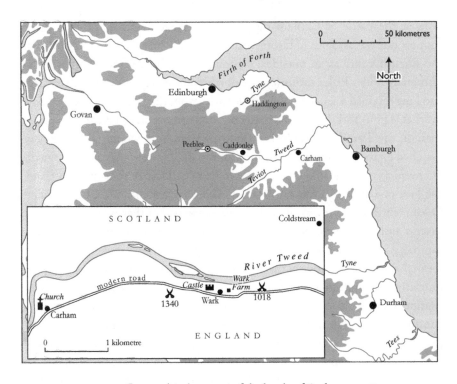

MAP 14 Geographical context of the battle of Carham, 1018

The political context

A detailed account of the battle of Carham has not survived, if indeed it was ever written. Twelfth-century Northumbrian chroniclers plainly regarded the battle as significant, but it receives no mention in Scottish, Irish or Welsh sources, nor indeed in the *Anglo-Saxon Chronicle*. Why it was fought and why it took place at a crossing-place on the Tweed are questions to which no easy answers are available. Máel Coluim and Owain were evidently the aggressors, for the battlefield lay in English lands beyond the borders of their kingdoms. Their main reasons for attacking Earl Eadwulf's domain were either economic or political or some combination of both. The fact that the Bamburgh forces stood alone, without aid from southern Northumbria, suggests that Eadwulf was not on friendly terms with Erik Haakonsson, the earl of York. Erik owed his position to Cnut, the king responsible for slaying Eadwulf's brother Uhtred, and the relationship between Erik and Eadwulf no doubt mirrored the relationship between Eadwulf and Cnut. Uhtred had chosen to support Cnut's rival Aethelred the Unready and Aethelred's son Edmund, and this was something that Cnut may have been unable to forgive. The absence of contingents from York at the battle of Carham suggests that Eadwulf not only lacked Erik's support but was also out of favour with Cnut.[27] He may have been regarded at the English court as an outsider. Although the whole of Northumbria was nominally under Erik's authority, the northernmost part above the River Tees had long retained a separate 'English' identity from the Danish-influenced part in what is now Yorkshire. If the battle of 1018 had occurred on the Tees rather than on the Tweed, an Anglo-Danish army from York would no doubt have marched up to confront the Scots and Cumbrians. However, because the northern invaders posed no immediate threat to Erik's earldom or to Cnut's heartland, the lord of Bamburgh was on his own. The very fact that Máel Coluim and Owain launched their assault at this time suggests that they were confident of success and were not expecting a response from Erik or Cnut. Indeed, their campaign is a further hint that Eadwulf was politically isolated. This does not mean that the chief motive of the allies was political, or that they were intent on unseating Eadwulf. In any case, they would have been aware that any move to capture Bamburgh or to obtain Eadwulf's homage was likely to provoke a confrontation with Cnut. Their campaign may have been primarily a raid for plunder, its main objective being the acquisition of portable loot in the form of livestock and human captives. Farms and villages would have been burned to reduce Eadwulf's resources, thus depriving him of the means for effective retaliation. Nevertheless, taking land in frontier districts may have been an addi-tional motive, especially if both Alba and Strathclyde hoped to extend their borders at Bamburgh's expense. This brings us to the matter of territory and to the question of where Carham-on-Tweed fitted into the political geography of the early eleventh century.

As we saw in Chapter 6, the English appear to have relinquished their long-standing possession of Edinburgh during the reign of the Scottish king Ildulb who reigned from 954 to 962. This presumably brought the south side of the Firth of Forth and some northern parts of Lothian into the kingdom of Alba. In the early 970s, Edgar of Wessex is said to have granted Lothian to Cináed mac Máel Coluim, but we do not know if this meant the whole region or only a portion of it. However, there is good reason to believe that the entire area from the Firth of Forth to the Haddingtonshire Tyne was in Scottish hands before the end of the tenth century.[28] Uhtred's victory over the Scots at Durham in 1006 may have regained some of this lost territory but another cession seems to have occurred after his death ten years later.[29] According to *De Obsessione Dunelmi*, Uhtred's brother and successor Eadwulf Cudel was anxious that the Scots might seek revenge for their defeat in 1006 and 'granted to them the whole of Lothian, for amends and steadfast peace'. We should probably place this transfer of English territory soon after Uhtred's death.[30] The absence of any mention of Cnut, or of his henchman Earl Erik of York, in these dealings is further support for the idea that Eadwulf governed the northern part of Northumbria as an autonomous earldom beyond the limit of Cnut's rule. If Eadwulf had been under Cnut's direct authority, holding Bamburgh as a royal lieutenant and as Erik Haakonsson's subordinate, he would not have been at liberty to cede territory without permission. In those circumstances, the trans-fer of land would surely have been made by Erik, acting on Cnut's behalf, or by Cnut himself. How much of Lothian was actually ceded by Eadwulf is a matter of debate, for *De Obsessione* might seem to imply that the region as a whole was handed over to Máel Coluim. In reality, the earldom of Bamburgh probably included only part of Lothian by 1016, the rest having been ceded to Alba in the 960s and 970s. Máel Coluim's actions in 1018 suggest that the portion of Lothian he received from Eadwulf two years earlier was not enough to prevent a renewal of hostilities. The course of the Anglo-Scottish border before the Carham campaign is unlikely to have lain on the Tweed and may have been some distance northward.[31] The battle was no doubt fought on the Tweed because Máel Coluim marched down from the existing border to claim the lands in between. This would be consistent with the idea that the earlier grants of 'Lothian', from the 960s onwards, involved parts of the region rather than all of it. Whichever portion Máel Coluim possessed before 1018, he was essentially staking a claim to the whole when he and Owain marched to Carham.

Although Owain barely gets a mention in the sources, his role in the Carham campaign should not be underestimated or ignored. As we have already seen, he was most likely an ally rather than a vassal of Máel Coluim. His motives for participating in an assault on Northumbria are likely to have been similar to those of the Scottish king. Eadwulf's isolation from powers further south may have encouraged Owain to relieve his domains of livestock and people. Nevertheless, just as Máel Coluim may have sought to push the Anglo-Scottish border south to the Tweed, so Owain may have hoped to grab English territory beyond his own borders. Prior to the battle of 1018, the frontier between the earls of Northumbria and the kings of Strathclyde probably lay in Tweeddale, perhaps in the vicinity of Peebles. An opportunity to annex lands further east along the valley may have been seized by the Cumbrian king.

Logistical considerations

The battle of Carham happened because a combined force of Scots and Cumbrians invaded Northumbria. A joint venture of this kind required considerable organisation in terms of planning, not least in co-ordinating a rendezvous for the allied armies. Máel Coluim and Owain would have led their respective forces to an agreed site, a place easily accessible to both and in a suitable location for an attack on Eadwulf's domains. It would have been in an area that the two armies could reach without the one infringing upon the other's territory, so it was most likely on 'neutral' ground along a shared frontier. If, as seems likely, the Scots already possessed parts of Lothian before the battle, a rendezvous with the Cumbrian army on the western flank of this region seems plausible. This was almost certainly where Alba's south-west border faced the eastern marchlands of Strathclyde in 1018. The same area, as we noted above, is probably where both kingdoms nudged against the domain of the earls of Bamburgh. Identifying the site of the rendezvous with any measure of certainty is impossible but a prime candidate is Caddonlee where Scottish armies of the thirteenth and fourteenth centuries assembled for raids on England.[32] Here, where the River Tweed is met by the Caddon Water flowing down from the north, Owain and Máel Coluim may have pooled their military forces. The Cumbrians would have entered Upper Tweeddale from the west before marching along the river to their eastern frontier, which may have lain quite near the river-junction at

Caddonlee. The Scots would no doubt have marched south from their lands around Edinburgh, following the Gala Water almost to its confluence with the Tweed. An alternative possibility is that the allied armies invaded Northumbria independently, each then making its way to a rendezvous where they eventually joined to form a single mighty force. In such a scenario, the Scots would probably have followed the old Roman highway of Dere Street as far as the crossing of the Tweed near Newstead, before turning east towards Carham. Owain's route in either case is likely to have remained unchanged: a direct eastward advance along Tweeddale. The total distance from his headquarters on the Clyde to the battle-site at Carham was nearly one hundred miles. At an average rate of twenty to twenty-five miles per day, the journey could have been completed in four or five days, plus a day or more to achieve a successful rendezvous with the Scots, as well as additional time spent on plundering, foraging and skirmishing.[33] Rest-periods for horses, to prevent saddle sores, would have meant further halts along the way. Taking these factors into account, a journey of seven to ten days for the Cumbrian army would not seem wide of the mark.

The aftermath of the battle

It is sometimes suggested that Owain the Bald perished at Carham. In the absence of any record of his survival after 1018 we may note that he may indeed have been slain in the battle but it is equally possible that he survived. The idea that he was among the casualties has been influenced by the entry in the Welsh Annals noting the killing of 'Owain, son of Dyfnwal' in 1015.[34] We have already considered an alternative interpretation which sees the Owain of 1015 not as Owain the Bald but as an older kinsman and predecessor. Nothing in our meagre sources for the battle of Carham suggests that any of the leading protagonists was slain. Another theory proposes that the current Anglo-Scottish border was fixed on the River Tweed as a result of the Northumbrian defeat.[35] This is a credible scenario which sits quite well with the historical circumstances. There seems little reason to doubt it. We might, in any case, regard the battle as a significant event in the history of northern Britain, even without the contemporary belief that its importance was presaged by a comet. To the Northumbrians of Eadwulf's time the defeat of the earl was a catastrophe in which their army sustained so many casualties that Bishop Ealdhun of Durham died soon afterwards, his spirit crushed under the weight of bereavement.[36] Incidentally, the bishop's death (in late 1018 or early 1019) supports the idea that the battle was not fought in 1016 but in the autumn of 1018, soon after the disappearance of the comet. To those Northumbrians south of the Tees, and likewise to the rest of the English, a battle on a distant frontier may have seemed of little concern. Its absence from the *Anglo-Saxon Chronicle* suggests that, in southern England at least, it was regarded as an event of local rather than of national importance.[37] To the Scots, however, it was surely a military triumph which finally completed their hitherto piecemeal annexation of Lothian. All of the previous cessions of Lothian to Scottish kings in the tenth and early eleventh centuries, up to and including Eadwulf's grant to Máel Coluim in 1016, had arguably involved portions of the region rather than the whole. It seems that the last remaining English part, perhaps an eastern district between the Haddington Tyne and the Tweed, was the victory-prize of the Scots in 1018.[38] For Máel Coluim, then, the principal benefit of his victory at Carham was probably a substantial enlargement of his kingdom. His ally Owain of Strathclyde may likewise have returned home not only with cattle and slaves but with something more valuable. The sources are silent on the nature of Owain's prize but it is likely that he, too, acquired new territory. A clue to the extent of his gains might be preserved in a twelfth-century survey of landholdings of the bishop of Glasgow, an exercise undertaken two or more generations after Strathclyde had been absorbed into the kingdom of Alba. This survey or 'Inquest' of episcopal possessions was mentioned in Chapter 1 where we noted that it was commissioned by the Scottish prince David, the future king David I, during the reign of his elder brother Alexander (1107–24). At that time, David held the title *Cumbrensis regionis princeps*, 'prince of the Cumbrian kingdom', which meant that he ruled what had once been the realm of the Clyde Britons.[39] His inquest was essentially a list of territories formerly held by the kings of Strathclyde. The old Cumbrian kingdom lay under his secular control but he intended that its ecclesiastical property should be given to the newly-established Scottish bishopric at Glasgow. The survey included Teviotdale, a major tributary valley of the Tweed and an integral part of Northumbria since the seventh century. Teviotdale's inclusion in a twelfth-century list of former Cumbrian lands suggests that it had been annexed by Strathclyde at some point in the recent past. One possible context for its transfer from Northumbrian to Cumbrian ownership is the aftermath of the battle of Carham, when Owain the Bald would have sought a suitable reward for his role in the victory. It is tempting to believe that this is indeed how Teviotdale came to be listed in David's inquest.[40] In a broader political context, the permanence of any transfer of English territory to the victors of Carham was in doubt while retaliation by Cnut remained a possibility. Indeed, according to the Burgundian chronicler Ralph Glaber, hostilities between Cnut and Máel

Coluim broke out in the early 1020s.[41] The seeds of this conflict may have been sown in the wake of Carham, either because Cnut hoped to regain English lands relinquished in 1018 or because the Scots were now in a better position to launch raids south of the Tweed. Ralph believed that the two sides eventually agreed a peace through the mediation of Duke Richard of Normandy, a descendant of Danish Vikings, who was Cnut's brother-in-law. The treaty, which must have been negotiated before Richard's death in 926, involved a formal ceremony at which Máel Coluim gave homage to Cnut. Nonetheless, the English territories lost in 1018 remained in Scottish hands, with Cnut seemingly being content to let Máel Coluim keep Lothian. Whether Strathclyde's putative acquisition of Teviotdale was similarly recognised by Cnut is unknown but, given the valley's inclusion in the twelfth-century inquest of Glasgow's episcopal possessions, this seems a likely scenario.

Cnut and the Cumbrians

If Owain the Bald had any further dealings with his neighbours after 1018, the sources fail to mention them. Nothing more is heard of him, not even the date of his death. The name of his successor is likewise unknown. By contrast, the sequence of eleventh-century kings in neighbouring Alba is well-documented, with Máel Coluim continuing to rule the Scots until his death in 1034. His submission to Cnut after the end of their war in the 1020s took place sometime between 1026 and 1034. It may have taken place in 1031, the year in which a royal meeting was noted by the northern 'D' and 'E' texts of the *Anglo-Saxon Chronicle*. Although the meeting took place on Scottish soil it was undoubtedly convened by Cnut, presumably while he was again campaigning against Máel Coluim. Two other kings were also present: 'King Cnut went to Rome, and the same year he went to *Scotlande*. The Scottish king Máel Coluim bowed to him, and two other kings, Maelbeth and Iehmarc.'[42]

If Cnut's journey to Scotland was not a purely ceremonial trip it may have been part of another round of his conflict with Máel Coluim. The context suggests that 'Scotland' here means Máel Coluim's kingdom in particular rather than northern Britain in general. Maelbeth is almost certainly Macbethad, Shakespeare's 'Macbeth'. Although not yet a king in any legitimate sense, Macbethad was a powerful lord of Moray who would eventually mount his own successful bid for the kingship of Alba. Iehmarc is likewise identifiable as Echmarcach, a Norseman from Ireland or the Hebrides, who later became a contender for the kingship of Dublin and a ruler of Galloway.[43] Given the northern venue, the presence of two Scottish rulers and the attendance of a Viking with northern connections, we might wonder why there is no mention of a representative from Strathclyde.[44] If the absence of a 'king of the Cumbrians' is not merely a chronicler's omission, it might tell us something about the political status of Strathclyde c. 1030. One possibility is that the kingdom had already ceased to exist as an independent entity and was under the rule of the Scots or of some other power.[45] Another is that the Cumbrian king was omitted from the list of attendees because he was not invited to the meeting. Cnut may have been openly hostile towards Strathclyde at this time, or the king of the Cumbrians might already have given homage in a separate ceremony. The attendance of Macbethad from distant Moray might imply that he was Máel Coluim's vassal, or that the relationship between these two was a cause of concern for Cnut. Both may have been regarded by England's king as key players in the politics of the far north, where long-established Norse colonies in Orkney and Caithness were also part of the mix. Echmarcach may have been invited to the meeting because Cnut saw him as a potential ally against other Viking warlords or as a useful counterweight to the ambitions of Máel Coluim and Macbethad.[46] In the late fourteenth century, John of Fordun stated that the meeting was held in Strathclyde but here, as in many other matters, his testimony cannot be trusted.[47] This is not to deny that a separate meeting might have taken place in the Cumbrian kingdom. Indeed, if Cnut was prepared to travel to Alba to deal with the Scots and to receive homage from their king, it would be surprising if he did not pursue a similar policy towards the Cumbrians. Máel Coluim's submission to Cnut followed a period of warfare in which his forces were undoubtedly on the losing side. A similar sequence of events may have occurred during Cnut's dealings with Strathclyde, with a treaty being imposed on the Cumbrians after a military campaign in which they were worsted. If hostilities did indeed occur, they might lie behind an entry in the Irish *Annals of Tigernach* under the year 1030: 'Ravaging of the Britons by the English and the Foreigners of Dublin.'[48]

As there is no mention of this raid in the Welsh Annals, the Britons in question are more likely to have been those of Strathclyde rather than of Wales.[49] A joint venture by English and Scandinavian forces may have taken the form of a two-pronged assault by land and sea, with the allied forces attacking Clydesdale just as the Anglo-Pictish coalition had done nearly three hundred years earlier. Such an alliance might have arisen from an agreement between Cnut and Echmarcach, with the latter using his influence among the Hiberno-Norse to provide ships and warriors from Dublin. If Echmarcach had already sworn an oath of fealty to Cnut, participation in a raid on the Cumbrians may have been among his obligations as a loyal vassal. It is possible that the raid led to a king of Strathclyde submitting to Cnut and paying homage at a ceremony that went unnoticed in the historical record. It is, however, equally possible that a Cumbrian ruler was present when Máel Coluim, Macbethad and Echmarcach submitted to Cnut when he came to 'Scotland'. We may note that another northern ruler, the earl of Bamburgh, is also absent from the list of rulers who submitted. The earl at that time was Ealdred, a nephew of Eadwulf Cudel. Ealdred's forces had been embroiled in sporadic warfare with neighbours from south of the Tees commanded by a Yorkshire nobleman called Carl.[50] This conflict, which is not mentioned in the surviving copies of *ASC*, is sometimes seen as a personal bloodfeud but is more likely to have arisen from Bamburgh's continuing refusal to acknowledge Cnut as king of England. Eventually, the fighting ended when Carl and Ealdred became 'sworn brothers'. Carl was an important royal officer in the north, so Ealdred's oath of brotherhood almost certainly accompanied a formal submission to Cnut, who in turn bestowed a gift of land on the community of St Cuthbert.[51] If this is the correct context, Ealdred and the king of Strathclyde may have made their submission to Cnut together, either alongside the other three rulers or in a separate ceremony at which the 'sworn brother' Carl was also present. We should perhaps note that Ealdred's submission raises the possibility that the English who joined the Dublin Norse in the raid on the Britons were his own Northumbrians, their participation proving his allegiance to Cnut. Other scenarios and permutations could no doubt be devised but the ones discussed here are as plausible as any. Needless to say, the patchy presentation of northern events in *ASC*, coupled with the selective accounts of later chroniclers, sufficiently explain our scant knowledge of Strathclyde in the first third of the eleventh century. The presence of the Cumbrians at the battle of Carham in 1018 seems certain, as does an Anglo-Scandinavian raid on their territory in 1030, but the years in between are a blank space, and the true political context of both events remains elusive.

THE FALL OF STRATHCLYDE

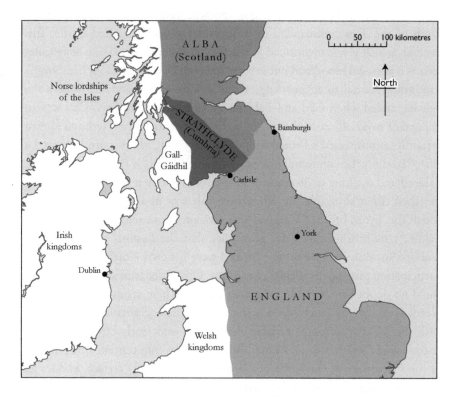

MAP 15 Kingdoms and peoples, c.1050

In 1038, eight years after the raid by a combined force of English and Vikings, the kingdom of Strathclyde endured yet another assault. This time, the attackers were the English alone, and their identity is not in doubt. The event was noted in *HRA*: 'After the death of his brother, Eadwulf was made earl of the Northumbrians. He, being exalted with pride, ravaged the Britons with sufficient ferocity.'[1]

The clear implication is that the raiders were Northumbrians commanded by the earl of Bamburgh, for their leader was Eadwulf, a son of the renowned Earl Uhtred who had defeated the Scots at Durham in 1006. Eadwulf was a namesake and nephew of Eadwulf Cudel, the man who most likely led the Northumbrians to disaster at Carham. The younger Eadwulf became earl of Bamburgh after the death of his brother Ealdred in 1038, three years after the passing of Cnut.[2] At the end of the previous chapter, we surmised that Ealdred had sworn allegiance to Cnut at the beginning of the 1030s, after a period of conflict with the royal officer Carl of York. In 1038, however, Carl murdered Ealdred, thereby renewing the old enmity between the northern and southern divisions of Northumbria. After Ealdred's death, his brother Eadwulf refused to bow to Cnut's son and successor Harthacnut.[3] The raid mentioned in *HRA* clearly took place after Ealdred's murder, when Eadwulf was earl of Bamburgh and at liberty to pursue his own interests rather than those of Carl and Harthacnut. Eadwulf may have launched the raid as a display of his military power, to send a message far and wide that Bamburgh's new earl was no pushover, or he might simply have been seeking to recapture former Northumbrian territory. There is no doubt that the Britons whom he attacked were those of Strathclyde, for the context is clearly northern.[4] What we cannot say with certainty is whether they were still ruled by their own kings at this date. However, with the sources making no mention of a Scottish takeover, nor any hint that the earlier raid of 1030 had led to an English conquest, we should probably assume that the Cumbrian kingdom was still independent in 1038. It may, however, have been in decline, its weakness perhaps being implied by the ease and confidence with which an earl of Bamburgh could ravage not only with 'sufficient ferocity' but without assistance from elsewhere. As far as we know, this was the first time a force from Bamburgh had attacked the Clyde Britons since 756, when King Eadberht and his Pictish ally Onuist launched their joint invasion. The difference in 1038 was that a Northumbrian army, drawn from a relatively small earldom north of the River Tees, was apparently able to do the job unaided. In other aspects the two campaigns may have been broadly similar, with Eadwulf's soldiers probably treading the same roads as their eighth-century ances-tors. Whether the raiders of 1038 assailed the Cumbrian heartlands in Clydesdale is, however, debatable. It is possible that the target was a frontier region seized from Northumbria in the tenth century when Strathclyde was at the height of its power, or a more recent territorial gain acquired by Owain the Bald in the wake of Carham. Eadwulf's troops may have recaptured one or more erstwhile Northumbrian districts at a time when Strathclyde's borders were already shrink-ing. Both the raid of 1038 and the earlier onslaught in 1030 imply that the kingdom was under pressure from neighbouring powers in the fourth decade of the eleventh century. There are, moreover, strong indications that a large area between the firths of Clyde and Solway had already been relinquished by the Cumbrians to a mysterious people known in the sources as the 'Foreigner Gaels'.

The Gall-Gáidhil

Under the year 1034, the Irish annals noted the death of Suibhne mac Cináeda, 'king of the Gall-Gáidhil'.[5] This individual is otherwise unknown but his people, the Gall-Gáidhil, later gave their name to Galloway in south-west Scotland. *Gall-Gáidhil* literally means 'Foreigner Gaels' and is thought to refer to warriors of Irish or Scottish heritage who had adopted the sea-raiding lifestyle of Vikings.[6] It is possible that the name actually had the intended meaning 'Viking Gaels' and that it was originally used to distinguish the Gall-Gáidhil from other Gaelic-speakers. The name first appears in reference to a number of military groups who were active in Ireland in the ninth century. In the tenth and eleventh centuries it seems to be applied to Gaelic-speaking Vikings in the isles and shorelands around northern parts of the Irish Sea. Some of these later Gall-Gáidhil, possibly from the Hebrides, began to seize territory between the firths of Clyde and Solway. One group evidently settled in the Rhinns of Galloway in the late tenth century, displacing local elites who were probably of Northumbrian or Cumbrian stock. By the twelfth century, an independent kingdom of Galloway had arisen in what later became the counties of Wigtownshire and Kirkcudbrightshire. Its rulers preserved their independence until the thirteenth century when their lands were absorbed into the kingdom of Scotland.[7] In Suibhne's time, however, the territory of the Gall-Gáidhil or 'Galwegians' was much greater than the later realm of Galloway. It comprised large parts of what is now south-west Scotland and, although it excluded Clydesdale, it encompassed many districts that had formerly belonged to the kingdom of Strathclyde. A hint of Gall-Gáidhil presence as far north as the River Gryfe in Renfrewshire, only ten miles from the Cumbrian royal centre at Govan, has prompted a suggestion that much of Strathclyde may have been under Suibhne's control.[8] An even more radical view sees Suibhne not as king of the Gall-Gáidhil but of the Cumbrians themselves, and also as a possible brother of the Scottish king Malcolm mac Cináeda.[9] Such theories are speculative, but the fact that they can be advanced at all shows how little we know about relations between Strathclyde and the Gall-Gáidhil. Nevertheless, there can be little doubt that this people played a key role in the eventual downfall of the Cumbrian kingdom. For example, the spread of the Gaelic language across south-west Scotland and the resulting displacement of Cumbric are largely due to the expansion of Gall-Gáidhil power. Many of the earliest Gaelic place-names in North Ayrshire, Renfrewshire and other districts undoubtedly testify to this expansion, even if we cannot chart its progress precisely.[10]

'Son of the king of the Cumbrians'

After Eadwulf's raid in 1038 we hear nothing of Strathclyde for more than a decade. The sources fall silent until the kingdom is mentioned in the context of wider political events around the middle of the century. The northern 'D' text of the *Anglo-Saxon Chronicle* sets the scene in its entry for 1054: 'At this time Earl Siward went with a great army into Scotland, with both a fleet and a land-force, and he fought against the Scots, and put to flight their king Macbethad, and he slew all that were best in the land, and brought back much plunder, such as no man had ever obtained . . .'[11]

Although the entry makes no reference to Strathclyde, it provides the backdrop for an account written by John of Worcester in the twelfth century. Drawing on information in an older Northumbrian chronicle, John tells us that Earl Siward 'put Macbethad to flight, and, as the king had commanded, set up as king Máel Coluim, son of the king of the Cumbrians'.[12]

One of the individuals named here by John is well-known, not just to historians but to anyone familiar with the works of William Shakespeare. Macbethad or 'Macbeth' was the ruler of Moray who had earlier submitted to Cnut. In 1040 he became king of Alba after defeating and destroying Donnchad (Shakespeare's 'Duncan'). Earl Siward, another character in Shakespeare's play, was a man of Scandinavian origin whom Cnut had appointed to the main Northumbrian earldom centred on York. Siward's marriage to a niece of Eadwulf, the earl of Bamburgh, greatly assisted his takeover of all Northumbria after Eadwulf's death in 1041.[13] The English king whom Siward served in 1054 was Edward the Confessor, one of the many sons of Aethelred the Unready and a stepson of Cnut. It was during Edward's reign that Siward marched north to confront Macbethad, whom he then defeated in battle. The 'D' text of *ASC* seems to regard the expedition as a raid for plunder, but John of Worcester asserts that it enabled Siward to install Máel Coluim 'son of the king of the Cumbrians' (*regis Cumbrorum filium*) as king. Máel Coluim was clearly a member of the royal family of Strathclyde and, although he bore a Gaelic name, there is no need to identify him as a Scot rather than as a Briton.[14] His name had previously occurred in the Cumbrian dynasty, having been borne by the tenth-century king Máel Coluim, son of Dyfnwal, who died in 997. Nonetheless, the strong Scottish connotations of the name have proved too alluring for many historians. As far back as the twelfth century, William of Malmesbury identified the Cumbrian Máel Coluim with a Scottish namesake, the 'Malcolm' of Shakespeare's play, who was a son of the deposed King Donnchad.[15] Although the Scottish Máel Coluim did indeed become king of Alba after the fall of Macbethad, it is hard to see why William associated him with the Cumbrians of Strathclyde. Such doubts have not prevented widespread acceptance of William's identification, nor have they deterred historians from identifying Donnchad as John of Worcester's 'king of the Cumbrians'.[16] The reasoning behind this entire scenario is that Donnchad ruled Strathclyde while his grandfather Máel Coluim mac Cináeda was king of Alba, Donnchad himself eventually succeeding to the Scottish throne when Máel Coluim died in 1034. This, we are led to believe, is how Donnchad's son Máel Coluim came to be described as 'son of the king of the Cumbrians'. What William of Malmesbury and his modern supporters have failed to explain is why Donnchad would be remembered by John of Worcester's source not for his well-documented reign over the Scots but for an otherwise unrecorded period of rule over the Cumbrians of Strathclyde.[17] Any notion that John's source would have regarded a Scottish king's supposed reign in Strathclyde as being of greater significance than a subsequent reign in Alba is extremely tenuous.[18] It is far simpler to identify the anonymous 'king of the Cumbrians' not as a Scottish crown-prince ruling a conquered province while awaiting his turn on the throne of Alba but as a member of the Strathclyde royal family.

After defeating and ousting Macbethad in 1054, Siward installed the Cumbrian Máel Coluim as king. The clear inference from John of Worcester's testimony is that the newcomer was placed on the Scottish throne, having been selected by Earl Siward and Edward the Confessor as their preferred candidate. Some historians have suggested that John's words might be ambiguous, and that the kingdom to which Máel Coluim was appointed was not Alba but Strathclyde.[19] While such a theory is certainly worth considering, the idea of a Briton obtaining the Scottish kingship is not without precedent. Looking back to the late ninth century we may recall that Eochaid, the half-Pictish son of King Rhun of Strathclyde, was described in the *Prophecy of Berchan* as king of Alba.[20] Like Eochaid, the Máel Coluim of 1054 may have been the son of a Cumbrian king and a mac Ailpín princess, his mother perhaps being a daughter of Máel Coluim mac Cináeda. Such a relationship would have given him a legitimate claim on the Scottish throne. He presumably also had a similar claim in Strathclyde, if indeed the kingdom still functioned as a separate entity in 1054.

Beyond suggesting that he may have replaced Macbethad as king of Alba we cannot draw much more from the sparse data. Moreover, the identity of his father, the 'king of the Cumbrians', is a mystery, for John of Worcester leaves no clues. Three unanswered questions are therefore left in the wake of the one brief mention of this king: what was his name, was he still reigning in 1054 and was he the last king of Strathclyde? The first question brings us back to Owain the Bald, the Cumbrian king who fought at Carham alongside his Scottish ally Máel Coluim mac Cináeda. Was Owain still reigning on the Clyde in 1054? There is no chronological objection to the idea of a king fighting a battle in 1018 and remaining in power nearly forty years later. In the first half of the previous century, Constantin mac Áeda had ruled the Scots for more than forty years, from his accession in 900 until his abdication in 942. If Owain the Bald did not die at Carham – and there is no reason to assume that he did – he might have had a similarly long reign, siring a prince who became Earl Siward's protege and ruling the Cumbrians in the early 1050s. He might have been a fairly young man when he fought at Carham, gaining his nickname because his hair-loss appeared at an unusually early age. It is therefore possible that Owain was still reigning in Strathclyde when Siward deposed Macbethad from the throne of Alba. Alternatively, the mysterious 'king of the Cumbrians' might not have been Owain himself but his successor, perhaps a son or nephew. Equally mysterious is Strathclyde's status in 1054 and whether or not it was still an independent kingdom. The extent of Siward's involvement in the affairs of the Cumbrian royal family becomes an important factor here, leading us to wonder if the kingdom had fallen under his control.[21] As earl of Northumbria he was well-placed to interfere in the affairs of Strathclyde, whether to further his own ambitions or those of the English king Edward. A hint of Northumbrian influence on Strathclyde in the 1050s comes not only from Siward's patronage of the Cumbrian prince Máel Coluim but also from a reference to ecclesiastical contacts. A twelfth-century source stated that Cynesige, the archbishop of York from 1055 to 1060, consecrated two bishops of Glasgow. These were named as John and 'Magsuen', the latter perhaps a garbled or mis-spelled form of a name in Cumbric or Gaelic. It is only a guess that they were Britons, but the important point is that they were consecrated by a senior Northumbrian cleric to a diocese in the heart of Strathclyde. As Glasgow seems to have been of minor importance at this time, the bishopric served by John and Magsuen might more realistically have been at Govan or Hoddom or some other significant place within the kingdom.[22] Nevertheless, there is a slight hint that Glasgow did play a role in the activities of the Cumbrian ecclesiastical elite. During recent archaeological excavations at

Glasgow Cathedral, the head of a stone cross decorated in Northumbrian style was discovered. Although this was originally thought to be of twelfth-century origin, a date in the mid-eleventh century now seems possible, in which case the cross may have been carved by Northumbrian masons in Siward's time.[23] What we may be seeing with both Siward and Cynesige is Northumbrian patronage of Cumbrian royalty and senior clergy in the 1050s. Whether such involvement by the secular and ecclesiastical elites of York implies Northumbrian political control over Strathclyde is hard to say. At the very least, it suggests that the Cumbrian kingdom had been drawn into a closer relationship with the English, a situation that would not have pleased the Scots.

If the Cumbrian Máel Coluim was placed upon the throne of Alba in 1054 he must have had supporters among the Scottish nobility who regarded him as preferable to Macbethad. Other Scots may have regarded him as Earl Siward's puppet, a usurper imposed upon them by the Northumbrian earl. John of Worcester states that Siward ousted Macbethad on the orders of Edward the Confessor, who presumably saw regime-change in Alba as a means of furthering his own interests. Máel Coluim of Strathclyde might have presented himself to the English king as an alternative to Macbethad, or he may have been nurtured for the role since childhood, as a fosterling in Siward's household. Although his paternal ancestry was Cumbrian, we cannot assume that he had spent much time in Strathclyde, or that he regarded it as his homeland. He might even have thought of himself as a Scot, not as a Briton, if his mother was Scottish and if he had been raised among her kin. Perhaps he sought English patronage as an exile from Alba, a fugitive forced out by Macbethad's supporters? We know nothing of his reign but it was certainly brief, for his patron Earl Siward died in 1055. By 1057, Macbethad was again on the Scottish throne, his restoration implying that Máel Coluim had been deposed. There is no record of English intervention to prevent Macbethad's return, nor is anything more heard of Máel Coluim.[24] Perhaps this Cumbrian prince failed to fulfil the hopes of his English patrons and was abandoned to his fate?

The conquest of Strathclyde

Macbethad continued to rule Alba until his death in 1058 when he was slain in battle by another Máel Coluim, the son of the earlier Scottish king Donnchad. This Máel Coluim ruled almost to the end of the century, to 1093, the year in which he was killed by English soldiers at Alnwick.[25] His reign witnessed the demise of England's Anglo-Saxon kings and their replacement by a Norman dynasty founded by William the Conqueror. William's victory over Harold Godwinesson at Hastings in 1066 heralded a period of change which profoundly affected the old pattern of political relationships in northern Britain. Anglo-Scottish relations, for instance, now had to accommodate the ambitions of William and his successors. In the shorter term, much of what had happened before 1066 continued to influence the years that followed, with the Scots raiding the Northumbrians and vice-versa. In 1070, the Northumbrian earl Gospatric led a counter-raid into Scottish territory. His target was *Cumbreland*, the land of the Strathclyde Britons, but this was no longer an independent realm ruled by its own kings. It had become part of the kingdom of Alba, having been seized by force at some point before Gospatric's raid: 'for at that time *Cumbreland* was under the dominion of King Máel Coluim, not through lawful possession, but through violent subjugation.'[26]

This information comes from *HRA* whose compiler must have found it in an older Northumbrian text. There is little doubt that the term *Cumbreland* has the same meaning here as in the *Anglo-Saxon Chronicle*. It means 'land of the Cumbrians' rather than 'the English county of Cumberland'.[27] The county did not yet exist in the eleventh century, nor had it come into being when *HRA* was compiled in the early twelfth. Whether Gospatric's raid targeted Cumbrian lands north or south of the Solway Firth is hard to say. Earlier in the same passage, the chronicler refers to a raid by 'an endless host of Scots' who plundered Teesdale and adjacent districts. The raiders, led by King Máel Coluim, passed through *Cumbreland* before turning east towards the valley of the Tees. Again, this is not a reference to an English county that had yet to come into being. It simply means that the Scots initially took a western route through Cumbrian territory rather than launching a direct assault across the Tweed. They may have used the Tyne Gap east of Carlisle or, if they advanced further south, the Stainmore Pass. The political context behind both this campaign and Gospatric's counter-raid is made clear a few lines later: *Cumbreland*, the former domain of the kings of Strathclyde, had already been conquered by Máel Coluim mac Donnchada 'through violent subjugation'. These words leave us in no doubt that the kingdom did not become part of Alba through treaty or negotiation but on the point of a Scottish sword. Aside from this brief notice and a similar one in a Durham text known as *Historia post Bedam*, the conquest left no trace in the documentary record.[28] It must, however, have occurred within the dozen or so years between Máel Coluim's accession in 1058 and Gospatric's raid in 1070. We cannot narrow this timespan any further.[29] In any case, the military aspect of the conquest may have been drawn out over several campaigning seasons, with the Scots meeting staunch Cumbrian opposition until a decisive battle paved the way for annexation. It is possible that Máel Coluim's chief adversary was the same 'king of the Cumbrians' whose son had been Earl Siward's protégé in 1054. An alternative is that the old native dynasty had already disappeared by c.1060, having been pushed aside by a Northumbrian elite that had infiltrated the kingdom in Siward's time.[30] The account in *HRA* challenges the legitimacy of Máel Coluim's takeover, an objection that makes sense if he was perceived as snatching Strathclyde away from Northumbrian influence. A Northumbrian chronicler had little to gain from saying that the Scots had unlawfully seized *Cumbreland* from the Cumbrians themselves, but may have regarded his own people as legitimate stakeholders in the kingdom.

It should be noted that a different interpretation of *HRA*'s testimony has also been proposed, with some modern historians seeing the *Cumbreland* of 1070 not as the former kingdom of Strathclyde in its entirety but only as the southern part, the later English county of Cumberland.[31] As noted above, such a view finds little justification in an eleventh-century context, for the county name is not recorded until 1177. In the tenth century, the term *Cumbreland* encompassed a very large territory stretching from Loch Lomond to the River Eamont. We cannot assume that its meaning had changed when the raid of 1070 was noted by *HRA*'s source. What does seem certain is that no part of *Cumbreland* still remained under Cumbrian control. The northern portion, including the Clydesdale heartlands, had been conquered by Máel Coluim sometime after 1058. As we shall see in the next section, the southernmost parts had probably been in English hands since Earl Siward's time.

Gospatric's Writ

HRA tells us that a certain Gospatric led a raid on *Cumbreland* in 1070. He is usually identified as the Northumbrian earl Gospatric, son of Maldred, who played a major role in northern affairs at the time of the Norman conquest of England.[32] How much of the former kingdom of Strathclyde was plundered by him is unknown but the first force of his assault would have been borne by frontier districts close to the English border. At that time, according to *HRA*, *Cumbreland* was under the authority of the Scottish king Máel Coluim, but he did not possess all of it. One portion had already been restored to English rule. This lay south of the Solway Firth and west of Carlisle. Gospatric's raid on *Cumbreland* must therefore have been directed at an area north of the Solway, perhaps in Dumfriesshire or even further north in Clydesdale itself.

The part of *Cumbreland* known to have been in English hands at the time of Gospatric's raid was Allerdale, an extensive lordship in the west of the later county of Cumberland. An eleventh-century charter granting various rights in Allerdale to a man called Thorfynn mac Thore refers to this lordship as one of 'the lands that were Cumbrian'. The charter was granted by a Gospatric whom some historians identify as the Northumbrian earl of 1070.[33] However, the name appears to have been quite popular in the eleventh century, so Thorfynn's benefactor may be a different Gospatric. He should, perhaps, be identified as the Gospatric who was a son of Earl Uhtred of Bamburgh, the same Uhtred whose brother Eadwulf Cudel was defeated at Carham in 1018.[34] This older Gospatric was the younger Gospatric's uncle and died in 1064, six years before his nephew's raid on *Cumbreland*, but he himself never attained the rank of earl. He served instead the formidable Earl Siward and probably played a role in the Scottish campaign which deposed Macbethad in 1054. Under the terms of the Allerdale charter, a document known today as 'Gospatric's Writ', Thorfynn mac Thore and other men received from Gospatric a guarantee of protection 'that Earl Siward and I have granted to them as freely as to any man living beneath the sky'. As Siward can only have granted protection in lands under his authority, this statement must mean that Allerdale had been one of his possessions. According to the Writ, it had previously been 'Cumbrian', a district under the rule of the kings of Strathclyde. If an area so far west had been seized by Siward then so, too, had other Cumbrian lands south of the Solway Firth, especially those lying closer to his earldom east of the Pennines. Indeed, frontier territories in the Pennine foothills and along the Eden Valley are likely to have fallen first to Siward's Northumbrian forces advancing from York, with Allerdale and other western districts being captured later. A logical inference from the Writ is that most if not all Cumbrian territory south of the Solway had been separated from Strathclyde, and had fallen under Siward's control, before his death in 1055.[35] These lands were thereafter no longer 'Cumbrian' in a political sense, even if their former status was still acknowledged by Gospatric. Indeed, the survival of the kingdom's English name *Cumberland* as the name of a later county indicates that the old political and cultural affiliations had left an indelible mark. Over time, the Cumbrian identity of the region between the Solway Firth and the River Eamont was slow to fade, long outlasting the deeds of Earl Siward and persisting even to the present day. In the next chapter, the origins of the county will be looked at more closely. For the moment, however, our focus returns to Gospatric's Writ. What can this fascinating document tell us about the end of Cumbrian rule in the lands south of the Solway?

Gospatric's Writ

Gospatrik greot ealle mine wassenas & hyylkun mann freo & ðrenge þeo woonnan on eallun þam landann þeo weoron Combres & eallun mine kynling freondlycc. & ic cyðe eoy þæt myne mynna/ is & full leof þæt Thorfynn mac Thore beo swa freo on eallan ðynges þeo beo myne on Alnerdall swa ænyg mann beo, oðer ic oðer ænyg myne wassenas, on weald, on freyð, on heyninga, & æt ællun ðyngan þeo by eorðe boenand & ðeoronðer, to Shauk, to Wafyr, to poll Waðoen, to bek Troyte & þeo weald æt Caldebek. & ic wille þæt þeo mann bydann mið Thorfynn æt Carðeu & Combeðeyfoch beo swa freals myð hem swa Melmor & Thore & Sygoolf weoron on Eadread dagan. & ne beo neann mann swa ðeorif þehat mið þæt ic heobbe gegyfene to hem neghar brech seo gyrth ðyylc Eorl Syward & ic hebbe getyðet hem se frelycc swa ænyg mann leofand þeo welkynn ðeoronðer. & loc hyylkun by þar byðann geyldfreo beo swa ic by & swa willann, Wallðeof & Wygande & Wyberth & Gamell & Kunyth & eallun mine kynling & wassenas. & ic wille þæt Thorfynn heobbe soc & sac, toll & theam, ofer eallun þam landan on Carðeu & on Combeðeyfoch þæt weoron gyfene Thore on Moryn dagan freols myð bode & wytnesmann on þy ylk stow.

'Gospatric greets all my dependants and every man, free and dreng, who dwell in all the lands that were Cumbrian, and all my kindred in friendly fashion. And I make known to you that my purpose and full agreement is that Thorfynn mac Thore be as free in all things that are mine in Allerdale as any man may be, whether I or any of my dependants, in the plain, in woodland, in enclosure, in all things that are above or beneath the earth, as far as the Chalk, the Waver, the Wampool, Wiza Beck and the plain at Caldbeck. And I desire that the men abiding with Thorfynn at Cardew and Cumdivock be as free in their persons as Melmor and Thore and Sygulf were in Eadred's days. And let no man be so bold as to withhold that which I have given to them, nor cause to be broken the guarantee of protection that Earl Siward and I have granted to them as freely as any man living under the sky. And let all whosoever are dwelling there be as free of royal taxation as I am and as Waltheof and Wygande and Wyberth and Gamell and Kunith may wish, and all my kindred and dependants. And I wish that Thorfynn has soke and sake, toll and team, over all the lands of Cardew and Cumdivock that were given to Thore in Moryn's days freely, with the right to claim bode and witnessman, in the same place.'[36]

Glossary:
'dreng' – Northumbrian term for a type of tenant whose obligations included military service on behalf of a lord
'soke and sake, toll and team' – a formulaic phrase encompassing various rights and privileges, including the right to exact tolls from travellers.
'bode and witnessman' – a legal right to send messengers and request witnesses
'Eadred' – an unidentified English lord or landowner

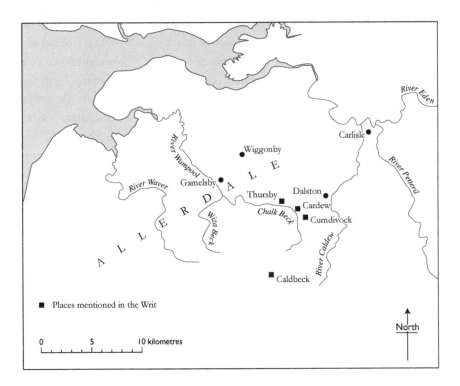

MAP 16 Gospatric's Writ

A glance at the Writ shows it to be a charter confirming rights and privileges already held by Thorfynn mac Thore in certain lands owned by Gospatric. Thorfynn was a landholding tenant, a person of considerable status, as was his father before him. His patronymic uses the Gaelic term *mac* ('son of') which suggests that Thorfynn himself was a Gaelic-speaker. His ancestry was most likely Hiberno-Norse, for both his name and that of his father are of Scandinavian origin.[37] Nonetheless, the terms of the charter are in Old English, a language Thorfynn presumably understood. Indeed, he might have considered himself an Englishman, regardless of his heritage, especially if it was socially and economically advantageous to do so. The name of his lord Gospatric is equally interesting, being neither English nor Scandinavian but Cumbric. It means 'servant of St Patrick' and was no doubt a fairly common name among the Cumbrians, especially in areas where they had close contact with the Hiberno-Norse.[38] Gospatric, son of Uhtred, was the first member of the house of Bamburgh to be given the name – as far as we know – so it might be an indicator of Cumbrian kinship or ancestry within this family. From the Writ we can infer that Gospatric was the lord of Allerdale, a large territorial unit west of Carlisle extending as far as the Irish Sea coast. He may have been granted this lordship by Earl Siward as a reward for military service following the restoration of Northumbrian rule. Although the Writ does not say if the region south of the Solway Firth was wrested from Britons or Scots, Gospatric's reference to 'lands that were Cumbrian' rather than 'lands that were Scottish' suggests that there was no interim period of Scottish rule between the periods of Cumbrian and Northumbrian ownership. As we have noted in earlier chapters, it was once widely believed that the kingdom of Strathclyde, with all its outlying provinces, fell under permanent Scottish control in the late ninth or early tenth century. Gospatric's Writ provides good evidence that this was not the case, and that Strathclyde's southernmost provinces remained in Cumbrian hands into the second millennium.[39] The Writ implies that the change to English ownership was a fairly recent event. It also suggests that the English takeover was achieved by Earl Siward, although it does not say if the lords whose lands he had seized were still answering to Clyde-based kings when he arrived. Perhaps Strathclyde was in such serious decline by c.1050 that it had already abandoned its southern territories in the face of Gall-Gáidhil expansion on the northern side of the Solway Firth? If this was the case, the Cumbrians on the southern side would have had to organise their own defence against Siward, with no prospect of aid from their compatriots in Clydesdale.

THE ANGLO-NORMAN PERIOD

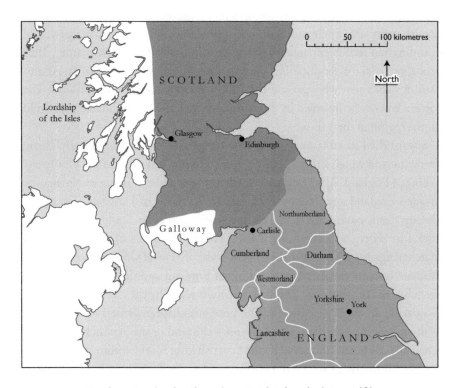

MAP 17 Southern Scotland and northern England in the late twelfth century

The county of Cumberland

Gospatric's Writ suggests that the southernmost portion of the kingdom of Strathclyde, the region between the Solway Firth and the River Eamont, was restored to English rule sometime around the middle of the eleventh century. Earl Siward, who was probably the architect of this reconquest, seems to have appointed Northumbrians such as Gospatric to positions of authority previously held by Cumbrian lords who answered to the kings of Strathclyde. The

English king Edward the Confessor thus gained a strategic foothold in the north-west, on the edge of the volatile Irish Sea zone. In the ensuing redistribution of estates, many of the boundaries established in the era of Cumbrian rule were respected and preserved. Gospatric's great lordship of Allerdale, for example, almost certainly originated as a British territorial unit in the tenth century. One change introduced by the English after their takeover was the splitting of large estates into smaller ones which were often named after the beneficiary of the division. This process has left its mark on modern maps, where the new estates are indicated by place-names in which a personal name is followed by the Danish suffix -*by*.[1] Such names do not appear to belong to an earlier period of Scandinavian settlement and are seen as creations of the eleventh century. They probably reflect a landholding pattern first introduced by Siward's Anglo-Danish henchmen who crossed the Pennines from the earldom of York. The pattern was later continued by the Normans when they consolidated their hold on the region in the 1100s.[2]

Siward died in 1055 and was succeeded as earl of Northumbria by Tostig Godwinesson whose brother Harold hoped to succeed Edward the Confessor as king of England. After Edward's death in 1066, Duke William of Normandy invaded England and destroyed Harold at the battle of Hastings. Tostig was already dead, having been slain three weeks earlier at Stamford Bridge in Yorkshire where, in alliance with King Harald Hardrada of Norway, he had marched against his own brother. In the wake of Harold Godwinesson's death, William became the first Norman king of England and the founder of a new French-speaking dynasty.[3] The raid on *Cumbreland* by the Northumbrian earl Gospatric, an event discussed in the previous chapter, came four years after William's victory. By then, *Cumbreland* – the land of the Strathclyde Britons – had already been conquered by the Scottish king Máel Coluim. South of the Solway, Strathclyde's southern provinces – described in the earlier Gospatric's charter as 'lands that were Cumbrian' – had probably been in English hands since Siward's time and must have lain outside the area conquered by Máel Coluim between 1058 and 1070.

William's grip on the English throne was hindered by unrest stirred up by rival claimants, the most persistent of these being Edgar the Aetheling, a great-grandson of Aethelred the Unready. Edgar's allies included his brother-in-law Máel Coluim of Alba, King Sweyn II of Denmark and various members of the English aristocracy. A series of revolts by Edgar's supporters in Northumbria eventually prompted William to launch a campaign of devastation, the so-called 'Harrying of the North', in the winter of 1069–70. In the ensuing years, the

Normans tightened their grip on northern England by building castles and establishing new lordships.[4] By consolidating their power in lands close to the Scottish border they seem to have unsettled Máel Coluim who, in 1091, crossed the River Tweed to invade Northumbria. He laid siege to Durham but withdrew in the face of a Norman counter-offensive and eventually agreed a peace treaty with William Rufus, the son and heir of William of Normandy.[5] In the following year, William Rufus came north with an army, his objective being to seize the old Roman city of Carlisle. The expedition was described in the *Anglo-Saxon Chronicle*:

> In this year King William with a great army went north to Carlisle and restored the town and built the castle; and drove out Dolfin, who ruled the land there before. And he garrisoned the castle with his vassals; and thereafter came south hither and sent thither a great multitude of peasants with women and cattle, there to dwell and till the land.[6]

Basing their ideas on an assumption that the district around Carlisle was the part of *Cumbreland* conquered by Máel Coluim before 1070 and raided by Earl Gospatric in that year, some historians see Dolfin as a subject of the Scottish king.[7] There is, in fact, no warrant for believing that Carlisle and its environs or any territory south of the Solway lay under Scottish rule in 1092, or that these erstwhile Cumbrian lands were ever conquered by Máel Coluim.[8] It is more likely that Dolfin was a rebellious Northumbrian lord who stubbornly refused to submit to William Rufus. His authority in the Carlisle district, like Gospatric's in Allerdale, had probably originated in Earl Siward's takeover of the 'lands that were Cumbrian'. Dolfin may have been the son or grandson of a Northumbrian nobleman to whom Siward had granted a unit of lordship formerly held by a Strathclyder. It has been suggested that he was the son of Gospatric of Bamburgh – the earl who raided *Cumbreland* in 1070 – but this is just a guess based on the fact that Gospatric did have a son of this name who fits the chronological context. Alternatively, Dolfin of Carlisle may have belonged to the family of an earlier Dolfin who is known to have fought and died in Siward's campaign against Macbethad in 1054.[9]

Norman control of the Carlisle area was strengthened by the granting of estates to new landowners whose names were of Continental origin. By the early 1100s, during the reign of King Henry I in England, a number of Anglo-Scandinavian *-by* place-names had become associated with this new elite. Examples include Botcherby and Rickerby which were granted, respectively, to Bochard and Richard – men with French names – who were responsible for maintaining two gates in Carlisle's city walls (Botchergate and Rickergate).[10] In Henry's time, the area known as the 'land of Carlisle' encompassed not only the city and its hinterland but also other lands as far west as Allerdale and as far south as Appleby. Henry granted this entire region to a powerful Norman nobleman, Ranulf le Meschin, who made his mark by establishing two baronies centred on Burgh by Sands on the Solway coast and at Liddel Strength on the Scottish border.[11] To each of these baronies Ranulf appointed one of his own henchmen. He seems to have tried to impose his brother William on an older barony at Gilsland, east of Carlisle, but failed to dislodge its incumbent lord. The latter was Gille, son of Boite, a mysterious figure of whom little is known. In 1120, Ranulf became Earl of Chester and returned the 'land of Carlisle' to direct royal control. King Henry then enlarged the area with the addition of the parish of Alston before splitting it into two sheriffdoms or 'shires' separated by the River Eamont. The northern shire was centred on Carlisle and was known as *Chaerlolium*, taking its name from the city. The southern shire was called *Westmarieland*, 'the land west of the moors', with an administrative centre at Appleby.[12] New baronies were created within the bounds of *Chaerlolium* and, in 1133, a bishopric was established at Carlisle. After Henry died in 1135 his nephew Stephen became king of England and a volatile period followed the accession. Stephen's hold on the crown was later contested by Henry's daughter Matilda in a bitter civil war but the first major crisis of his reign was an invasion by the Scottish king David I, one of the sons of Máel Coluim, in late December 1135. David seized Carlisle and much adjacent territory and managed to hold onto these gains under the terms of a peace treaty negotiated with Stephen.[13] David's son, Prince Henry, was made earl of Carlisle and David himself died there in 1153. Four years after David's death, his grandson King Máel Coluim IV was forced to relinquish the new earldom to Henry II of England.[14] It was during Henry's long reign (1133– 87) that the shire of *Chaerlolium* became known as the county of *Cumberland*, being first recorded under this name in 1177.[15]

The prince of the Cumbrians

The Scottish king Máel Coluim, conqueror of Strathclyde, died in 1093 in a battle against Anglo-Norman forces at Alnwick. His death sparked a power-struggle which eventually brought his son Edgar to the throne. Edgar's designated heir was his brother, Alexander, to whom he gave an earldom in lands north of the River Forth. To David, his youngest brother, Edgar allocated a substantial territory south of the Forth–Clyde isthmus, intending that David should take control of it when Alexander succeeded to the Scottish throne.[16] At that time, however, David was based in England, having fled there with his brothers in 1093 after their uncle Domnall Bán had seized the throne in the wake of their father's death. David remained in England long after Edgar and Alexander returned home. He became close to the court of Henry I, his brother-in-law, and was regarded as a prominent member of the Anglo-Norman aristocracy. When Edgar died in 1107, Alexander succeeded him as king but was reluctant to honour his bequest to their younger sibling, perhaps fearing that the wealth of a large lordship in the southern part of the kingdom might give David too much power.[17] David was probably in no position to demand his inheritance at that time, for his patron Henry I was embroiled in a long-running war in Normandy which dragged on until 1113. With Henry's attention distracted by the war, David would have had little hope of backing up any demands he might make on his brother. Moreover, David himself was part of Henry's entourage and would have been obliged to take part in the Normandy campaign.[18] It is possible that he had to wait six years before being in a position to claim the lands bequeathed to him by Edgar. By then, Henry was able to support the claim by threatening to invade Alexander's kingdom if it was refused. Alexander was left with little choice, so David came home to take his inheritance. Edgar's generous bequest placed David in control of a very large domain which he ruled as an autonomous province within the Scottish realm.[19] He was not given one of the usual titles, such as earl, but was known instead as *princeps Cumbrensis*, 'prince of the Cumbrians' and *Cumbrensis regionis princeps*, 'prince of the Cumbrian kingdom'. The lands under his control comprised much of what is now south-west Scotland, from Loch Lomond to the Solway Firth, with the exception of Galloway and some other territories. What his elder brother had in fact bequeathed to him was the former heartland of Strathclyde.

David's principality stretched along the River Tweed from its source in the hills of Dumfriesshire to Teviotdale. Other parts of Tweeddale further east also lay within his domain but his authority was more limited there because Alexander ruled more directly. To the south-west, David's domain bordered the 'land of Carlisle' which was then part of England. This region, although once ruled by the kings of Strathclyde, was not part of David's inheritance. The exclusion of this erstwhile Cumbrian territory south of the Solway Firth was mentioned in one of his charters, where a scribe observed that he 'was not, in truth, lord of the whole Cumbrian kingdom'.[20] What David did have in common with the Cumbrian kings of old was a long frontier with the English. In the tenth and eleventh centuries, this border had frequently been crossed by armies intent on plunder or conquest. In the early twelfth century it may have been somewhat less volatile, for Henry I knew that his Scottish friend David now controlled the northern side.[21] The bond between the two men, already strengthened by Henry's marriage to David's sister, was now reinforced by David's own marriage to Matilda de Senlis, a wealthy Anglo-Norman widow who happened to be Henry's second cousin. As a granddaughter of Earl Siward by his son Waltheof, Matilda had a family connection which gave David a potential advantage in future dealings with Northumbria. Through her, for instance, he could make a valid claim on the former Cumbrian lands south of the Solway, these having been part of the enlarged Northumbrian earldom held by Siward and Waltheof in the second half of the eleventh century. Although the earldom itself, as a formal rank or title, had been phased out in 1095 its territorial bounds were not forgotten.

David's rule had a significant impact on what had once been the kingdom of Strathclyde. In 1113, soon after taking up his inheritance, he established a monastery at Selkirk in Tweeddale, granting it to monks of the Tironensian Order whose headquarters lay in France.[22] The following year saw another ecclesiastical development: the revival of a bishopric at Glasgow in the heart of the old Cumbrian realm. This bishopric had evidently been defunct for a long time and was described in one contemporary text as 'old but decayed'.[23] The description suggests that the last Cumbrian bishop had been ousted during the Scottish conquest in the previous century and had followed his royal patrons into oblivion. In resurrecting the bishopric, David claimed to be restoring spiritual and moral guidance to the inhabitants of his principality. While such pious intentions might indeed have played a role, they were undoubtedly accompanied by political motives. The revived bishopric strengthened David's hold on the Cumbrian lands by creating a spiritual authority which mirrored and supported his secular rule.[24] He had good reason to consolidate his position in this way for, although he had the favour of the English king, he had less influence at the Scottish court at that time and was not yet his brother's designated heir.

David's inquest

Reviving the defunct bishopric of Glasgow necessitated a survey of its former possessions. To gather this information, David commissioned an *inquisitio* or 'inquest' of ecclesiastical landholdings within his principality. The resulting document, compiled between 1117 and 1124, was essentially a survey of church property within the old kingdom of Strathclyde. Indeed, the bishops later made an explicit link between their diocese and the Cumbrian kingdom by

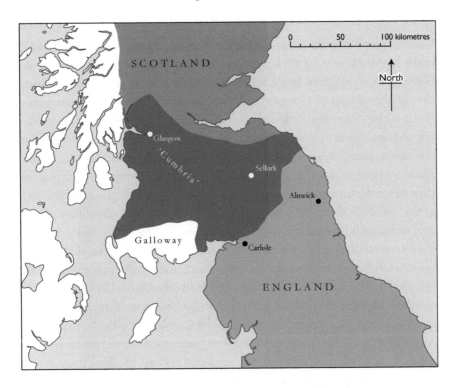

MAP 18 David's principality: 'Cumbria' in the Scottish kingdom, c.1120

promoting themselves as the legitimate successors of its royal dynasty.[25] The geographical limits of the inquest are a useful indicator of the extent of the kingdom, with the exclusion of Renfrewshire and Ayrshire suggesting that these areas were not part of it at the time of the Scottish takeover.[26] They may have been seized from the Cumbrians by a neighbouring power, perhaps the Gall-Gáidhil, during the kingdom's final phase. However, the inclusion of both areas within David's wider domain indicates that they were in Scottish hands when King Edgar created the bequest for his younger brother, so they had probably been annexed during or after Máel Coluim's conquest of Strathclyde. Unsurprisingly, the inquest excludes any territory south of the Solway Firth, despite the likelihood that the authority of bishops on the Clyde had formerly extended to the River Eamont in the days of the Cumbrian kings. In the early twelfth century, the spiritual needs of this region were already being met by Anglo-Norman clerics whose secular lord was the king of England. David obviously regarded it as belonging to Henry I and therefore made no claim on it while Henry lived, perhaps because any such claim would have required him to give homage to Henry.[27] The inquest also sheds light on dealings between Cumbrian and English clergy after the collapse of Anglo-Saxon Northumbria in the late ninth century. It identifies the monastery of Hoddom, an important Northumbrian religious house from the seventh century onwards, as a possession of the bishop of Glasgow and thus, by implication, as an ecclesiastical centre within Strathclyde. Hoddom's fate in the Viking period is undocumented but archaeological evidence suggests continuity into the tenth century when the surrounding area was certainly under Cumbrian rule. In the inquest, Hoddom heads a list of places in Annandale which were probably its dependent churches at the time of the Scottish conquest in the eleventh century.[28] Nowhere in the inquest is there any sense that an ethnically distinct Cumbrian population remained identifiable within David's domain. This is consistent with the scant survival of Cumbric place-names in the core territory of the old kingdom. Even in Clydesdale such names are quite scarce, their rarity suggesting a major upheaval in which the Cumbric language was swiftly replaced by Gaelic.[29] If any members of the Cumbrian aristocracy managed to retain their lands into the twelfth century they can only have done so by assimilating with the Scottish and Anglo-Norman lords to whom David now granted substantial estates between the firths of Clyde and Solway. If any residual Cumbric-speaking communities still existed in this region in the early 1100s, their days were undoubtedly numbered. Two or three generations had probably passed since the fall of Strathclyde and there was no longer any incentive for anyone to maintain the Cumbric language or a Cumbrian identity. All important matters were now conducted in Gaelic, the language of the Scottish royal family and of the new landholding elite. 'Scottishness' therefore replaced 'Britishness' as the preferred cultural affiliation for people of ambition and was eventually adopted by everyone. There is thus no need to regard a contingent of *Cumbrenses* who fought in the Scottish army in 1138 as a remnant of the Britons.[30] These soldiers may have been Englishmen from the part of 'Cumberland' around Carlisle, marching under David's banner after his seizure of the city three years earlier. Nor should we take at face value the statement, made by an English archbishop of Canterbury in 1119, that the Glasgow diocese was served by a 'bishop of the Britons'. While this shows awareness of the former existence of the kingdom of Strathclyde, it does not imply that anyone living within the new Scottish diocese still spoke Cumbric or maintained a Cumbrian identity.[31]

The Cumbrian legacy

Cumberland, the English county, continued in existence until a major reorganisation of local government in the United Kingdom in 1974. Since then, together with neighbouring Westmorland, it has been subsumed within the larger county of Cumbria. Both the older name and the new are found in medieval texts as synonyms for the kingdom of Strathclyde. Ironically, neither is preserved in the landscape of Clydesdale, the core of the kingdom, nor is there a general awareness that this was once the very heart of 'Cumbrian' territory. There are, of course, a number of place-names of Cumbric origin around Glasgow and in other parts of south-west Scotland, each a reminder of the language spoken in these districts a thousand years ago, but place-names commemorating the Cumbrians themselves are rare. The most familiar is probably 'The Cumbraes', a collective name for a pair of islands off the coast of North Ayrshire, which derives from Old Norse *Kumreyiar* ('isles of the Cumbrians').[32] Cumbernauld in North Lanarkshire and Cummertrees in Dumfriesshire seem, at first glance, to have names derived from Old English *Cumber* ('Cumbrian' in the sense of 'North Briton') but the first element in both names is more likely to mean 'confluence' (Gaelic *comar* and the Cumbric equivalent of Welsh *cymer* respectively).[33] To find Old English *Cumber* in place-names we must look across the Solway Firth to the lands around Carlisle. Here, the Cumbric-speaking settlers of the tenth century are still remembered by the continuing use of 'Cumbrians' to describe the inhabitants of the post-1974 county. The term now encompasses not only the people of the former county of Cumberland but those who dwell in the erstwhile Westmorland south of the River Eamont, together with neighbouring communities in the Cartmel and Furness peninsulas that were formerly within Lancashire. Another reminder of the Viking Age survives on the southern outskirts of Carlisle, where the village of Cummersdale has a name in which Old English *Cumber* is attached to Old Norse *dalr* to denote 'the valley of the Britons'.[34]

Although present-day Cumbrians are indistinguishable from folk in other parts of England, in terms of language and national identity, they maintain a sense of regional distinctiveness in which memories of the ancient kingdom play a role. The local legends of King Dunmail and Ewen Caesarius have already been mentioned, but other links with the distant past might also be preserved. One possible 'survival' is a system of counting which uses numbers that appear to derive from a Brittonic language. In the nineteenth century, when it was first documented, this was used as a method for counting sheep in the Lake District and in other parts of the old counties of Cumberland and

Westmorland. Observers noted that the numbers or 'scores' were not only used by shepherds but were also found in children's rhyming games. Certain linguistic similarities with Welsh and Cornish numerical systems were identified and the idea of a connection with the ancient past soon arose. In truth, the situation is rather more complex. Variant forms of the counting system have been found in other parts of northern England – both east and west of the Pennines – and also in Scotland, with a few examples from southern England. Nonetheless, although their precise history is unknown, the numbers have been seen as originating in northern Britain in areas where the Cumbric language was once spoken. This might turn out to be the best explanation, in spite of a more sceptical idea that they were brought to English and Scottish sheep-farming districts by itinerant shepherds from Wales. How and why such a counting system would have survived the otherwise complete disappearance of Cumbric speech are questions that remain unanswered.

Sheep-counting in Cumbric?

The numbers in the left-hand column below were recorded in the Lake District valley of Borrowdale in the nineteenth century.

	Modern Welsh
1 = yan	1 = un
2 = tyan	2 = dau
3 = tethera	3 = tri
4 = methera	4 = pedwar
5 = pimp	5 = pump
6 = sethera	6 = chwech
7 = lethera	7 = saith
8 = hevera	8 = wyth
9 = devera	9 = naw
10 = dick	10 = deg

11

CONCLUSIONS

This book has presented a narrative history of relations between the Cumbrians of Strathclyde and their Anglo-Saxon neighbours during the Viking period of the ninth to eleventh centuries. The book's chronological coverage has been slightly wider, starting with contacts between the two peoples in the sixth century and ending with the creation of the English county of Cumberland in the twelfth. This extended span has given extra depth and context to the core narrative, which has been chiefly concerned with a period of some two hundred years from the fall of Alt Clut in 870 to the Scottish conquest of Strathclyde. Throughout the book, the source-materials have been handled cautiously and with due acknowledgement of their limitations. In some instances, especially when the source gives ambiguous or contradictory information, a particular interpretation has been chosen from one or more alternatives. Whenever this has occurred, the alternatives have usually been acknowledged in the main text or in the chapter endnotes. The intention all along has not been to assess the relative merits of the sources themselves, but rather to present a continuous narrative which attempts to weave together the scattered threads of a fragmented history.

This book has had three main objectives. The first was to finally lay to rest the notion that the Strathclyde Britons were permanently subjugated by their Scottish neighbours before the eleventh century, or that their kings were princes of the royal dynasty of Alba. The second was to remove any doubt that, in early medieval times, the terms 'Cumbria' and 'Cumberland' referred to an extensive kingdom centred on Clydesdale and not just to one small part of it lying south of the Solway Firth. The term 'Cumbrians', whenever we encounter it in an early medieval context, should therefore be assumed to refer to the inhabitants of this large realm rather than to those of the later English county. The book's third objective was to highlight the important role played by the kings of Strathclyde in the creation of the countries we know today as Scotland and England. This role has often been overlooked, minimised or ignored, leaving the Cumbrians and their rulers on the sidelines of history. What this book has shown is that

Strathclyde was one of the major powers in Britain during the Viking Age, an important kingdom whose status was acknowledged by contemporary observers on both sides of the Irish Sea.

The book has challenged a number of modern misunderstandings about Strathclyde by showing them to be completely unsupported by older sources such as the *Anglo-Saxon Chronicle*. It has also tackled controversial topics where the sources are more ambiguous and where certainty is less evident. A number of events in the history of Strathclyde are, in fact, caught up in scholarly debates which show little sign of being resolved in the near future. A particular view on such matters has sometimes been taken in this book, as in the case of the battle of Brunanburh. The location of this great clash of arms remains tantalisingly elusive and continues to exercise the minds of many folk, not just within academic circles but elsewhere. Attempts to pinpoint the battlefield on a modern map have produced various theories, some of which were mentioned in Chapter 5. In the same chapter a particular stance was adopted and a case was made for Lancashire, with two sites being highlighted as potential candidates. It is unlikely that readers who strongly support other sites, such as Bromborough in Cheshire or Lanchester in County Durham, will be swayed by the arguments presented here. The main reason for making a case for one particular area is that the overall purpose of this book – to present a continuous narrative history – requires something more definite than a mere list of theories. Another battle at the centre of a mystery is Carham-on-Tweed where both the year and the name of the English commander are uncertain. In Chapter 8, support was given to 1018 for the former and to Eadwulf Cudel for the latter, with arguments put forward to justify both. As with the stance taken on Brunanburh, readers will judge the merits of the case for themselves and can draw their own conclusions. Such is the nature of objective debate. Agreement is likewise absent on the origin of Gospatric's Writ, a document whose eponymous grantor might be a nephew of Eadwulf Cudel or a later namesake who led a raid on *Cumbreland* in 1070. Here, support has been given to the view that the 'older' Gospatric made the grant, but not all readers will be convinced.

Amid all the uncertainties and controversies it is worth noting that we are not wholly reliant on snippets of information scattered among the textual sources. The story of the kingdom of Strathclyde is not preserved in manuscripts alone but also, and more tangibly, in sculptured monuments bequeathed to later ages. These magnificent relics, far from being mute sandstone blocks, speak forcefully of the wealth and power that lay behind their making. They connect us to the era of the Cumbrian kings. Thus, when we cross the threshold of the old parish church at Govan, we enter the very heart of an ancient realm. Walking among the ornate memorials of people who worshipped in that same place a thousand years ago, we soon realise that these folk were not the subjugated vassals of Gaelic-speaking neighbours, desperately clinging to the last vestige of independence. They were an ambitious and confident elite, the royal and noble kindreds of the North Britons or 'Strathclyde Welsh'. After the destruction of their former stronghold in 870 they created a new centre of power and rebuilt the fortunes of their kingdom. Within a generation they had regained their status as a potent political and military force. Over the next hundred years they not only preserved their territory but expanded its frontiers. Whether as friends or foes of English, Scottish or Scandinavian neighbours they successfully steered a path through one of the most volatile periods in European history. It is a curious irony that the destruction of their ancient fortress and the subsequent expansion of their power were both largely due to the Vikings. The fall of Dumbarton to Hiberno-Norse warlords in 870 occurred at roughly the same time as the Danish incursions into England, which in turn led to the collapse of Anglo-Saxon Northumbria. The Danes created an opportunity for the rulers of Strathclyde, who pushed southward across the Solway Firth to take control of erstwhile Northumbrian lands. The tenth century was thus a golden age for the Cumbrians, the time of their greatest achievements. Like the Norse of Dublin, they began to lose their power as the second millennium dawned. In the eleventh century, the royal dynasties of both Strathclyde and Dublin were eventually overthrown by enemies. This was probably more than coincidence. It may have been the inevitable fate awaiting two powerful kingdoms whose stories belonged to the Viking Age.

NOTES

Chapter 1

1 On the Govan sculpture, see the papers in Ritchie 1994. For a useful overview, see Ritchie 1999.

2 Clancy 2006. The modern Welsh form is Ystrad Clud.

3 Jackson 1955, 77. The name 'Cumbri' appears in a tenth-century English chronicle in the dative plural *Cumbris* (Aethelweard, *Chronicon*, s.a. 975).

4 Broun 2004, 112–13; Jackson 1963.

5 *AU* 872.

6 Clancy 2006. On Alt Clut, see below (Chapter 2).

7 *ASC* 875.

8 Note also the form *Kumbraland* in the Norse saga *Heimskringla*, referring to Viking raids in the late 900s.

9 Oram 2008, 63.

10 On the inquest, see below (this chapter) and Chapter 10.

11 *Registrum Episcopatus Glasguensis*, i, 1: *seniores homines et sapientiores totius Cumbriae.*

12 e.g. Kirby 1962, Summerson 1993, Phythian-Adams 1996

13 On Fordun's ideas about Strathclyde and Cumbria, see below.

14 Wilson 1966.

15 McKitterick 1999.

16 Woolf 2007a, 312–50.

17 On the poem *Armes Prydein*, see Bollard and Haycock 2011.

18 Downham 2007, xv–xx.

19 John of Fordun, *Chronicle*, 163–4.

20 Anderson 1922, i, lviii.

21 See below, Chapter 6.

22 Broun 2004, 130–5; Sellar 1985, 34–5; Macquarrie 1993, 15.

23 Broun 1997, 18–20.

24 On *CKA*, see below.

25 On the origin of *ASC*, see Swanton 1996.

26 *ASC* 'A': Cambridge, Corpus Christi College, MS 173, fols 1–32.

27 *ASC* 'D': British Library, MS Cotton Tiberius B.iv.

28 *ASC* 'E': Bodleian Library, MS Laud misc. 636.

29 Aethelweard, *Chronicon*: Henry Savile's edition of 1596 is the basis of modern editions such as Campbell 1962.

30 John of Worcester, *Chronicon*: edition and translation in Darlington and McGurk 1995. Selected translations in Anderson 1908.

31 On the reliability of John of Worcester's chronicle, see Brett 1981 and Darlington and McGurk 1982.

32 On the cult of St Cuthbert, see Rollason 1987.

33 The full title is *Libellus de exordio atque procursu istius, hoc est Dunhelmensis, ecclesie* ('Tract on the Origins and Progress of this the Church of Durham').

34 Rollason 2000.

35 *Historia Regum Anglorum et Dacorum*: edition in Hinde 1868. English translation in Stevenson 1858. Selected translations in Anderson 1908. For a useful comparison of *HRA* with the northern versions of *ASC*, see Downham 2003, 36–9.

36 Rollason 1998. On the relationship between the Durham chronicles and other twelfth-century sources, see Darlington and McGurk 1982, lxxi–lxxii.

37 William of Malmesbury, *Gesta Regum Anglorum* ('History of the English Kings'): edition and translation in Mynors, Thomson and Winterbottom 1998–9; Henry of Huntingdon, *Historia Anglorum* ('History of the English'): edition and translation in Greenway 1996. Selected translations from both chroniclers appear in Anderson 1908.

38 On the works of William of Malmesbury and Henry of Huntingdon, see Gransden 1996.

39 Roger of Wendover, *Flores Historiarum*: edition in Coxe 1841–2; English translation in Giles 1849. Selected translations in Anderson 1908. Other English texts of this period, such as Ranulf Higden's *Polychronicon* and the *Chronicle of Crowland*, are not cited in the following chapters.

40 The late Geoffrey Barrow considered that 'the identity of Cumbria or the larger Strathclyde was becoming forgotten' by c.1150 (Barrow 1960, 38).

41 On the *Vita Kentigerni* of Jocelin of Furness see Macquarrie 1986, Macquarrie 1997a, 117–44 and Birkett 2010.

42 *Y Gododdin*, stanza B1/A78: see Dunshea 2014.

43 *AU*: Mac Airt and Mac Niocaill 1983; *AT*: Stokes 1895. Selected translations from both sets of annals appear in Anderson 1922.

44 Dumville 1982; Mac Airt and Mac Niocaill 1983; Dumville 1985; Evans 2010.

45 *AClon*: Murphy 1896. Selected translations in Anderson 1922.

46 *AFM*: O'Donovan 1856. Selected translations in Anderson 1922.

47 *Annals of Inisfallen*. Mac Airt 1951: *FAI*: Radner 1978.

48 Radner 1978, xix–xxi. Wainwright (1959, 1956) regarded *FAI* as 'an Irish source which preserves much interesting information in an unconvincing setting'.

49 *CKA*: Hudson 1998.

50 Dumville 2000; Woolf 2007a, 88–93.

51 *Prophecy of Berchan*; edition and translation in Hudson 1996.

52 On the historical value of this poetry, see the papers in Woolf 2013.

53 Gruffydd 1990.

54 *Annales Cambriae*: edition and translation in Morris 1980. See also Dumville 2002 and Hughes 1973.

55 *Historia Brittonum*: edition and translation in Morris 1980. See also Dumville 1986.

56 On the Welsh pedigrees, see Bartrum 1966. Rhun's pedigree is shown in the Genealogies section above and is discussed in Miller 1976. See also Chapter 2.

57 On hagiography in general, see Heffernan 1992. On the hagiography of medieval Scotland, see Macquarrie 1997a, 1–14.

58 Macquarrie 1997a, 117–44; Birkett 2010, 171–99.

59 Macquarrie 1997a, 199–210 and Dumville 2001. See also Downham 2003, 26–7.

60 *Aberdeen Breviary*: Bannatyne Club edition, 1854. For discussion, see Macquarrie 1997a, 6–10.

61 Ralph Glaber, *Historiarum Libri Quinque*, ed. J. France 1989.

62 Woolf 2007a, 277–85. 'In general, they provide an imaginative and deceptively detailed account of the past, invented to fit with earlier legends and skaldic poetry' (Downham 2003, 28).

63 Sawyer 1968.

Chapter 2

1 For a useful summary of the Roman conquest of Britain, see Breeze 1996.

2 On the Roman walls, see Breeze 1982.

3 On the North Britons in Roman times, see Clarkson 2010a, 9–16.

4 On the names and locations of the four groups, see Rivet and Smith 1979.

5 Watson 1926, 33.

6 Alcock and Alcock 1990, 101–3.

7 Alcock and Alcock 1990, 113–16.

8 The barbarian raids on Late Roman Britain are discussed in Esmonde-Cleary 1989.

9 For a recent discussion of these processes, see Halsall 2013, 253–99.

10 On the early Anglo-Saxon settlements, see Bassett 1989.

11 See Higham 2007b and Halsall 2013, 221–52.

12 Gildas, *de Excidio,* 27.

13 On the early Anglo-Saxon settlements in Yorkshire, see Higham 1993, 62–70. On the origins of Deira, see Higham 1993, 78–81.

14 On the *Historia Brittonum*, see Dumville 1986. On Bede, see Wallace-Hadrill 1988.

15 Higham 1993, 78–9.

16 *HB*, 61.

17 Andrew Breeze suggests that *Din Guoaroy* might mean 'theatre fort', in reference to a wooden auditorium like the one discovered at the Bernician royal settlement of Yeavering (Breeze 2009).

18 Driscoll and Forsyth 2004, 4.

19 See Watson 1926, 33, on the place-name.

20 Miller 1976.

21 *VC*, i, 15. On the two versions of Rhydderch's pedigree, see Miller 1976.

22 Jarman 1978.

23 *HB*, 63. For discussion, see Lovecy 1976.

24 Clarkson 2010a, 67–8.

25 On the location of Rheged, see Clarkson 2010a, 68–75.

26 Partick: Jocelin, *Vita Kentigerni,* 45. On the likelihood that Partick was an early royal estate, see Barrow 1999, 72. On the oldest burials at Govan, see Dalglish and Driscoll 2009, 35–6.

27 On the origins of Dál Riata, see Clarkson 2012a, 50–5.

28 Clarkson 2012b, 72.

29 On the Picts, see Clarkson 2010b.

30 For a useful discussion of Áedán's battles, see Macquarrie 1997a, 103–16. On the Miathi, see Clarkson 2012b, 63–8.

31 For the text of the poem and an English translation, see Fraser 2002, Appendix 6.

32 On Aethelfrith's conquests of British territory, see *HE*, i, 34.

33 See *HE*, iii, 1–2 on this sequence of events.

34 *AU* 638: *obsesio Etin*. For discussion, see Clarkson 2010a, 126–8.

35 *Maserfelth*: *HE*, iii, 9; Stancliffe 1995; Thacker 1995.

36 *HB*, 65; *HE*, i, 2; *HE*, iii, 24; Fraser 2008.

37 *AU* 642. For a discussion of this battle, see Clarkson 2010a, 133–8.

38 *AU* 643.

39 On the extent of Oswiu's hegemony, see Clarkson 2010a, 143.

40 Fraser 2002, 22.

41 *HE*, v, 23.

42 Fraser 2005, 108; Clarkson 2010a, 150–1.

43 Bede, *Continuatio*, s.a. 750.

44 *AU* 750: *bellum catohic*; *AC* 750: *gueith mocetauc*; Clarkson 2010a, 154.

45 *AU* 744.

46 *HRA* 756: *Anno ab incarnatione Dominica DCCLVI Eadberht rex xviii. anno regni sui, et Unust rex Pictorum, duxerunt exercitum ad urbem Alcwith. Ibique Brittones inde conditionem receperunt, prima die mensis Augusti. Decima autem die eiusdem mensis interiit exercitus poene omnis quem duxit de Ovania ad Niwanbirig, id est ad Novam Civitatem.* The English translation is from Forsyth 2000, 29, which is based on Anderson 1908, 57.

47 *HE*, i, 12. See also *HE*, i, 1: 'a very strongly fortified British town called *Alcluith*.'

48 Clancy 1998.

49 Dalglish and Driscoll 2009, 45.

50 Dalglish and Driscoll 2009, 37.

51 On the place-name, see Macquarrie 1997b; Clancy 1998; Koch 2000; Breeze 1999. On the sculpture see Ritchie 1994 and Ritchie 1999. On Govan's status as a royal and religious site, see Driscoll 1998, 2003 and 2004.

52 Kirby 1967, 60; Duncan 1975, 66; Fraser 2009, 317.

53 Bede, *Continuatio*, s.a. 761. The translation used here is by B. Colgrave in his edition (with R.A.B. Mynors) of Bede's *Ecclesiastical History of the English People* (Oxford, 1969).

54 *AU* 741: *percutio Dáil Riatai la hÓengus mac Forgusso*. The wider context of the *percutio* is discussed by Fraser 2009, 298–305. On the possible Gaelic origin of *HRA*'s obituary of Onuist, see Forsyth 2000, 27.

55 Clancy 1998.

56 Jackson 1955, 85: 'a crushing defeat inflicted on Eadbert by the Britons as he was retiring from Dumbarton.' See also Breeze 1999, 137: '. . . disaster overtook Eadbert's troops somewhere between Clyde and Tyne. Perhaps they were ambushed by British troops at an unknown place in the Border Hills . . .' It may be no more than coincidence that 10 August, a Tuesday in 756, is the feast-day of Blane (or Blaan), a saint known in later tradition as 'triumphant Blaan of the Britons'.

57 See Hodgson-Hinde 1868, 20, n4: 'Niwanbirig is no doubt Newburgh on the Tay'.

58 Newbrough was proposed by Kirby 1991, 150 and Breeze 1999, 134. More recently, Andrew Breeze has noted that the idea was doubted by the late Geoffrey Barrow (Breeze 2014, 191). On the place-name, see Ekwall 1960, 339: *Nieweburc* (1203). Its late attestation was noted by Breeze 1999, 134 and Woolf 2005, 38.

59 Woolf 2005, 39.

60 On troop numbers in this period see Clarkson 2001, 132–5.

61 Breeze 1999, 136: '. . . Ovania must be the place where Eadberht's troops began their withdrawal to their destination at "Newburgh"'.

62 Margary 1973, 470.

63 Suggested to me by Peta Glew, to whom I am grateful for discussion of her research on early medieval Cathcart.

Chapter 3

1 Portland: *ASC* 789; Lindisfarne: *ASC* 793; Monkwearmouth-Jarrow: *ASC* 794.

2 Iona: *AU* 795. The raids on Ireland are discussed in Woolf 2007a, 45–7.

3 *ASC* 865.

4 *ASC* 879.

5 Fraser 2005.

6 *AU* 839. On Cináed mac Ailpín, see Woolf 2007a, 93-106.

7 *AU* 870: *Obsesio Ailech Cluathe a Norddmannis, .i. Amlaiph & Imhar, duo reges Norddmannorum obsederunt arcem illum & distruxerunt in fine .iiii. mensium arcem & predauerunt.*

8 See Downham 2007 on the Dublin Norse in this period.

9 Clarkson 2010a, 160.

10 *AU* 872: *Artghal, rex Britanorum Sratha Cluade, consilio Custantini filii Cináedho occisus est.*

11 Clancy 2006.

12 See the papers in Ritchie 1994.

13 Ritchie 1999, 10. For a detailed study of the Govan Sarcophagus, see Spearman 1994.

14 Partick: *VK: Pertnech.* For discussion, see Dalglish and Driscoll 2009, 47–8.

15 Dalglish and Driscoll 2009, 40–5.

16 On *thing*-sites, see Darville 2004 and Owen 2013.

17 Woolf 2007a, 110.

18 Woolf 2007a, 111.

19 Hudson 1994, 38.

20 Woolf 2007a, 125–6.

21 *Prophecy of Berchan*, ed. Hudson, 84: *cath Luaire, for ri m-Bretan m-bratuaine.*

22 Carlowrie was suggested by Skene 1867, cxxxv.

23 For discussion, see Clarkson 2010a, 165.

24 The Hebridean sites are Dun Guaidhre on Mull (recorded as 'Dun Guaire' in 1878) and Dun Guaidhre on Islay. It should be noted that Dun Guaidhre might mean 'goat-fort' rather than 'fort of Guaire' (Gough-Cooper 2001).

25 *ASC* 875: *Her for se here from Hreopedune, & Healfdene for mid sumum þam here on Norþhymbre. & nam wintersetl be Tinan þære ea, & se here þæt lond geeode. & oft Hergade on Peohtas, & on Straecledwalas* ('The army went from Repton, and Halfdan went with part of the army into Northumbria and set up winter quarters by the River Tyne, and the army conquered the land and they often ravaged among the Picts and the Strathclyde Welsh'). Aethelweard's account of these events refers to the Strathclyders as *Cumbrenses* (Aethelweard, *Chronicon*, ed. Campbell, 41).

26 Clarkson 2010a, 161.

27 Woolf 2007a, 117–21; Hudson 1994, 55–7.

28 *Prophecy of Berchan*, ed. Hudson, 85: *an Britt a Cluaide, mac mna a Dhun Guaire.*
29 *AU* 889.
30 Hudson 1994, 57–8; Woolf 2007a, 155–6.

Chapter 4

1 On Alfred's and Edward's campaigns, see, respectively, Abels 1998 and Foot 2011, 12–17.
2 Wainwright 1959, 54.
3 *AU* 902.
4 Downham 2007, 84–5.
5 On Ingimund, see Wainwright 1948.
6 Downham 2007, 30.
7 Downham 2007, 31.
8 *FAI* 918: *Do rigne Edeldrída tría na gliocas féin sidh fria Fiora Alban, & re Breathnuibh, gibé tan tiugfáidís an cineadh cédna da h-ionsoighidh-si, gur ro eirghidis sin do congnamh lé. Damadh chuca-somh nó tháosdaois, gur ro eirgeadh-si leo-sumh. Céin ro bhás ime sin, ro lingsiot Fir Alban & Breatan fo bhailibh na Lochlannach, ra mhilliod & rá airgsiod íad. Tainig rí Lochlannach iar t-tain, & ra airg Sraith Cluaidhe, & ra airg an tír. Acht ní ro cumaing namaid do Sraith Chluaidhe.* Some scholars have wondered if this is fiction rather than history (e.g. Davidson 2001, 203; Downham 2007, 95 nn198 and 164), but there seems no compelling reason to doubt that such an alliance or treaty actually happened.
9 Wainwright 1959, 65.
10 Note also the suggestion by Collingwood (1920) that the kingdom of Strathclyde may have extended as far south as the Mersey in Aethelflaed's time. This seems very unlikely.
11 *CKA: Doneualdus rex Britanniorum et Dunenaldus filius Ede rex elig.*
12 Anderson 1922, 445–6.
13 Hudson 1988.
14 *AU* 915: *Domnall m. Aedho, ri Ailigh, uerno equinoctio in penitentia moritur.*
15 Jackson 1963.
16 e.g. Bispham in Amounderness, where the Anglo-Norse hybrid *Biscopheyma* supplanted an earlier English name *Biscopham* after 1086 (Watson 2011, 136). See also O'Sullivan 1984, 151.
17 Fellows-Jensen 1985, 80–1. See also Edmonds 2014 for a recent study of cultural interaction in the Furness Peninsula (I am grateful to Daniel Elsworth for this reference).
18 Higham 1986, 323.
19 Jackson 1963, 83; Smyth 1984, 227–8.
20 On these names, see Armstrong (1952, xxi), Jackson (1963, 82–3) and Higham (1986, 318).
21 An alternative view, which sees all Cumbric names south of the Solway as pre-English survivals, is not widely held. Its case is set out in Phythian-Adams 1996, 77–87 and Todd 2005, 96–7.
22 Collingwood 1920, 58; Jackson 1955, 86; Wilson 1966, 73–4; O'Sullivan 1984, 144; Higham 1985, 39–42; Breeze 2006, 331; Downham 2007, 161; Charles-Edwards 2013, 570.
23 Phythian-Adams 1996, 77–87; Todd 2005, 96–7.
24 Paterson *et al.* (2014). I am grateful to Diane McIlmoyle for this reference.
25 Higham 1986, 321.

26 Collingwood 1923, 127; Higham 1986, 320.

27 *HSC*, 21 (Tilred) and 22 (Alfred). See also Higham 1986, 322 and Woolf 2007a, 143.

28 Jackson 1958, 316. Phythian-Adams 1996, 72–3. On the date of the Kentigern dedications, see also Davies 2009, 75–83.

29 *AU* 918.

30 Woolf 2007a, 142.

31 *HSC*, 22. A second mention of the same battle in *HSC* (Chap. 24) has led to an erroneous belief that there were two separate battles (Wainwright 1950). See Downham 2007, 91–5 for a useful explanation of how this arose.

32 Rollason 2003, 213.

33 *ASC* 918.

34 *HRA* 919. Some versions of *ASC*, evidently drawing on Mercian tradition, assert that the people of York (i.e. the Northumbrians) submitted to Aethelflaed shortly before her death in June 918, but the political context is unclear (see Wainwright 1959, 65).

35 *ASC* 919.

36 *ASC* 920: *Her on þysum gere foran to middum sumera for Eadweard cyning mid fierde to Snotingaham, & het gewyrcan þa burg on suþhealfe þære eas, ongean þa oþre, & þa brycge ofer Treontan betwix þam twam burgum; & for þa þonan on Peaclond to Badecanwiellon, & het gewyrcan ane burg þær on neaweste, & gemannian; & hine geces þa to fæder & to hlaforde Scotta cyning & eall Scotta þeod; & Rægnald, & Eadulfes suna, & ealle þa þe on Norþhymbrum bugeaþ, ægþer ge Englisce, ge Denisce, ge Norþmen, ge oþre; & eac Stræcledweala cyning, & ealle Stræcledwealas.*

37 Davidson 2001; Downham 2007, 97.

38 Smyth 1984, 228: Clarkson 2001, 202–5.

39 Davidson 2001, 203; Rollason 2003, 262.

40 Alternatively, the Strathclyde attendee may have been Dyfnwal himself (Clarkson 2010a, 174).

41 Higham 1993, 188.

Chapter 5

1 *ASC* 924. This chapter has benefited from Kevin Halloran's comments on a draft version.

2 *ASC* 926.

3 *ASC* 927.

4 William of Malmesbury, i, 147.

5 *ASC* 927: *Her oðeowdon fyrena leoman on norðdæle þære lyfte. & Sihtric acwæl, & Æþelstan cyning feng to Norðhymbra rice. & ealle þa cyngas þe on þyssum iglande wæron he gewylde, ærest Huwal Westwala cyning, & Cosstantin Scotta cyning, & Uwen Wenta cyning, & Ealdred Ealdulfing from Bebbanbyrig, & mid wedde & mid aþum friþ gefæstnodon on þære stowe þe genemned is æt Eamotum on .iiii. Idus Iulii, & ælc deofolgeld tocwædon, & syþþam mid sibbe tocyrdon.*

6 Stenton 1971, 332; Woolf 2007a, 151–2.

7 *ASC* 927. Foot 2011, 163–4.

8 Foot 2011, 162 n15; Woolf 2007a, 151.

9 Downham 2007, 101.

10 Halloran 2011.

11 Woolf 2007a, 152.

12 *Dacor*: William of Malmesbury, i, 147. Ekwall (1960, 155) suggested that the meeting took place at the junction of the Dacre Beck and River Eamont.

13 The case for Brougham was proposed by Lapidge 1981, 91 n140.

14 Woolf 2007a, 158.

15 Sawyer 1968, S407.

16 Downham 2007, 103.

17 *ASC* 934.

18 *AClon* 928 (for 934).

19 Woolf 2007a, 164.

20 *HRA* 934: *Scotiam usque Dunfoeder et Wertermorum terrestri exercitu vastavit, navali vero usque Catenes depopulatus est.*

21 On the identification of Fortriu, see Woolf 2006.

22 Sawyer 1968, S426.

23 *HDE* 934; William of Malmesbury, i, 147.

24 John of Worcester, *Chronicon*, 388. See also Hill (2004), 127. In an unpublished paper ('The Invasion of Scotland, 934') Kevin Halloran takes a different view: 'There is no convincing evidence that Causantin had ever given his word to Athelstan let alone broken it in 934.'

25 Kapelle 1979, 36.

26 Sawyer 1968, S407.

27 The charters witnessed by Owain are S1792 (Cirencester, 935) and S435 (Dorchester, Dorset, 21 December 935). See Sawyer 1968.

28 Woolf 2007a, 166–7.

29 Downham 2007, 104.

30 John of Worcester (*Chronicon*, 392) describes Constantin as Anlaf's father-in-law.

31 On the attendance of the Welsh kings at the English court in this period, see Halloran 2011.

32 *AU* 937: *Bellum ingens lacrimabile atque horribile inter Saxones atque Norddmannos crudeliter gestum est, in quo plurima milia Nordmannorum que non numerata sunt, ceciderunt, sed rex cum paucis euassit, .i. Amlaiph. Ex altera autem parte multitudo Saxonum cecidit. Adalstan autem, rex Saxonum, magna uictoria ditatus est.*

33 Text based on Murphy's edition (1896, 150–1). Anlaf Guthfrithsson ('Awley McGodfrey') is the only identifiable figure in the list of names. For the other names, I have not followed the identifications suggested in Livingston 2011a, 153.

34 The translation here is based on Anderson 1908, 70–1 and Livingston 2011a, 55.

35 *CKA: et bellum Duinbrunde in xxxiiii eius anno ubi cecidit filius Constantini.*

36 On the matter of Strathclyde's involvement in the battle, see Downham 2007, 165–6.

37 *ASC* 937.

38 Livingston 2011b, 19.

39 Paul Cavill sees *dinges mere* as a place-name meaning 'wetland of the *thing*', where *thing* is a Norse word for assembly or parliament (Cavill 2011, 337; Cavill, Harding and Jesch 2004). Andrew Breeze (2014) thinks that *dinges mere* might not be a place-name at all, but an error for *dingles mere* ('sea of the abyss').

40 Aethelweard erroneously dates the battle to 939.

41 John of Worcester, *Chronicon*, 392. The error was noted long ago by A.O. Anderson (2008, 69, n3).

42 River Browney: Breeze 2014, 191. Brinsworth: Wood 1980 (although see Wood 2013 for his more recent argument in favour of a site on the River Went, south of Pontefract).

43 On the case for Bromborough, see Higham 1997 and Cavill 2008. The etymological case has recently been restated (Cavill 2011), but note Halloran's important observation: 'It is sometimes wrongly assumed that there exists a recorded OE form *Brunanburh* for Bromborough' (2010, 249).

44 Woolf 2007a, 171.

45 On the lack of evidence for Lancashire estates, see Foot 2011, 177. Against this we may note that Amounderness, presented by Athelstan to the archbishop of York as a royal gift, can hardly have been an unproductive wasteland. See Abels 1997 on the provisioning role of West Saxon fortresses and Higham 1988, 213, on the presumed *burh* at Penwortham.

46 Halloran 2005, 139.

47 On the case for Burnswark, see Halloran 2005 and 2010. Halloran (2005, 143) argues that the coalition may have raided in Athelstan's lands before retreating to a defensive position beyond the Solway Firth, thus drawing the English forces northward.

48 On Bruneberh, see Flaxington 2001, 30. Recorded forms of the name include *Bronneberh* (1253) and *Bruneberh* (c.1270). In the case of Bourne Hill, attention tends to focus on the name of the nearby settlement of Bourne which was recorded as *Brune* in 1086 (Ekwall 1922, 157). Mention can be made here of Broom Hill, a possible Bronze Age tumulus on the north-west edge of Garstang, which has also been linked to the battle of Brunanburh. On the landscape of the Fylde in the tenth century, see Watson 2011.

49 The case for the River Brun was proposed by Wilkinson (1857).

50 Halloran 2005, 135-6.

51 Ekwall 1922, 164.

52 The survey is described in the 'Digs' section of the Wyre Archaeology website: http://www.wyrearchaeology.org.uk [last verified 14 July 2014].

53 Taylor 1902, 200.

54 Gelling and Cole 2000, 164.

55 Michael Livingston overstated the case for Bromborough when he wrote that it is currently 'so firm that many scholars are engaged not with the question of whether Brunanburh occurred on the Wirral, but where on the peninsula it took place' (Livingston 2011b, 19).

56 Halloran 2005 is one of the few studies to consider the part played by Constantin and Owain and the logistical issues they faced in 937.

57 Downham 2007, 105; Woolf 2007a, 174.

58 Foot 2011, 155.

59 *ASC* 939.

60 Downham 2007, 110.

61 *AClon: Awley McGodfrey king of Danes died.*

62 *ASC* 'D': 'In this year the Northumbrians abandoned their allegiance, and chose Anlaf of Ireland for their king.' On the dating of this sequence of events, see Downham 2003, 33–4.

63 Downham 2007, 108–11.

64 On the relationship between *Armes Prydein Vawr* and the battle of Brunanburh, see Bollard and Haycock 2011, 245–62. Andrew Breeze (2011) suggests 940 as the date of composition.

Chapter 6

1 *AFM* 940. Downham 2007, 244.

2 *Life of St Cathroe*, ed. Colgan.

3 Macquarrie 1997a, 201; Watson 1926, 310–12.

4 Macquarrie 1997a, 203–4.

5 Anderson 1922, 441; Busse 2006.

6 *Life of St Cathroe: usque Loidam civitatem, quae est confinium Normannorum atque Cumbrorum; ibique excipitur a quodam viro nobili Gunderico, a quo perducitur ad regem Erichium in Euroacum urbem: qui scilicet rex habebat conjugem, ipsius domini Kaddroe propinquam.*

7 The name Gunderic was borne by two fifth-century kings, respectively of the Vandals and Burgundians.

8 Leeds: *Loidis: HE*, ii, 14. On the identification of Loida with Leeds, see Anderson 1922, 441 and Downham 2007, 160. Carlisle has also been suggested (McCarthy 1993).

9 *Loedria* (c.1092–5) in a charter of King William Rufus. Later forms include *Lauuedra* (1174), *Lodre* (1197) and *Lauder* (c.1180). The origin of the name may be Cumbric (Phythian-Adams 1996, 100).

10 Phythian-Adams 1996, 98.

11 Phythian-Adams 1996, 98, 150.

12 On the term *civitas*, see Niermeyer 1976.

13 Downham 2007, 112–15.

14 Downham 2004; Downham 2007, 116–19.

15 But note Halloran's suggestion that Anlaf Sihtricsson, not Anlaf Guthfrithsson, was the king of Northumbria between 939 and 941 (Halloran 2013).

16 Macquarrie 1997a, 205. On the chronological problem, see also Downham 2003, 27.

17 *ASC* 943.

18 *ASC* 945: *Her Eadmund cyning oferhergode eal Cumbra land & hit let to eal Malculme Scotta cyninge on þæt gerad þæt he wære his midwyrhta ægþer ge on sæ ge on lande.* Old English *midwyrhta* has the literal meaning 'together-worker'.

19 *AC* 946 (for 945): *Strat Clut vastata est a Saxonibus.*

20 Henry of Huntingdon: *Sequenti vero anno totam Cumberland, quia gentem provinciae illius perfidam et legibus insolitam ad plenum domare nequibat, praedavit et contrivit; et commendavit eam Malculmo regi Scotiae hoc pacto, quod in auxilio sibi foret terra et mari.*

21 Roger of Wendover: *Eodem anno rex Eadmundus, adjutorio Leolini regis Demetiae fretus, Cumbriam totam cunctis opibus spoliavit, ac duobus filiis Dunmail, ejusdem provinciae regis, oculorum luce privatis, regnum illud Malcolmo, Scotorum regi, de se tenendum concessit, ut aquilonales Angliae partes terra marique ab hostium adventantium incursione tueretur.*

22 Woolf 2007a, 183.

23 Ritual blinding of kings and princes is also recorded from tenth-century Ireland: 'Áed grandson of Máel Sechnaill was blinded by his kinsman, Donnchad, king of Mide' (*AU*, 919). See also Boyle 2006 for an eleventh-century example from England.

24 Anderson 1922, 449 n3.

25 Sir John's amended version, quoted by A.O. Anderson, is *o'r Bryttaniaid ac a berthynai ydynt.*

26 *AU* 945.

27 Woolf 2007a, 183.

28 *HSC* 945. The translation here is from Anderson 1908, 73.

29 Kapelle 1979, 247 n34.

30 The ravaging of 945 'ensured that Strathclyde would be too weak to support a Viking campaign against Northumbria' (Downham 2007, 166) but the ensuing period of Scottish

dominance was brief and 'the native line of Cumbrian kings' soon regained control (Kapelle 1979, 36). On the Dunmail folklore, see below.

31 *ASC* 946.

32 *ASC* 947.

33 *ASC* 948.

34 *ASC* 949. Halloran 2013.

35 Woolf 2007a, 187.

36 *CKA*: 'In the 7th year of his reign he plundered the English as far as the River Tees and carried off many people and many droves of cattle . . .'

37 *AU* 952: *Cath for Firu Alban & Bretnu & Saxonu ria Gallaibh.*

38 Woolf 2007a, 188.

39 Useful discussions can be found in Downham 2003, 26–32 and Downham 2007, 115–20.

40 *ASC* 952.

41 Woolf 2007a, 189.

42 Downham 2007, 155.

43 Clarkson 2010a, 181.

44 *ASC* 952.

45 *ASC* 954.

46 Downham 2007, 121.

47 Woolf 2007a, 190.

48 For discussion of the name Ildulb, see Woolf 2007a, 192-3 and Hudson 1994, 89.

49 Woolf 2007a, 194.

50 John of Worcester, *Chronicon,* 406.

51 *Prophecy of Berchan,* ed. Hudson, 88.

52 Hudson 1994, 89.

53 Woolf 2007a, 194–5.

54 Late Cumbric names in Lothian include Loquhariot (Breeze 2002, 106) and *Lyntun Ruderic* (Woolf 2007a, 205 n40).

55 On the early history of Edinburgh Castle Rock, see Driscoll and Yeoman 1997.

Chapter 7

1 *ASC* 959.

2 *AU* 966.

3 Charter S779; summary in Sawyer 1968. Text and translation in Robertson 1939, 98–103 (for discussion, see 345–7). See also Charles-Edwards 2013, 544. In the charter, Edgar says that God 'has now reduced beneath my sway Scots and Cumbrians and likewise Britons [i.e. Welsh] and all that this island contains'.

4 Macquarrie 1993, 16.

5 *AU* 971: *Culen m. Illuilb, ri Alban, do marbad do Bretnaibh i r-roi catha* ('Cuilén son of Ildulb, king of Alba, was killed by the Britons in a battle-rout').

6 Abington: Anderson 1922, 476. Abingdon: Gelling 1957, 62.

7 An example of a late Cumbric place-name in Lothian is *Lyntun Ruderic,* now West Linton, where a Cumbric personal name *Ruderic* (Rhydderch) has been attached to an Old English name, probably indicating 'a settlement founded by Northumbrians which came into the hands of a Strathclyder' (Woolf 2007a, 205).

8 Woolf 2007a, 209.

9 On the etymology of Loquhariot, see Breeze 2002. On the spelling Uacoruar in the manuscript of *CKA*, see Anderson 1973.

10 Woolf 2007a, 210; Hudson 1994, 95–6.

11 *ASC* 973: *Her wæs Eadgar æþeling gehalgod to cyninge on Pentecostenes mæssedæg on .v. Idus Maias, þy .xiii. geare þe he on rice feng, æt Haþabaþum, & he wæs þa ane wana .xxx. wintre. & sona æfter þam se cyning gelædde ealle his scipfyrde to Leiceastre, & þær him comon ongean .vi. cyningas, & ealle wið hine getreowsodon þæt hi woldon efenwyrhtan beon on sæ & on lande.* This event is also reported in *ASC* 'E'. The Old English word *atheling* means 'prince'.

12 John of Worcester, *Chronicon*, 422.

13 Charles-Edwards 2013, 545.

14 *Brut y Tywysogion*, s.a. 971 and 972.

15 On the identification of Maccus, see Thornton 1997.

16 Thornton 2001 66–7; Woolf 2007a, 208; Downham 2007, 124.

17 Barrow 2001. Matthews 2009, 73: 'the consensus now is that the "regatta" did take place even if some of the details may have been added'.

18 Smyth 1984, 228; Thornton 2001, 78–9; Breeze 2007, 157; Williams 2004; Charles-Edwards 2013, 545.

19 *AU* 975: *Domnall m. Eogain, ri Bretan, i n-ailithri, Foghartach, abbas Daire, mortui sunt.* ('Dyfnwal son of Owain, king of the Britons, while on pilgrimage, and Fogartach, abbot of Daire, both died'); *Brut y Tywysogion*: 'and then died Edgar, king of England; and Dyfnwallawn, king of Strathclyde, went to Rome'.

20 Stancliffe 1983.

21 *ASC* 978.

22 *ASC* 991.

23 *AC* 995; Downham 2007, 131.

24 *AU* 997: *Máel Coluim m. Domnaill, ri Bretan Tuaiscirt, moritur* ('Máel Coluim son of Dyfnwal, king of the North Britons, dies').

25 *AC* (Version B) s.a. 1015: *Owinus filius Dunawal occisus est* ('Owain son of Dyfnwal was killed').

26 Broun 2004, 128 n66.

27 *ASC* 1000: *Her on þissum geare se cyning ferde into Cumberlande & swiðe neah eall forhergode, & his scypu wendon ut abutan Lægceaster, & sceoldon cuman ongean hyne, ac hi ne meahton, þa gehergodon hi Monige.*

28 Woolf 2007a, 222.

29 Hudson 1994,106. It remains a possibility that the original targets included the Norse of Man and the Isles as well as the Cumbrians of Strathclyde: 'both kingdoms had long proved troublesome to the English' (Williams 2003, 52).

30 Woolf 2007a, 222–3; Clarkson 2010a, 187–8.

31 Henry of Huntingdon, iv, 35: 'Therefore King Aethelred went with a very powerful army into Cumberland, which was the chief abode of the Danes. And he conquered the Danes in a very great battle, and raided and wasted almost the whole of Cumberland.'

32 Bailey 1994; Macquarrie 2006.

33 Driscoll, O'Grady and Forsyth 2005.

34 Craig 1991.

35 Crawford 1994; Ritchie 2004; Crawford 2005.

36 Davies 1994.

37 Collingwood 1923.

38 Collingwood 1920.

39 Hutchinson 1794, 328–34.

40 Clare 1979.

Chapter 8

1 *AU* 1005.

2 *ASC* 1013.

3 *ASC* 1016.

4 Kapelle 1979, 15–16.

5 *AU* 1002.

6 *Cogadh Gaedhel re Gallaibh*, ed. Todd, 136–7.

7 Anderson 1922, 525 n.3.

8 Hudson 1994, 114.

9 *Cogadh Gaedhel re Gallaibh*, ed. Todd, clix n1.

10 *De Obsessione Dunelmi*, ed. Arnold, 215–16. See also Morris 1992.

11 *AU* 1006.

12 Woolf 2007a, 236; Broun 2004, 128 n66 and 133–5.

13 *HDE*, ed. Arnold, 84.

14 *HRA* 1018: *Ingens bellum apud Carrum gestum est inter Scottos et Anglos, inter Huctredum filium Waldef comitem Northymbrorum, et Malcolmum filium Cyneth regem Scottorum. Cum quo fuit in bello Eugenius Calvus rex Lutinensium.*

15 *Clutenses*: Ritson 1828, 185. *Clutienses*: Woolf 2010, 235. Asser's *Stratcluttenses* is in Chap. 47 of his *Life of Alfred*.

16 Graham 1976.

17 *ASC* 1016.

18 Kapelle 1979, 22; Fletcher 2002, 111.

19 Stenton 1970, 412.

20 See note 13 above.

21 e.g. AU 1018: 'A comet appeared this year for the space of a fortnight in the autumn season.'

22 Kronk 1999, 168–70.

23 John of Worcester, *Chronicon*, 494.

24 Duncan 1976, 27–8.

25 Anderson 1960, 104.

26 Kapelle 1979, 243 n49.

27 Fletcher 2002, 113.

28 Hudson 1992, 358.

29 Anderson 1960, 111; Meehan 1976, 5.

30 Anderson 1960, 110; Anderson 1963, 7.

31 Woolf 2007a, 237; Anderson 1960, 111.

32 Woolf 2007a, 238. On Caddonlee as a muster-site in the twelfth and thirteenth centuries, see Barrow 2006, 88.

33 A march-rate of twenty to twenty-five miles per day is a realistic estimate for armies of this period (Clarkson 2001, 143–6; Nesbitt 1963).

34 Macquarrie 1993, 17: 'It is a possible inference that he [Owain the Bald] was killed at Carham.' On the *AC* entry for 1015, see Broun 2004, 128 n66.

35 Meehan 1976.

36 Kapelle 1979, 24.

37 Meehan 1976, 14.

38 Hudson 1992, 358.

39 Oram 2008, 63.

40 Broun 2004, 139 n117. Kapelle (1979, 266–7 n37) suggests that Teviotdale had already fallen to Strathclyde in the tenth century.

41 Ralph Glaber, ii, 3 (ed. J. France 1989, 54–6). See also Fletcher 2002, 133.

42 *ASC*, 1031.

43 Hudson 1994, 118; Downham 2007, 171.

44 Woolf 2007a, 248.

45 Duncan 2002, 29.

46 Hudson 1992.

47 John of Fordun, *Chronica*, iv, 41.

48 *AT* 1030: *Orguin Bretan o Saxanaib & o Gallaib Atha Cliath.*

49 Broun 2004, 137.

50 Fletcher 2002, 119.

51 Kapelle 1979, 25.

Chapter 9

1 Anderson 1922, 583.

2 *ASC* 1035; Kapelle 1979, 25.

3 Fletcher 2002, 137.

4 Woolf 2007a, 254.

5 *AU* 1034.

6 Downham 2007, 17; Woolf 2007a, 253 n45.

7 On the medieval lords of Galloway, see Oram 2001.

8 Broun 2004, 136.

9 On the identity of Suibhne, see Woolf 2007a, 253–4.

10 Broun 2004, 136.

11 *ASC* 'D' 1054.

12 John of Worcester, Chronicon, 574: *et Malcolmum, regis Cumbrorum filium, ut rex jusserat, regem constituit.*

13 Kapelle 1979, 29.

14 Duncan 2002, 41; Broun 2004, 134; Clancy 2006, 1820.

15 Duncan 2002, 40.

16 Broun 2004, 134.

17 Duncan 2002, 40.

18 See, for example, William Kapelle who, while noting that 'king of the Cumbrians' was for Donnchad 'an unlikely title', nevertheless suggested that it 'probably reflects what seemed important about him to the English' (1979, 43).

19 Duncan 2002, 41; Oram 2008, 20.

20 See Chapter 3 above.

21 Edmonds 2009, 53.

22 The bishops are mentioned by Hugh the Chanter in his *History of the Church of York* (c.1130). See Durkan 1999, 89. On their possible connection with Hoddom, see Scott 1991, 40. [23]

23 Driscoll 2002, 85–7; Woolf 2007a, 263 n65.

24 The fate of Máel Coluim is discussed in Clarkson 2013.

25 *ASC* 'E' 1093.

26 *HRA: enim eo tempore Cumbreland sub regis Malcolmi dominio, non jure possessa sed violenter subjugata.*

27 Woolf 2007a, 270.

28 Broun 2004, 138 n116.

29 Woolf 2007a, 271.

30 Broun 2004, 138.

31 Duncan 2002, 44–5.

32 Kapelle 1979, 124.

33 Kirby 1962, 93; Phythian-Adams 1996, 175–81.

34 Harmer 1952, 419–22; Kapelle 1979, 44; O'Sullivan 1984, 144.

35 Fletcher 2002, 147. See also Edmonds 2009, 53–4.

36 English translation based on Armstrong 1952, xxix. For detailed discussion of the Writ, see Harmer 1952, 419–24 and 531–6.

37 Broun 2004, 139; Charles-Edwards 2013, 577.

38 Edmonds 2009.

39 Broun 2004, 140.

Chapter 10

1   Phythian-Adams 1996, 149.

2   Phythian-Adams 1996, 150.

3   For an overview of the Norman Conquest, see Morris 2012.

4   Kapelle 1979, 142–5.

5   *ASC* 1091.

6   *ASC* 'E' 1092: *On þisum geare se cyng Willelm mid mycelre fyrde ferde norð to Cardeol. & þa burh geæðstaþelede. & þone castel arerde. & Dolfin utadraf þe æror þær þes landes weold. & þone castel mid his mannan gesette. & syððan hider suð gewænde. & mycele mænige Eyrlisces folces mid wifa & mid orfe þyder sænde. þær to wunigenne þæt land to tilianne.*

7   e.g., Armstrong 1952, xxxi.

8   Oram 2008, 35. For a different view, see Kapelle 1979, 150–2.

9   Kapelle 1979, 151. Dolfin is a name of Scandinavian origin (*Dolgfinnr*).

10 Phythian-Adams 1996, 150.

11 Armstrong 1952, xxxiv–xxxv. For a useful study of Anglo-Norman policy in the lands at the eastern end of the Solway Firth, see Scott 1997.

12 Armstrong 1952, xxxv.

13 Oram 2008, 122.

14 Oram 2008, 202.

15 Armstrong 1952, xxxv. On medieval Cumberland (the county), see Winchester 1987.

16 Oram 2008, 60.

17 Oram 2008, 60.

18 Oram 2008, 62.

19 Oram 2008, 64.

20 Lawrie 1905, 46: *non vero toti Cumbrensi regione dominabatur.*

21 Oram 2008, 64.

22 Barrow 1999, no.14.

23 Oram 2008, 68.

24 Oram 2008, 66.

25 Broun 2004, 141.

26 Broun 2004, 139 n117. The claim by a thirteenth-century bishop of Glasgow that his diocese extended to the Rey (or Rere) Cross on Stainmore probably has no bearing on the extent of Strathclyde (Broun 2004, 173–80).

27 Wilson 1966, 90.

28 On the archaeology of Hoddom, see Lowe 2006.

29 Grant 2007.

30 Wilson 1966, 92.

31 Shead 1969, 223–4; Broun 2004, 119–20.

32 Hines 2001, 13, 27.

33 Cummertrees might mean 'confluence of turbulent water' (Breeze 2005, 91). Cumbernauld is probably 'confluence of brooks' (Watson 1926, 243).

34 Armstrong 1950, Part 1, 130.

BIBLIOGRAPHY

Part 1 Primary Sources: Editions and Translations

Aberdeen Breviary: Breviarium Aberdonense. Bannatyne Club edition (London, 1854)

AC Annales Cambriae (Welsh Annals). J. Morris (ed. and trans.) *Nennius: British History and the Welsh Annals* (Chichester, 1980)

ASC Anglo-Saxon Chronicle. A. Savage (ed.) *The Anglo-Saxon Chronicles* (Godalming, 1997)

AClon Annals of Clonmacnoise. D. Murphy (ed.) *The Annals of Clonmacnoise* (Dublin, 1896). Reprinted by Llanerch Publishers in 1993

AFM Annals of the Four Masters. J. O'Donovan (ed.) *Annala Rioghachta Eireann: Annals of the Kingdom of Ireland, by the Four Masters, from the Earliest Period to the Year 1616*. 2nd edn. (Dublin, 1856)

Annals of Inisfallen. S. Mac Airt (ed. and trans.) *The Annals of Inisfallen (MS. Rawlinson B.503)* (Dublin, 1951)

AT Annals of Tigernach. W. Stokes (ed.) 'The Annals of Tigernach, 1 – the Fragment in Rawlinson B.502', *Revue Celtique* 16: 374–419. Selected English translations in A.O. Anderson (ed.) *Early Sources of Scottish History, AD 500 to 1286*. Vol. 1 (Edinburgh, 1922)

AU Annals of Ulster. S. Mac Airt and G. Mac Niocaill (eds and trans.) *The Annals of Ulster to AD 1131* (Dublin, 1983)

Aethelweard, *Chronicon*. A. Campbell (ed.) *The Chronicle of Aethelweard* (London, 1962).

Bede, *Continuatio*. English translation in J. McClure and R. Collins (eds) *Bede: The Ecclesiastical History of the English People* (Oxford, 1994)

Bede, *Historia Ecclesiastica Gentis Anglorum*. See *HE*

Berchan's Prophecy. B.T. Hudson (ed.) *The Prophecy of Berchan* (Westport, 1996)

Brut y Tywysogion. J. Williams ab Ithel (ed. and trans.) *Brut y Tywysogion or the Chronicle of the Princes* (London, 1860). Selected English translations in A.O. Anderson (ed.) *Early Sources of Scottish History, AD 500 to 1286*. Vol. 1 (Edinburgh, 1922)

CKA Chronicle of the Kings of Alba. W.F. Skene (ed.) *Chronicles of the Picts, Chronicles of the Scots, and Other Early Memorials of Scottish History* (Edinburgh, 1867). Selected English translations in A.O. Anderson (ed.) *Early Sources of Scottish History, AD 500 to 1286*. Vol. 1 (Edinburgh, 1922)

Cogadh Gaedhel re Gallaibh. J.H. Todd (ed.) *Cogadh Gaedhel re Gallaib – The War of the Gaedhil with the Gaill*. Rolls Series, 48 (London, 1867)

De Obsessione Dunelmi. T. Arnold (ed.) *Symeonis Monachi Opera Omnia*. Vol. 1 (London, 1882), 215–20.

FAI Fragmentary Annals of Ireland. J. Radner (ed. and trans.) *The Fragmentary Annals of Ireland* (Dublin, 1978)

Gildas, *De Excidio Britanniae*. M. Winterbottom (ed.) *Gildas: the Ruin of Britain and Other Works* (Chichester, 1978)

Henry of Huntingdon, *Historia Anglorum*. D. Greenway (ed.) *Historia Anglorum: History of the English People* (Oxford, 1996)

HB Historia Brittonum. J. Morris (ed. and trans.) *Nennius: British History and the Welsh Annals* (Chichester, 1980)

HDE Historia Dunelmensis ecclesiae. T. Arnold (ed.) *Symeonis Monachi Opera Omnia*. Vol. 1 (London, 1882). Selected English translations in A.O. Anderson (ed.) *Scottish Annals from English Chroniclers, AD 500 to 1286* (London, 1908). See also D. Rollason (ed.), *Libellus de exordio atque procursu istius, hoc est Dunhelmensis, ecclesie = Tract on the Origins and Progress of this the Church of Durham* (Oxford, 2000)

HE Bede, *Historia Ecclesiastica Gentis Anglorum*. J. McClure and R. Collins (eds) *Bede: the Ecclesiastical History of the English People* (Oxford, 1994)

HRA Historia Regum Anglorum. J.H. Hinde (ed.) *Symeonis Dunelmensis Opera et Collectanea* (Durham, 1868). English translation J. Stevenson (ed.) *Simeon of Durham: a History of the Kings of England* (London, 1858)

HSC Historia de Sancto Cuthberto. T. Johnson-South (ed. and trans.) *Historia de Sancto Cuthberto: a History of Saint Cuthbert and a Record of His Patrimony* (Cambridge, 2002)

John of Fordun, *Chronica Gentis Scotorum*. W.F. Skene (ed.) *John of Fordun's Chronicle of the Scottish Nation* (Edinburgh, 1871).

John of Worcester, *Chronicon*. R. Darlington and P. McGurk (eds) *The Chronicle of John of Worcester, Vol. 2: The Annals from 450 to 1066*. (Oxford, 1995) [with an English translation by J. Bray]

Life of St Cathroe. J. Colgan (ed.) *Acta Sanctorum Hiberniae*. Vol. 1 (Leuven, 1645). Partly reproduced in Skene (1867), 106–16. Selected English translations in A.O. Anderson (ed.) *Early Sources of Scottish History, AD 500 to 1286*. Vol. 1 (Edinburgh, 1922)

Ralph Glaber, *Historiarum Libri Quinque*: J. France (ed.) *Rodulfus Glaber Opera* (Oxford, 1989)

Registrum Episcopatus Glasguensis. C. Innes (ed.) *Registrum Episcopatus Glasguensis*. 2 vols. (Edinburgh, 1843)

Roger of Wendover, *Flores Historiarum*. H. Coxe (ed.) *Rogeri de Wendover, Chronica sive Flores Historiarum*. 4 vols. (London, 1841–2). English translation by J. Giles, *Roger of Wendover's Flowers of History*. 2 vols (London, 1849)

VC Adomnán, *Vita Sancti Columbae*. R. Sharpe (ed.) *Adomnán of Iona: Life of Saint Columba* (London, 1995)

VK Jocelin of Furness, *Vita Sancti Kentigerni* (Life of St Kentigern). A.P. Forbes (ed.) *The Historians of Scotland: V – Lives of St Ninian and St Kentigern* (Edinburgh, 1874)

William of Malmesbury, *Gesta Regum Anglorum*. R. Mynors, R. Thomson and M. Winterbottom (eds) *Gesta Regum Anglorum: the History of the English Kings*. 2 vols. (Oxford, 1998–9)

Part 2 Modern Scholarship

Abels, R. (1997) 'English Logistics and Military Administration, 871–1066: the Impact of the Viking Wars', pp. 257–65 in A.N. Jorgensen and B.L. Clausen (eds) *Military Aspects of Scandinavian Society in a European Perspective, AD 1–1300* (Copenhagen)

Abels, R. (1998) *Alfred the Great: War, Kingship and Culture in Anglo-Saxon England*. (London)

Alcock, L. and Alcock, E. (1990) 'Reconnaissance Excavations . . . 4: Excavations at Alt Clut, Clyde Rock, Strathclyde, 1974–5', *Proceedings of the Society of Antiquaries of Scotland* 120: 95–149

Anderson, A.O. (ed.) (1908) *Scottish Annals from English Chroniclers, AD 500 to 1286* (London)

Anderson, A.O. (ed.) (1922) *Early Sources of Scottish History, AD 500 to 1286*. Vol. 1 (Edinburgh)

Anderson, A.O. (1963) 'Anglo-Scottish Relations from Constantine II to William', *Scottish Historical Review* 42: 1–20

Anderson, M.O. (1960) 'Lothian and the Early Scottish Kings', *Scottish Historical Review* 39: 98–112

Anderson, M.O. (1973) *Kings and Kingship in Early Scotland* (Edinburgh)

Armstrong, A.M., Mawer, A., Stenton, F.M. and Dickins, B. (1950) *The Place-Names of Cumberland*. Parts 1 and 2 (Cambridge)

Armstrong, A.M., Mawer, A., Stenton, F.M. and Dickins, B. (1952) *The Place-Names of Cumberland*. Part 3 (Cambridge)

Bailey, R.N. (1994) 'Govan and Irish Sea Sculpture', pp. 113–22 in Ritchie (1994)

Barrow, G.W.S. (1960) (ed.) *The Acts of Malcolm IV, King of Scots 1153–65*. Regesta Regum Scottorum, vol. 1 (Edinburgh)

Barrow, G.W.S. (1999) (ed.) *The Charters of David I* (Woodbridge)

Barrow, G.W.S. (2006) *Robert Bruce and the Community of the Realm of Scotland* (Edinburgh)

Barrow, J. (2001) 'Chester's Earliest Regatta? Edgar's Dee-Rowing Revisited' *Early Medieval Europe* 10: 81–93

Bartrum, P.C. (ed.) (1966) *Early Welsh Genealogical Tracts* (Cardiff)

Bassett, S. (ed.) (1989) *The Origins of Anglo-Saxon Kingdoms* (Leicester)

Birkett, H. (2010) *The Saints' Lives of Jocelin of Furness: Hagiography, Patronage and Ecclesiastical Politics* (York)

Bollard, J.K. and Haycock, M. (2011) 'The Welsh Sources Pertaining to the Battle', pp. 245–68 in Livingston (ed.) (2011).

Boyle, E. (2006) 'A Welsh Record of an Anglo-Saxon Political Mutilation', *Anglo-Saxon England* 35: 245–9.

Breeze, A. (1999) 'Simeon of Durham's Annal for 756 and Govan, Scotland', *Nomina* 22: 133–7

Breeze, A. (2002) 'St Kentigern and Loquhariot, Lothian', *Innes Review* 54: 103–7

Breeze, A. (2005) 'Brittonic Place-Names from South-West Scotland – Part 6: Cummertrees, Beltrees, Trevercarcou' *Transactions of the Dumfriesshire & Galloway Natural History & Antiquarian Society* 79: 91–3

Breeze, A. (2006) 'Britons in the Barony of Gilsland, Cumbria', *Northern History* 43: 327–32

Breeze, A. (2009) 'Din Guoaroy: the Old Welsh Name for Bamburgh' *Archaeologia Aeliana,* 5th Series 38: 123–8

Breeze, A. (2011) 'Durham, Caithness, and *Armes Prydein*' *Northern History* 48: 147–52

Breeze, A. (2014) 'Review of *Wales and the Britons, 350–1064*, by T. Charles-Edwards', *Northern History* 51: 190–2

Breeze, D. (1982) *The Northern Frontiers of Roman Britain* (London)

Breeze, D. (1996) *Roman Scotland* (London)

Bromwich, R. (ed.) (1961) *Trioedd Ynys Prydein: the Welsh Triads* (Cardiff)

Brooke, D. (1991a) 'The Northumbrian Settlements in Galloway and Carrick: an Historical Assessment', *Proceedings of the Society of Antiquaries of Scotland* 121: 295–327

Brooke, D. (1991b) 'Gall-Gáidhil and Galloway', pp. 97–116 in R.D. Oram and G.P. Stell (eds) *Galloway: Land and Lordship* (Edinburgh)

Broun, D. (1997) 'The Birth of Scottish History', *Scottish Historical Review* 76: 2–22.

Broun, D. (2004) 'The Welsh Identity of the Kingdom of Strathclyde, c.900–1200', *Innes Review* 55: 111–80

Busse, P.E. (2006) 'Catroe/Cadroe', p.356 in J.T. Koch (ed.) *Celtic Culture: an Historical Encyclopedia*. Vol. 1 (Santa Barbara)

Cavill, P. (2008) 'The Site of the Battle of Brunanburh: Manuscripts and Maps, Grammar and Geography', pp. 303–19 in O. Padel and D. Parsons (eds) *A Commodity of Good Names: Essays in Honour of Margaret Gelling* (Donnington)

Cavill, P. (2011) 'The Place-Name Debate', pp. 327–49 in Livingston (2011a)

Cavill, P., Harding, S. and Jesch, J. (2004) 'Revisiting *Dingesmere*', *Journal of the English Place-Name Society* 36: 25–38

Charles-Edwards, T.M. (2013) *Wales and the Britons, 350–1064* (Oxford)

Clancy, T.O. (1998) 'Govan, the Name, Again', *Report of the Society of Friends of Govan Old* 8: 8–13

Clancy, T.O. (2006) 'Ystrad Clud', pp.1818–20 in J.T. Koch (ed.) *Celtic Culture: an Historical Encyclopedia*. Vol. 5 (Santa Barbara)

Clancy, T.O. (2008) 'The Gall-Ghaidheil and Galloway', *Journal of Scottish Name Studies* 2: 19–50

Clare, T. (1979) *Interim Report on Excavations at Castle Hewen 1978–79 and the Question of Arthur* (Kendal)

Clarkson, T. (2001) *Warfare in Early Historic Northern Britain*. Unpublished PhD thesis, University of Manchester.

Clarkson, T. (2010a) *The Men of the North: the Britons of Southern Scotland* (Edinburgh)

Clarkson, T. (2010b) *The Picts: a History* (Edinburgh)

Clarkson, T. (2012a) *The Makers of Scotland: Picts, Romans, Gaels and Vikings* (Edinburgh)

Clarkson, T. (2012b) *Columba* (Edinburgh)

Clarkson, T. (2013) 'The Last King of Strathclyde', *History Scotland* 13 (6) (Nov/Dec): 24–7

Collingwood, W.G. (1920) 'The Giant's Thumb', *Transactions of the Cumberland & Westmorland Antiquarian & Archaeological Society*, Second Series 20: 53–65

Collingwood, W.G. (1923) 'The Giant's Grave, Penrith', *Transactions of the Cumberland & Westmorland Antiquarian & Archaeological Society*, Second Series 23: 115–28

Craig, D. (1991) 'Pre-Norman Sculpture in Galloway: Some Territorial Implications', pp. 45–62 in R.D. Oram and G.P. Stell (eds) *Galloway: Land and Lordship* (Edinburgh)

Crawford, B.E. (1994) 'The Norse Background to the Govan Hogbacks', pp. 103–12 in Ritchie (1994).

Crawford, B.E. (2005) *The Govan Hogbacks and the Multi-Cultural Society of Tenth-Century Scotland*. Friends of Govan Old Lecture Series. (Govan)

Dalglish, C. and Driscoll, S.T. (2009) *Historic Govan: Archaeology and Development* (Edinburgh)

Darlington, R. and McGurk, P. (1982) 'The *Chronicon ex Chronicis* of Florence of Worcester and its Use of Sources for English History before 1066', *Anglo-Norman Studies* 5: 185–96.

Darville, T. (2004) 'Tynwald Hill and the "Things" of Power', pp. 217–32 in A. Pantos and S. Semple (eds) *Assembly Places and Practices in Medieval Europe* (Dublin)

Davidson, M.R. (2001) 'The (Non-)Submission of the Northern Kings in 920', pp. 200–11 in N.J. Higham and D.H. Hill (eds) *Edward the Elder, 899–924* (London)

Davies, J.R (2009) 'Bishop Kentigern among the Britons', pp. 67–99 in S. Boardman, J.R. Davies and E. Williamson (eds) *Saints' Cults in the Celtic World* (Woodbridge)

Davies, W. (1994) 'Ecclesiastical Centres and Secular Society in the Brittonic World in the Tenth and Eleventh Centuries', pp. 92–101 in A. Ritchie (ed.) *Govan and its Early Medieval Sculpture* (Stroud)

Downham, C. (2003) 'The Chronology of the Last Scandinavian Kings of York, AD 937–954', *Northern History* 40: 25–51

Downham, C. (2004) 'Erik Bloodaxe – Axed? The Mystery of the Last Viking King of York', *Medieval Scandinavia* 14: 51–77

Downham, C. (2007) *Viking Kings of Britain and Ireland: the Dynasty of Ivarr to AD 1014* (Edinburgh)

Driscoll, S.T. (1998) 'Church Archaeology in Glasgow and the Kingdom of Strathclyde', *Innes Review* 49: 94–114

Driscoll, S.T. (ed.) (2002) *Excavations at Glasgow Cathedral, 1988–1997*. Society for Medieval Archaeology monograph 18 (Leeds)

Driscoll, S.T. (2003) 'Govan: an Early Medieval Royal Centre on the Clyde', pp. 77–85 in R. Welander, D. Breeze and T.O. Clancy (eds) *The Stone of Destiny: Artefact and Icon* (Edinburgh)

Driscoll, S.T. (2004) *Govan from Cradle to Grave*. Friends of Govan Old Lecture Series. (Glasgow)

Driscoll, S.T. and Forsyth, K. (2004) 'The Late Iron Age and Early Historic Period', *Scottish Archaeological Journal* 26: 4–11

Driscoll, S.T., O'Grady, O. and Forsyth, K. (2005) 'The Govan School Revisited: Searching for Meaning in the Early Medieval Sculpture of Strathclyde', pp. 135–58 in S.M. Foster and M. Cross (eds) *Able Minds and Practised Hands: Scotland's Early Medieval Sculpture in the Twenty-First Century* (Leeds)

Driscoll, S.T. and Yeoman, P. (1997) *Excavations within Edinburgh Castle, 1988–91* (Edinburgh)

Dumville, D.N. (1977) 'Sub-Roman Britain: History and Legend', *History* 62: 173–92

Dumville, D.N. (1982) 'Latin and Irish in the Annals of Ulster, AD 431–1050', pp. 320-41 in D. Whitelock, R. McKitterick and D.N. Dumville (eds) *Ireland in Early Medieval Europe: Studies in Memory of Kathleen Hughes* (Cambridge)

Dumville, D.N. (1985) 'On Editing and Translating Medieval Irish Chronicles: the *Annals of Ulster*', *Cambridge Medieval Celtic Studies* 10: 67–86

Dumville, D.N. (1986) 'The Historical Value of the *Historia Brittonum*', *Arthurian Literature* 6: 1–26

Dumville, D.N. (2000) 'The Chronicle of the Kings of Alba', pp. 73–86 in S. Taylor (ed.) *Kings, Clerics and Chronicles in Scotland, 500–1297: Essays in Honour of Marjorie Ogilvie Anderson on the Occasion of her Ninetieth Birthday* (Dublin)

Dumville, D.N. (2001) 'St Cathroe of Metz and the Hagiography of Exoticism', pp. 172–88 in J. Carey, M. Herbert and P. O'Riain (eds) *Studies in Irish Hagiography: Saints and Scholars* (Dublin)

Dumville, D.N. (ed.) (2002) *Annales Cambriae, AD 682–954: Texts A–C in Parallel* (Cambridge)

Duncan, A.A.M. (1975) *Scotland: the Making of the Kingdom* (Edinburgh)

Duncan, A.A.M. (1976) 'The Battle of Carham, 1018', *Scottish Historical Review* 55: 20–8

Duncan, A.A.M. (2002) *The Kingship of the Scots, 842–1292: Succession and Independence* (Edinburgh)

Dunshea, P. (2014) 'The "Strath Caruin" *awdl* and the Welsh Annals', *The Medieval Journal* (forthcoming)

Durkan, J. (1999) 'The Glasgow Diocese and the Claims of York', *Innes Review* 50: 89–101

Edmonds, F. (2009) 'Personal Names and the Cult of Patrick in Eleventh-Century Strathclyde and Northumbria', pp. 42–65 in S. Boardman, J.R. Davies and E. Williamson (eds), *Saints' Cults in the Celtic World*. Studies in Celtic History 25 (Woodbridge)

Edmonds, F. (2013) 'The Furness Peninsula and the Irish Sea Region: Cultural Interactions from the Seventh Century to the Twelfth', pp. 17–44 in C. Downham (ed.) *Jocelin of Furness: Essays from the 2011 Conference* (Donnington)

Ekwall, E. (1922) *The Place-Names of Lancashire* (Manchester)

Ekwall, E. (1960) *The Oxford Dictionary of English Place-Names*. 4th edn. (Oxford)

Esmonde-Cleary, S. (1989) *The Ending of Roman Britain* (London)

Evans, N. (2010) *The Present and the Past in Medieval Irish Chronicles* (Woodbridge)

Fellows-Jensen, G. (1985) 'Scandinavian Settlement in Cumbria and Dumfriesshire: the Place-Name Evidence', pp. 65–82 in J.R. Baldwin and I.D. Whyte (eds) *The Scandinavians in Cumbria* (Edinburgh)

Flaxington, D. (2001) *The History of Heysham* (Heysham)

Fletcher, R. (2002) *Bloodfeud: Murder and Revenge in Anglo-Saxon England* (London)

Foot, S. (2011) *Athelstan: the First King of England* (London)

Forsyth, K. (2000) 'Evidence of a Lost Pictish Source in the *Historia Regum Anglorum* of Symeon of Durham', pp. 19–32 in S. Taylor (ed.) *Kings, Clerics and Chronicles in Scotland, 500–1297: Essays in Honour of Marjorie Ogilvie Anderson on the Occasion of her Ninetieth Birthday* (Dublin)

Fraser, J.E. (2002) *The Battle of Dunnichen, 685* (Stroud)

Fraser, J.E. (2005) 'Strangers on the Clyde: Cenél Comgaill, Clyde Rock and the Bishops of Kingarth', *Innes Review* 56: 102–20

Fraser, J.E. (2008) 'Bede, the Firth of Forth and the Location of *Urbs Iudeu*', *Scottish Historical Review* 87: 1–25

Fraser, J.E. (2009) *From Caledonia to Pictland: Scotland to 795* (Edinburgh)

Gelling, M. (1957) 'The Hill of Abingdon', *Oxonensia* 22: 54–62.

Gelling, M. and Cole, A. (2000) *The Landscape of Place-Names* (Stamford)

Gough-Cooper, H. (2001) 'Dun Guaire', *SPNS Newsletter*, Autumn 2001 [http://www.spns.org.uk/oldnotes2.html]

Graham, F. (1976) *The Castles of Northumberland* (Newcastle-upon-Tyne)

Gransden, A. (1996) *Historical Writing in England, 1: c.550 to c.1307* (London)

Grant, A. (2007) 'Lordship and Society in Twelfth-Century Clydesdale', pp. 98–124 in H. Price and J. Watts (eds) *Power and Identity in the Middle Ages: Essays in Memory of Rees Davies* (Oxford)

Gruffydd, R.G. (1990) 'Where was Rhaeadr Derwennydd (*Canu Aneirin*, Line 1114)?', pp. 261–6 in A. Matonis and D. Melia (eds) *Celtic Language, Celtic Culture: a Festschrift for Eric P. Hamp* (Van Nuys)

Halloran, K. (2005) 'The Brunanburh Campaign: a Reappraisal', *Scottish Historical Review* 84: 133–48

Halloran, K. (2010) 'The Identity of Etbrunnanwerc', *Scottish Historical Review* 89: 248–53

Halloran, K. (2011) 'Welsh Kings at the English Court, 928–956', *Welsh History Review* 25: 297–313

Halloran, K. (2013) 'Anlaf Guthfrithsson at York: a Non-Existent Kingship?', *Northern History* 50: 180–5

Halsall, G. (2013) *Worlds of Arthur: Facts and Fictions of the Dark Ages* (Oxford)

Harmer, F. (1952) *Anglo-Saxon Writs* (Manchester)

Heffernan, T. (1992) *Sacred Biography: Saints and their Biographers in the Middle Ages* (Oxford)

Higham, N.J. (1985) 'The Scandinavians in North Cumbria', pp. 37–52 in J.R. Baldwin and I.D. Whyte (eds) *The Scandinavians in Cumbria* (Edinburgh)

Higham, N.J. (1986) *The Northern Counties to AD 1000* (London)

Higham, N.J. (1988) 'The Cheshire Burhs and the Mercian Frontier to 924', *Transactions of the Lancashire and Cheshire Antiquarian Society* 85: 193–222

Higham, N.J. (1993) *The Kingdom of Northumbria, AD 350–1100* (Stroud)

Higham, N.J. (1997) 'The Context of Brunanburh', pp. 144–56 in A.R. Rumble and D. Mills (eds) *Names, Place and People: an Onomastic Miscellany in Memory of John McNeal Dodgson* (Stamford)

Higham, N.J. (2007a) (ed.) *Britons in Anglo-Saxon England* (Woodbridge)

Higham, N.J. (2007b) 'Historical Narrative as Cultural Politics', pp. 68–79 in N.J. Higham (ed.) *Britons in Anglo-Saxon England* (Woodbridge)

Hill, P. (2004) *The Age of Athelstan: Britain's Forgotten History* (Stroud)

Hines, J. (2001) *Old Norse Sources for Gaelic History* (Cambridge)

Hodgson-Hinde, J. (ed.) (1868) *Symeonis Dunelmensis Opera et Collectanea*. Vol.1 (Durham)

Hudson, B.T. (1988) '*Elech* and the Scots in Strathclyde', *Scottish Gaelic Studies* 15: 145–9

Hudson, B.T. (1992) 'Cnut and the Scottish Kings', *English Historical Review* 107: 350–60

Hudson, B.T. (1994) *Kings of Celtic Scotland* (Westport)

Hudson, B.T. (1996) (ed.) *Prophecy of Berchan: Irish and Scottish High-Kings in the Early Middle Ages* (Westport)

Hudson, B.T. (1998) 'The Scottish Chronicle', *Scottish Historical Review* 77: 129–61

Hughes, K. (1973) 'The Welsh Latin Chronicles: *Annales Cambriae* and Related Texts', *Proceedings of the British Academy* 59: 233–58. Reprinted on pp. 67–85 in K. Hughes, *Celtic Britain in the Early Middle Ages* (Woodbridge, 1980)

Hutchinson, W. (1794) *The History of the County of Cumberland* (Carlisle)

Jackson, K.H. (1955) 'The Britons in Southern Scotland', *Antiquity* 29: 77–88

Jackson, K.H. (1958) 'The Sources for the Life of St Kentigern', pp. 273–357 in N.K. Chadwick et al. *Studies in the Early British Church* (Cambridge)

Jackson, K.H. (1963) 'Angles and Britons in Northumbria and Cumbria', pp.60–84 in H. Lewis (ed.) *Angles and Britons* (Cardiff)

Jarman, A.O.H. (1978) 'Early Stages in the Development of the Merlin Legend', pp. 335–48 in R. Bromwich and R.B. Jones (eds) *Astudiaethau ar yr Hengerdd* (Cardiff)

Kapelle, W.E. (1979) *The Norman Conquest of the North: the Region and its Transformation, 1000–1135* (London)

Kirby, D.P. (1962) 'Strathclyde and Cumbria: a Survey of Historical Development to 1092', *Transactions of the Cumberland & Westmorland Antiquarian & Archaeological Society*, Second Series 62: 71–94

Kirby, D.P. (1967) *The Making of Early England* (London)

Kirby, D.P. (1991) *The Earliest English Kings* (London)

Koch, J.T. (2000) 'Appendix' in Forsyth (2000)

Kronk, G.W. (1999) *Cometography: a Catalog of Comets*. Vol. 1: Ancient – 1799 (Cambridge)

Lapidge, M. (1981) 'Some Latin Poems as Evidence for the Reign of Athelstan', *Anglo-Saxon England* 9: 61–98

Lawrie, A.C. (ed.) (1905) *Early Scottish Charters prior to AD 1153* (Glasgow)

Livingston, M. (ed.) (2011a) *The Battle of Brunanburh: a Casebook* (Exeter)

Livingston, M. (2011b) 'The Roads to Brunanburh', pp. 1–26 in Livingston (2011a).

Lovecy, I. (1976) 'The End of Celtic Britain: a Sixth-Century Battle Near Lindisfarne', *Archaeologia Aeliana*, Fifth Series 4: 31–45

Lowe, C. (2006) *Excavations at Hoddom, Dumfriesshire: an Early Ecclesiastical Site in South-West Scotland* (Edinburgh)

Mac Airt, S. and Mac Niocaill, G. (eds) (1983) *The Annals of Ulster to AD 1131* (Dublin)

McCarthy, M. R. (1993) *Carlisle: History and Guide* (Stroud)

McKitterick, R. (1999) 'Paul the Deacon and the Franks', *Early Medieval Europe* 8: 319–39.

Macquarrie, A. (1986) 'The Career of St Kentigern of Glasgow: Vitae, Lectiones and Glimpses of Fact', *Innes Review* 37: 3–24

Macquarrie, A. (1993) 'The Kings of Strathclyde, c.400–1018', pp. 1–19 in A. Grant and K.J. Stringer (eds) *Medieval Scotland: Crown, Lordship and Community* (Edinburgh)

Macquarrie, A. (1997a) *The Saints of Scotland: Essays in Scottish Church History, AD 450–1093* (Edinburgh)

Macquarrie, A. (1997b) 'The Name Govan, the Kirk and the Doomster Hill', *Annual Report of the Society of Friends of Govan Old* 7: 1–3

Macquarrie, A. (2006) *Crosses and Upright Monuments in Strathclyde: Typology, Dating and Purpose*. Friends of Govan Old Lecture Series. (Govan)

Margary, I.D. (1973) *Roman Roads in Britain*. 3rd edn. (London)

Matthews, S. (2009) 'King Edgar and the Dee: the Ceremony of 973 in Popular History Writing', *Northern History* 46: 61–74

Meehan, B. (1976) 'The Siege of Durham, the Battle of Carham and the Cession of Lothian', *Scottish Historical Review* 55: 1–19

Miller, M. (1976) 'Historicity and the Pedigrees of the Northcountrymen', *Bulletin of the Board of Celtic Studies* 26: 255–80

Mills, D. (1976) *The Place-Names of Lancashire* (London)

Morris, C. J. (1992), *Marriage and Murder in Eleventh-Century Northumbria: a Study of 'De Obsessione Dunelmi'*. Borthwick Paper No. 82. (York)

Morris, J. (1973) *The Age of Arthur* (London)

Morris, M. (2012) *The Norman Conquest* (London)

Nesbitt, W. (1963) 'The Rate of March of Crusading Armies in Europe: a Study and Computation', *Traditio* 19: 167–81

Niermeyer. J. F. (1976) *Mediae Latinitatis Lexicon Minus* (Leiden)

O'Sullivan, D.M. (1984) 'Pre-Conquest Settlement Patterns in Cumbria', pp. 143–54 in M. Faull (ed.) *Studies in Late Anglo-Saxon Settlement* (Oxford)

Oram, R. (2001) *The Lordship of Galloway, c.900–c.1300* (Edinburgh)

Oram, R. (2008) *David: the King Who Made Scotland* (Stroud)

Owen, O. (ed.) (2013) *Things in the Viking World* (Lerwick)

Paterson, C., et al. (2014) *Shadows in the Sand: Excavation of a Viking-Age Cemetery at Cumwhitton* (Oxford)

Phythian-Adams, C. (1996) Land of the Cumbrians: a Study in British Provincial Origins, AD 400–1120 (Aldershot)

Radner, J. (ed.) (1978) *The Fragmentary Annals of Ireland* (Dublin)

Ritchie, A. (ed.) (1994) *Govan and its Early Medieval Sculpture* (Stroud)

Ritchie, A. (1999) *Govan and its Carved Stones* (Balgavies)

Ritchie, A. (2004) *Hogback Gravestones at Govan and Beyond* Friends of Govan Old Lecture Series. (Govan)

Ritson, J. (1828) *Annals of the Caledonians, Picts, and Scots*. Vol. 2 (London)

Rivet, A.L.F. and Smith, C. (1979) *The Place-Names of Roman Britain* (London)

Robertson, A.J. (1939) *Anglo-Saxon Charters* (Cambridge)

Rollason, D. (1987) (ed.) *Cuthbert: Saint and Patron* (Durham)

Rollason, D. (1998) (ed.) *Symeon of Durham: Historian of Durham and the North* (Stamford)

Rollason, D. (2000) (ed.) *Symeon of Durham: Libellus de exordio atque procursu istius, hoc est Dunhelmensis, Ecclesie – Tract on the Origins and Progress of this the Church of Durham* (Oxford)

Rollason, D. (2003) *Northumbria, 500–1100: Creation and Destruction of a Kingdom* (Cambridge)

Sawyer, P.H. (1968) *Anglo-Saxon Charters: an Annotated List and Bibliography* (London)

Scott, J.G. (1991) 'Bishop John of Glasgow and the Status of Hoddom', *Transactions of the Dumfriesshire & Galloway Natural History & Antiquarian Society* 66: 37–45

Scott, J.G. (1997) 'The Partition of a Kingdom: Strathclyde, 1092–1153', *Transactions of the Dumfriesshire & Galloway Natural History & Antiquarian Society* 72: 11–40

Sellar, W.D.H. (1985) 'Warlords, Holy Men and Matrilinear Succession', *Innes Review* 36: 29–43

Sharpe, R. (ed.) (1995) *Adomnán of Iona: Life of St Columba* (London)

Shead, N.F. (1969) 'The Origins of the Medieval Diocese of Glasgow', *Scottish Historical Review* 48: 220–5

Skene, W.F. (ed.) (1867) *Chronicles of the Picts, Chronicles of the Scots, and Other Early Memorials of Scottish History* (Edinburgh)

Smyth, A.P. (1984) *Warlords and Holy Men: Scotland, AD 80–1000* (London)

Spearman, R.M. (1994) 'The Govan Sarcophagus: an Enigmatic Monument', pp. 33–45 in A. Ritchie (ed.) *Govan and its Early Medieval Sculpture* (Stroud)

Stancliffe, C. (1983) 'Kings who Opted Out', pp. 154–76 in P. Wormald (ed.) *Ideal and Reality in Frankish and Anglo-Saxon Society: Essays Presented to J. M. Wallace-Hadrill* (Oxford)

Stancliffe, C. (1995) 'Where Was Oswald Killed?', pp. 84–96 in C. Stancliffe and E. Cambridge (eds) *Oswald: Northumbrian King to European Saint* (Stamford)

Stenton, F.M. (1970) *Preparatory to Anglo-Saxon England* (Oxford)

Summerson, H.R.T. (1993) *Medieval Carlisle: the City and the Borders from the Late Eleventh to the Mid-Sixteenth Century*. Vol. 1. (Kendal)

Swanton, M. (1996) *The Anglo-Saxon Chronicle* (New York)

Taylor, H. (1902) 'The Ancient Crosses of Lancashire: the Hundred of Amounderness', *Transactions of the Lancashire and Cheshire Antiquarian Society* 20: 145–213

Thacker, A. (1995) '*Membra Disjecta*: the Division of the Body and the Diffusion of the Cult', pp. 97–127 in C. Stancliffe and E. Cambridge (eds) *Oswald: Northumbrian King to European Saint* (Stamford)

Thornton, D.E. (1997) 'Hey Mac! The Name *Maccus*, Tenth to Fifteenth Centuries', *Nomina* 20: 67–94

Thornton, D.E. (2001) 'Edgar and the Eight Kings, AD 973', *Early Medieval Europe* 10: 49–80

Todd, J.M. (2005) 'British (Cumbric) Place-Names in the Barony of Gilsland, Cumbria', *Transactions of the Cumberland & Westmorland Antiquarian & Archaeological Society*, Third Series 5: 89–102

Wainwright, F.T. (1948) 'Ingimund's Invasion', *English Historical Review* 63: 145–69.

Wainwright, F.T. (1950) 'The Battles at Corbridge', *Saga-Book of the Viking Society* 13: 156–73

Wainwright, F.T. (1959) 'Aethelflaed, Lady of the Mercians', pp. 53–69 in P. Clemoes (ed.) *The Anglo-Saxons: Studies in Some Aspects of their History* (London)

Wallace-Hadrill, J.M. (1988) *Bede's Ecclesiastical History of the English People: a Historical Commentary* (Oxford)

Watson, R. (2011), 'Viking-Age Amounderness: a Reconsideration', pp. 125–141 in N.J. Higham and M.J. Ryan (eds) *Place-Names, Language and the Anglo-Saxon Landscape* (Woodbridge)

Watson, W.J. (1926) *A History of the Celtic Place-Names of Scotland* (Edinburgh)

Wilkinson, T.T. (1857) 'On the Battle of Brunanburh and the Probable Locality of the Conflict', *Transactions of the Historic Society of Lancashire and Cheshire* 9: 21–41

Williams, A. (2003) *Aethelred the Unready: the Ill-Counselled King* (London)

Williams, A. (2004) 'An Outing on the Dee: King Edgar at Chester, AD 973', *Medieval Scandinavia* 14: 229–44

Wilson, P.A. (1966) 'On the Use of the Terms "Strathclyde" and "Cumbria"', *Transactions of the Cumberland & Westmorland Antiquarian & Archaeological Society*, Second Series 66: 57–92

Winchester, A.L. (1987) *Landscape and Society in Medieval Cumbria* (Edinburgh)

Wood, M. (1980) 'Brunanburh Revisited', *Saga-Book of the Viking Society* 20: 200–17

Wood, M. (2013) 'Searching for Brunanburh: the Yorkshire Context of the "Great War" of 937', *Yorkshire Archaeological Journal* 85: 138–59

Woolf, A. (2005) 'Onuist Son of Uurguist: Tyrannus Carnifex or a David for the Picts?', pp. 35–42 in D. Hill and M. Worthington (eds) *Aethelbald and Offa: Two Eighth-Century Kings of Mercia*. BAR British Series 383. (Oxford)

Woolf, A. (2006) 'Dun Nechtain, Fortriu and the Geography of the Picts', *Scottish Historical Review* 85: 182–201

Woolf, A. (2007a) *From Pictland to Alba, 789–1070* (Edinburgh)

Woolf, A. (2007b) *Where was Govan in the Early Middle Ages?* Friends of Govan Old Lecture Series. (Govan)

Woolf, A. (2010) 'Reporting Scotland in the Anglo-Saxon Chronicle', pp. 221–39 in A. Jorgensen (ed.) *Reading the Anglo-Saxon Chronicle* (Turnhout)

Woolf, A. (ed.) (2013) *Beyond the Gododdin: Dark Age Scotland in Medieval Wales* (St Andrews)

INDEX

Aberdeen Breviary 17

Abernethy 41, 103

Adomnán 27, 30–2,

Áedán mac Gabráin 31–2

Aethelflaed, ruler of Mercia 58–62, 70, 76, 178n, 179n

Aethelfrith 33

Aethelred the Unready, English king 125–7, 131, 133

Aethelred, ruler of Mercia 56, 58

Aethelweard, English chronicler 9, 88–9, 98, 173n, 177n

Alba, origins of 5–6, 52

Alexander I, king of Alba 162–3

Alfred, Northumbrian layman 67, 69–70

Alfred the Great 57, 99

Allerdale 155–8, 160

Alt Clut 15, 27–47; *see also* Dumbarton

Amounderness 80, 82, 93, 95, 99, 181n

Anglo-Saxon Chronicle
  manuscripts 8–9
  references to Strathclyde/Cumbria 4, 72, 76–7, 80, 108, 111, 126

Anglesey 58, 123

Anglo-Saxons, origins of 5, 23–4

Anlaf 'Conung' 46

Anlaf Guthfrithsson 83–9, 92, 94, 97, 101, 106,

Anlaf Sihtricsson ('Cuarán') 101, 106, 108, 110, 113–16, 123–5

Annales Cambriae; *see* annals, Welsh

annals
  Irish 12–13, 37
  Welsh 14–15, 108

Annals of Clonmacnoise 12–13, 80, 84

Annals of the Four Masters 12–13, 103

Annals of Inisfallen 12–13

Annals of Tigernach 12, 144

Annals of Ulster 12, 84

Antonine Wall 20, 24

Argyll; *see* Scots

Armes Prydein Vawr (Welsh poem) 6, 102

Artgal, king of Alt Clut 15, 47, 50–2

Athelstan 75–95, 97, 100–2

Ayrshire 8, 29, 37, 63, 128, 149, 165

Bakewell 72–3

Bamburgh 26, 34, 53, 63, 70, 80, 114, 131, 158, 175n

Bede 10, 25, 33–4, 36, 38, 104, 176n

Berchan's Prophecy; *see Prophecy of Berchan*

Bernicia 25–6, 28–36; *see also* Bamburgh

Brian Bóruma 132

Brindle 95–6

Brinsworth 89, 95

Britons (North) 22, 46–7, 60; *see also* Strathclyde *and other named kingdoms*

Bromborough 91, 95, 99, 181n

Brougham 78–9

Brun (river) 95, 97

Bruna Hill 95, 98–9

Brunanburh, battle of 84–100, 170

Brut y Tywysogion 56, 109, 123

Burnswark 95, 181n

Bute, Isle of 45

Caddonlee 140–1

Cadwallon 33–4

Caithness 81, 144

Carham-on-Tweed, battle of 133–43, 170

Carl, Northumbrian nobleman 145, 147

Carlisle 154, 161–2, 166, 182n

Carman Hill 21

Cathroe (saint) 16, 103–7

Cenél nGabráin 31, 33, 46, 52

charters 18–19, 78, 120, 155–8

Chester 58–9, 122–4

Chester-le-Street 10, 67, 82, 110

Chronicle of the Kings of Alba 8, 13, 51, 61–2, 69, 85, 117, 121–2

Cináed mac Ailpín 46, 51–2

Cináed mac Duib, king of Alba 127, 131

Cináed mac Maíl Coluim, king of Alba 121–4

Clyde (river) 1–2, 47–9

Cnut 131, 133–4, 142–5, 149

Columba (saint) 27, 30–2,

comets 135–6

Constantin mac Áeda 61, 69–70, 73–4, 76–82, 97, 101, 103, 106

Constantin mac Cináeda 50–3

Corbridge 69–70, 73–4, 82, 179n

Cowal 31, 45

Cuilén, king of Alba 120–1

Cumberland (English county) 153–4, 162, 167, 169

Cumbraes (islands) 45, 167

Cumbria (medieval term) 3–5, 7, 47

Cumbric language 3, 39, 60–1, 64–5, 118, 149, 158, 166–8

Cumwhitton 65–6

Cuthbert (saint) 10, 67

Cutheard (bishop) 67, 69

Cynesige, archbishop of York 151–2

Dacre 78, 180n

Dál Riata 31, 35, 40, 45, 52; *see also* Scots

Damnonii 21, 26–7

Danes 6, 44–5, 57, 58, 64, 125, 131; *see also* Vikings

David I, king of Scotland 4–5, 19, 142, 162–6

De Obsessione Dunelmi 11, 132–3, 139

Dee (river) 122–4

Deira 25–6, 33

Dere Street 110, 141

Derwent (Lake District river) 14, 66

dinges mere 88, 180n

Dolfin 161, 187n

Domnall, son of Constantin (died 900) 8, 52, 54, 61

Donnchad mac Maíl Coluim, king of Alba 149–50

Doomster Hill 1, 39, 49–50

Dublin 46–7, 51, 58–9, 102, 143–4

Dumbarton 4, 15, 21–3, 27, 38, 41, 46–7; *see also* Alt Clut

Dumfriesshire 64, 66, 128, 167

Dunmail, legendary king 112–13

Dunmail Raise (cairn) 112–13

Durham 10–11, 132–3, 141, 161

Dyfnwal, king of Alt Clut (mid eighth century) 38, 40

Dyfnwal, king of Strathclyde (early tenth century) 8, 61–2, 179n

Dyfnwal, king of Strathclyde (died 975) 101, 103–13, 115–18, 120, 122–3, 125

Eadberht, king of Northumbria 37–8, 40–2

Eadred, English king 113–17

Eadwig, English king 117–18

Eadwulf 'Evil Child' 122

Eadwulf Cudel 135–42

Eadwulf, earl of Bamburgh (eleventh century) 146–7, 149

Ealdred, lord of Bamburgh (tenth century) 69–70, 73, 76–7, 79–80

Ealdred, earl of Bamburgh (eleventh century) 145

Eamont (river) 64–6, 76–80, 105, 162

East Anglia 45, 57

Ecgfrith 35–6

Echmarcach 143–4

Edgar, English king 119–25

Edgar, king of Alba 162–5

Edinburgh 34, 117–18

Edmund, English king 101, 107–13, 115

Edmund Ironside 135, 138

Edward the Confessor 149–52, 160

Edward the Elder 57, 58, 70, 72–4, 75

Edwin 25, 33

English; *see* Anglo-Saxons *and individual kingdoms by name*

English language; *see under* languages

Eochaid, son of Rhun 53–4, 61

Erik, king of Northumbria 104, 106, 113–14
Erik Bloodaxe 106, 114–17
Erik Haakonsson, earl of York 135–9

Fordun; *see* John of Fordun
Forth (river) 121, 162
Fortriu 81; *see also* Moray
Fragmentary Annals of Ireland 12–13, 59–60, 174n
Frew, Fords of 121

Gaelic language; *see under* languages
Gall-Gáidhil 148–9, 158, 165
Galloway 128, 148
Garstang 95, 98, 181n
genealogies 15, 25–7, 35, 51
Giant's Grave 129–30
Gildas 24
Giric 54, 61
Glasgow (bishops of) 16, 49, 142, 151–2, 164–6, 188n
Gododdin (kingdom) 30, 33–5
Gosforth 129–30
Gospatric, earl of Northumbria 153–4, 160–1
Gospatric, lord of Allerdale 18, 155–60
Gospatric's Writ 18, 155–8, 170
Govan 1, 30, 38–9, 41–2, 47–50, 127–9, 148, 151, 171
Gunderic 104–5
Guthfrith, grandson of Ivar 76, 81–3
Gwynedd 33, 56, 81, 124

Hadrian's Wall 20, 24
hagiography 15–16
Halfdan 45, 53
Harald Hardrada 92, 160
Harold Godwinesson 153, 160
Harthacnut 147
Hastings, battle of 153, 160
Henry I, king of England 161–5
Henry of Huntingdon 11, 108, 127
Hereford 77–8
Heversham 67
Heysham 95
Hiberno-Norse; *see* Norsemen/Norse

Historia Brittonum 15, 25, 28–9, 34
Historia Dunelmensis ecclesiae 10, 81, 85, 133
Historia Regum Anglorum et Dacorum 10–11, 38, 81, 134–7, 146, 153–4
Historia de Sancto Cuthberto 11, 67, 69–70
Hoddom 151, 166
Humber 89, 92, 94
Hywel the Good (Hywel Dda) 76–7, 81, 83, 109

Iceland 17, 44
Ida 26, 29
Iehmarc; *see* Echmarcach
Ildulb, king of Alba 117–18, 120
Ingimund 58–9
Iona 12, 31, 33, 44, 125
Ireland 44, 46, 58–9, 82, 84, 132, 148, 182n
Irish annals; *see* annals, Irish
Iudeu 34–5
Ivar, king of Dublin (ninth century) 46–7

Jarrow 10, 44
Jocelin of Furness 16, 49
John of Fordun 5, 7–8, 55, 62, 144
John of Worcester 9, 89, 122–4, 149–52

Kentigern (saint) 33, 69
    vitae 12, 16, 30, 33, 49
Kintyre 31, 46, 52
Kyle 37–8

Lancashire 80, 95, 167
Lanchester 89, 95
languages
    Brittonic (British) 3; *see also* Cumbric language
    English 24, 158
    Gaelic 23, 52, 149, 157, 166
Leeds 104, 130
Lennox 21, 121, 132
Libellus de exordio; *see Historia Dunelmensis ecclesiae*
Limerick 84, 123
Lindisfarne 10, 44
Loida 104–5
Lothian 117–18, 121, 139, 142–3

Lowther (river) 78, 105
Lowther Church 105
Lune (river) 80, 93

Macbethad ('Macbeth') 143–4, 149–52
Maccus Haraldsson 122–4
Maeatae 32
Maelbeth; *see* Macbethad
Máel Coluim mac Cináeda, king of Alba
    131–4, 138–45, 148, 150–1
Máel Coluim mac Domnaill, king of Alba
    101, 108, 111, 114–17
Máel Coluim mac Donnchada, king of Alba
    150, 152–4, 161–2, 165
Máel Coluim, son of Dyfnwal, king of
    Strathclyde 120–6
Máel Coluim, 'son of the king of the
    Cumbrians' 149–52
Man, Isle of 59, 125–6
Manchester 72–3, 93
Manau 32
Mercia 34, 45, 57–8, 76, 94
Mersey (river) 58, 72, 80, 178n
Metz 16, 103
Miathi; *see* Maeatae
Moin Uacoruar, battle of 121–2
Moray 143; *see also* Fortriu
Mugdock, battle of 37–8
Mungo (saint); *see* Kentigern

Neithon of Alt Clut 32–3
Niwanbirig 40–2
Normandy 131, 143, 163
Normans 160–2
Norsemen/Norse, 6, 58–61, 63–9; *see also*
    Vikings
Norse sagas 17, 106, 173n, 175n
North Britons; *see* Britons
Northumbria; *see also* Bernicia *and* Deira
    origins 36
    relations with Alt Clut 36–8, 40–3
    relations with Picts 35–8, 40–3
    relations with Scots 69–70, 114–15,
        117–18, 133–42, 153–5, 161
    relations with Strathclyde 61, 64–67,
        104–6, 133–43, 154–5

    relations with West Saxons 70, 72–4, 76,
        79, 101, 110, 113–15, 131, 133
    Viking raids 44–5
Nottingham 72, 82

Óengus; *see* Onuist
Olaf; *see* Anlaf
Onuist, son of Urguist 37–8, 40–2, 45
Orkney 115, 144
Oswald 33–5
Oswine, king of Deira 34–5
Oswiu 34–6
Oswulf, lord of Bamburgh 115–16
Owain, son of Beli 33, 35
Owain, king of Strathclyde (early tenth
    century) 62, 73, 76–9, 82–4, 97, 100–1,
    130
Owain, son of Dyfnwal (early eleventh
    century) 126, 133, 141
Owain, son of Urien Rheged 130
Owain the Bald, king of Strathclyde 133–4,
    138–43, 151

Partick 30, 47–9
pedigrees; *see* genealogies
Peebles 42, 140
Penda 34–5, 37
Penrith 67, 129–30
Penwortham 93
Picts
    language 32
    relations with Alt Clut 37–8, 40–3
    relations with Northumbria 35–8, 40–3
    relations with Scots 32, 40, 52
    relations with Strathclyde 50–5
    relations with Vikings 45–6
place-names 60, 63–6, 118, 160–1, 167, 178n,
    183n
poetry
    Welsh 12, 14, 27–8, 102
    Anglo-Saxon 85–8, 92
Prophecy of Berchan 14, 52–4, 117
Ptolemy, Greek geographer 21, 26

Ragnall, king of York (died 921) 59–60,
    69–70, 72–4, 75

Ragnall Guthfrithsson 108, 110
Ralph Glaber 17, 143
Renfrewshire 38, 148–9, 165
Rheged 30, 33, 35, 130
Rhun, son of Artgal 15, 27, 47, 50–3, 61
Rhydderch Hael 27–33, 47
Rhydderch, son of Dyfnwal 120–1
Ribble (river) 80, 93, 97
Roger of Wendover 11, 108–9
Romans 20–1, 23

sagas; *see* Norse sagas
Saxons; *see* Anglo-Saxons
Scots
    origins 31
    relations with Alt Clut 31–2, 35
    relations with Northumbria 69–70,
        114–15, 117–18, 133–42, 153–5, 161
    relations with Picts 32, 40, 52
    relations with Strathclyde 81–5, 108–11,
        115–16, 121–2, 134, 149–54
    relations with Vikings 45, 114
    relations with West Saxons 72–4, 76–88,
        108–11
sculpture
    of the Anglo-Saxons 73, 105, 128–30, 152
    of the Britons 1, 48, 127–8, 170–1
Sihtric, grandson of Ivar 59–60, 75–6
Siward 149–52, 155–61, 164
Solway Firth 64, 148, 153–5, 158
sources 7–19
Stainmore 105, 108, 116, 122, 153, 188n
stones (carved); *see* sculpture
Strathcarron, battle of 35–6
Strathclyde
    expansion in tenth century 63–9, 121
    name 2, 4
    origins 47–8
    relations with Mercia 59–62, 178n
    relations with Northumbria 61, 64–67,
        104–6, 133–43, 154–5
    relations with Picts 50–5
    relations with Scots 81–5, 108–11, 115–6,
        121–2, 134, 149–54
    relations with Vikings 60, 74, 81–5, 125–6,
        144

relations with West Saxons 62, 72–4,
    76–85, 92–4, 100–1, 108–11, 123–4,
    126–7, 133, 149–51
Strathearn 54, 103
Suibhne, king of the Gall-Gáidhil 148
Sweyn Forkbeard 125–7, 131

Tamworth 70, 76
Tees (river) 114, 138, 153
Teudubr 37
Teviotdale 142–3, 163–4
Thorfynn mac Thore 155–8
Tilred, Northumbrian abbot 67, 69
Tweed (river) 138–40, 143, 161, 163
Tyne (English river) 45, 53, 69,
Tyne (Scottish river) 139, 142
Tyninghame 101

Uhtred, earl of Bamburgh 132–9, 155
Urien Rheged 29–30, 130

Vikings 6, 39, 44–7, 57, 58–60, 63–4, 81–5,
    131; *see also* Norsemen/Norse, Danes
    and named individuals
Vita Kaddroe 103–4
Vita Sancti Kentigerni 12, 30
vitae 15–16, 103
Votadini 21, 30; *see also* Gododdin (kingdom)

Wales 35, 56, 59, 77, 102, 122, 124, 168
Waltheof, earl of Bamburgh 131–2
Waterford 59, 69
Wearmouth–Jarrow; *see* Jarrow
Welsh annals; *see* annals, Welsh
West Saxons
    relations with Northumbria 70, 72–4, 76,
        79, 101, 110, 113–15, 131, 133
    relations with Scots 72–4, 76–88, 108–11
    relations with Strathclyde 62, 72–4, 76–85,
        92–4, 100–1, 108–11, 123–4, 126–7,
        133, 149–51
    Viking raids 45
Westmorland 162, 167
Whithorn 128
William the Conqueror 153, 160

William of Malmesbury 11, 76, 78, 80–2, 94,
     124, 150
William Rufus, king of England 161
Winchester 82, 107
Winwaed, battle of 35
Wirral 91, 95, 181n

Wulfstan, archbishop of York 80, 83, 101,
     108, 113, 116

York 45, 76, 97, 101, 104, 106, 111, 113–14,
     117, 131